Dipl.-Ing. Arsitek

German-trained Indonesian Architects from the 1960s

Dipl.-Ing. Arsitek
German-trained Indonesian Architects from the 1960s

Edited by Moritz Henning and
Eduard Kögel

DOM
publishers

WEST BERLIN

Kurfürstendamm in the glow of neon signs.

Cafe Kranzler on Kurfürstendamm.

Office building on Kurfürstendamm.

Women clearing war debris in front of the almost-completed Congress Hall.

Visitors at the 1957 Interbau building exhibition in Berlin.

A square with a kiosk for international magazines, fashion journals, and traffic tower.

Visitors at the 1957 Interbau building exhibition in Berlin.

Street scene with a Mercedes Benz.

Photos: SLUE Dresden, Deutsche Fotothek, Fritz Eschen

HANOVER

The former Leineschloss palace, which was destroyed during the war, was rebuilt and supplemented as the seat of the Lower Saxony Parliament. Architect: Dieter Oesterlen (1957–1962).

Funkhaus Hannover. Architects: Friedrich Wilhelm Kraemer with Gerd Lichtenhahn and Dieter Oesterlen (1949–1952).

The Hanover nurses' home.

The 'Blauer See' (Blue Lake) petrol station, Hanover. Architect: Dieter Oesterlen (1953).

Photos: bpk, Heinrich Heidersberger

AACHEN

Katschhof in Aachen with the Dom in the background, around 1960.

Photo: Technische Universität, Berlin Architekturmuseum, Inv. Nr. TBS 701,03, photographer unknown

The interior of the Dom in Aachen.

Photo: Bildarchiv Foto Marburg, Harald Busch, 1957

The Catholic Parish Church of Saint Elisabeth in Aachen. Architect: Eduard Endler (1904–1907).

Photo: Bildarchiv Foto Marburg, Karl Franz Keller, 1953/1970

The Catholic Parish Church of St. Michael in Geistingen near Bonn, rebuilt by architect Willy Weyres after destruction during the war until 1961.

Photo: Rheinisches Bildarchiv, rba_059076

Notkirche by Otto Bartning in Aachen, 1948.

Photo: Bildarchiv Foto Marburg, Karl Franz Keller, 1953/1979

Pilgrimage Church of Mary, Queen of Peace, Neviges, 1970.
Architect: Gottfried Böhm.

Photo: Greven Archiv Digital, Arved von der Ropp, undated

Catholic Parish Church of St. Nicholas in Düren-Rölsdorf. Architect: Hans Peter Fischer, 1929.

Photo: Bildarchiv Foto Marburg, Karl Franz Keller, 1953/1967

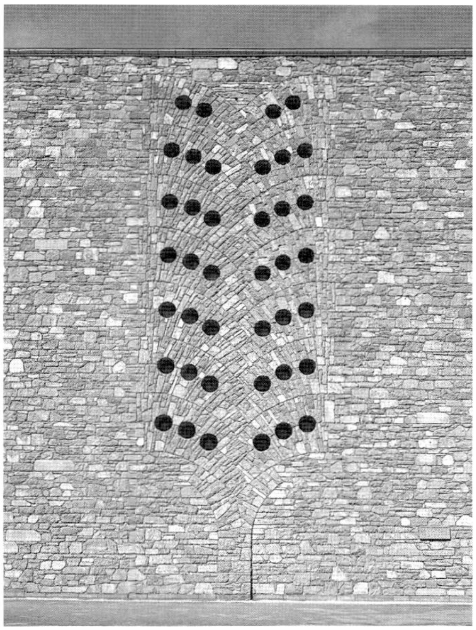

Decorative wall openings (*Tree of Life*) in the Catholic Parish Church of St. Anna in Düren (1954–1956). Architect: Rudolf Schwarz.

Photo: Bildarchiv Foto Marburg, Helga Schmidt-Glassner, 1960

Gottfried Böhm, 24 December 1955, Isometry Mission Church Ching Liau [Jiangliao], Taiwan, pencil on transparent.

Source: Gottfried Böhm-Archiv, Deutsches Architekturmuseum, Frankfurt am Main, Inventarnummer 028-017-002

JAKARTA

The Monumen Nasional (Monas) under construction, 1967.

The Monument of the Proclamator Heroes Sukarno and Hatta was constructed on the site where the Indonesian Proclamation (declaration) of Independence was read on 17 August 1945. The monument features statues of Sukarno, the first president of Indonesia, with vice president Mohammad Hatta. Photo: 1970–1985.

The West Irian Liberation Monument, symbolising the liberation of Papua after the conflict between the Netherlands and Indonesia over the territory. Photo: 1960–1969.

DPR/MPR (National Parliament) Builcing,
partly under construction, 1971.

DPR/MPR (National Parliament) Building,
partly under construction, 1971.

Entry to the National Parliament Building. Photo: 1970–1985.

Ministry of Information, under construction, 1967.

JAKARTA

Gelora Bung Karno Sports Palace (completed 1961), located in Gelora Bung Karno Sports Complex. The People's Congress meeting was held here in 1967.

All Chinese shops and business premises closed their doors after violent riots against the Chinese in 1967.

The People's Congress in session in the Gelora Bung Karno Sports Palace, 1967.

The Gedung Pola building under construction, 1963. After its completion, the most important construction projects initiated by the government of Indonesia were shown here.

New West German embassy in Jakarta, 1967.

Skyline of Jakarta, 1985.

New Dutch embassy in Jakarta, 1967

Jakarta high-rise buildings photographed from the Hotel Indonesia, 1985.

Contents

Introduction

In August 2019, we sat down in Berlin with Avianti Armand and Setiadi Sopandi, the curators of *Occupying Modernism*, the Indonesian contribution to our joint project *Encounters with Southeast Asian Modernism*. One of the topics we spoke about was German-Indonesian relations in architecture. We knew that Soejoedi Wirjoatmodjo and Han Awal, two architects who were instrumental in shaping modern Indonesian architecture since the 1960s, had studied in West Germany, but little else. So, the idea was born to pursue this topic. Indeed, we discovered photographic documentation in the archives of Technische Universität Berlin of the final projects of nine Indonesian students who graduated with a degree in architecture (*Diplom-Ingenieur Architektur*; in Indonesian: *Dipl.-Ing. Arsitek*) in 1960 and 1961. Among them were designs by Soejoedi Wirjoatmodjo and Han Awal (who went by his birth name HAN Hoo Tjwan), as well as Eddy Heryadie, Herianto Sulindro (then KHO Lin Hek), Jan Beng Oei, King-Han Oei, Mustafa Pamuntjak, Po Hin Thung (then THUNG Pohin), and Hoemer Tjokrodiatmo. Many of them transferred from Delft in the Netherlands to German universities around 1957/1958. Their final diploma projects were the inspiration and starting point for this publication, the exhibition of the same name in Jakarta, as well as two accompanying symposia.

Dipl.-Ing. Arsitek: German-trained Indonesian Architects from the 1960s provides the first insights into a little-known aspect of German-Indonesian relations in the field of architecture. Starting in the 1950s, a growing number of young Indonesians went to study in West Germany (and a few in East Germany) – with some budding architects among them. Indonesia's independence from the former colonial power, the Netherlands, which was finally achieved with the official transfer of power in 1949, as well as the postwar period in Germany, resulted in new academic ties between the two countries. The establishment of diplomatic relations between them in 1952 played an important role. Some of the students from that time went on to have distinguished careers in their native country. Still, there are not many traces of their time as students in Germany, although that experience seems to have been formative for their later work. Han Awal once said: 'It was only in Germany that I learned about the great concepts of architecture.'[1] According to Laksmi Pamuntjak, the daughter of the architect Mustafa Pamuntjak: 'To me, my father had always been more German than anything else.'[2]

This book now focuses on eight architects whose successful careers had their roots in Germany.[3] In addition to Han Awal, Soejoedi Wirjoatmodjo, Herianto Sulindro, Jan Beng Oei, and Mustafa Pamuntjak, who studied in Berlin, they include Bianpoen (then Liem Bian Poen) and Suwondo Bismo Sutedjo (then Soewondo Bismo Sutedjo), who earned their degrees in Hanover in 1961. They are joined in this book by the priest Yusuf Bilyarta Mangunwijaya, who in 1960 was sent to the Rheinisch-Westfälische Technische Hochschule Aachen by the Catholic Church in Bandung, Indonesia, to study church building.

After receiving their degrees, most of the graduates returned to Indonesia, where they became influential figures in their field. At that time, the country was seeking forms of built expression that marked a clear break with the architecture of the colonial era and could represent a modern civil society with contemporary structures. During this highly dynamic period, the young architects quickly became influential voices in Indonesian architecture. They contributed significantly to the country's architectural and aesthetic expression, engaged in education, and laid the foundation for contemporary

1 'Han Awal: Artisek Pemugar Bangunan Tua', *Tokoh Indonesia*, 7 September 2007 <https://tokoh.id/biografi/2-direktori/arsitek-pemugar-bangunan-tua/> accessed 1 November 2022.

2 Laksmi Pamuntjak, 'My Late Father, the German-Indonesian: Trauma and Historical Memory in Germany and Indonesia', *The Globalist*, 26 May 2021 <https://www.theglobalist.com/my-late-father-the-german-indonesian/> accessed 1 November 2022.

3 The exact number of Indonesian architecture students in Germany in the 1950s and 1960s is not known. We do know of the following additional students in German universities at that time: the only woman, Oei Giok Lan (1954, Germany); Harisanto (1955, Universität Stuttgart); H.A. Go Kian Dijen (1955, Technische Hochschule Karlsruhe); Lie Eng Hong (1961, Technische Universität Braunschweig); and Burhan Amongpradja (1962, Technische Hochschule Hanover).

Indonesian architecture with their work. They drew on their learnings from West Germany, influenced by the legacy of *Neues Bauen* ('New Objectivity') in the 1920s and ideas about organic architecture championed by Hans Scharoun in Berlin. Their embrace of rational functionalism, as well as more free-form architecture that engaged in dialogue with the landscape and its complexity, are reflected to an extent in the final diploma projects by the students in Berlin and their buildings in Indonesia. Returning to their homeland, they built on the promise of modernity, hoping to promote harmony and social justice with a well-designed environment. They looked to transcend regional circumstances and characteristics through international design principles, even as they evolved their own architectural language, informed over the years by shifting political conditions and architectural discourses. This also applies to the graduates who did not return to Indonesia; they are represented in this book by Jan Beng Oei, who found a new home in southern Germany and success as an architect through numerous public competitions.

The presentation in this book must inevitably remain fragmentary. Although the work of architects in Germany has been exhibited, collected, and archived in public institutions and private galleries for decades, this is by no means the case in Indonesia. For example, many of the documents held in their private estates, presented here in part for the first time, were not systematically collected and archived. For some of their buildings, no documents could be found, and for some of the architects, there was little information to reconstruct their lives and career paths. While several of the individuals featured in this book are considered protagonists of an independent architectural development in Indonesian circles today, there is little documentation about their work, especially its German origins. Similarly, the successful paths taken by these graduates are virtually unknown in Germany. In this respect, we hope that this book will not only provide insights into the life and work of these architects, but also stimulate further research.

Acknowledgements
Our thanks go to those who contributed to this project and publication, especially Avianti Armand and Setiadi Sopandi in Jakarta and Sally Below in Berlin. Without their support, this book would not have become a reality. In Jakarta, a fantastic team worked to access private archives, some of which had been dormant for many years: Adelia Andani Djarot, Adetania Pramanik, Angeline Basuki, Bangkit Mandela, Febriyanti Suryaningsih, Fernisia Winnerdy, Gregorius Jasson, Hedista Rani Pranata, Setiap Gedung Punya Cerita, Jesslyn Amanda, Nadia Purwestri, Nadira Adiswari, Rifandi Nugroho, Siti Arfah Annisa, Trisha Karina Lahu, and Warda Lutfiah Roihana, as well as the Pusat Dokumentasi Arsitektur (Indonesian Centre for Architecture Documentation, PDA).
In Berlin, we received essential support from Sarah Reiche and Joanna Jurkiewicz.
We would like to thank the families of the featured architects for sharing the valuable information about their past that informed this project: Yori Antar Awal, Maria Daryati Awal, Daisy Gandasubrata, Carla Bianpoen, Mirah Bianpoen, Maruto and Cecilia Soetedjo, Endang Pamuntjak, Laksmi Pamuntjak, Sharmi Ranti, Santoso Soejoedi, Hadijanto Soejoedi, Arya Abieta, Linda Hoemar, Linda Lochmann, Jan Beng Oei, and Steffen Thomas, and Marc Oei.
The University Archives and the Architecture Museum at Technische Universität Berlin supported our research on the Indonesian architects' time in Berlin.
Wonderful new photographs were taken by William Sutanto and Moritz Bernoully.
Last but not least, we would like to thank the German Federal Foreign Office, whose willingness to engage with this topic and provide funding made the project possible in the first place.

Moritz Henning and Eduard Kögel

CONTEXT

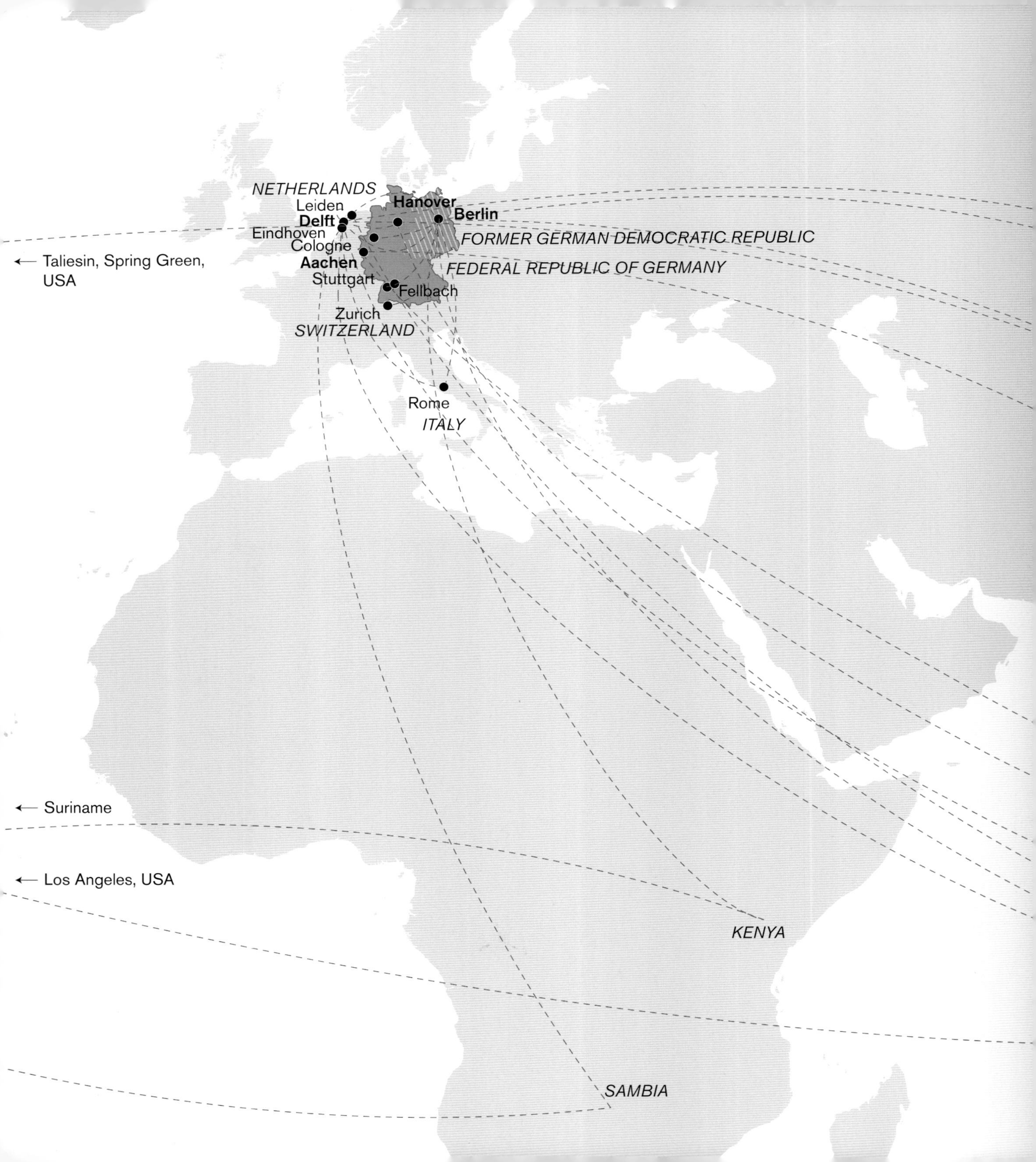

NETHERLANDS
Leiden
Delft
Eindhoven
Cologne
Aachen
Stuttgart
Hanover
Berlin
FORMER GERMAN DEMOCRATIC REPUBLIC
FEDERAL REPUBLIC OF GERMANY
Fellbach
Zurich
SWITZERLAND
Rome
ITALY
← Taliesin, Spring Green, USA
← Suriname
← Los Angeles, USA
KENYA
SAMBIA

Jakarta
Semarang
Sukabumi
Surabaya
Bandung
Purwokerto
Solo
Ambarawa
Yogyakarta
FORMER PAPUA
REPUBLIC OF INDONESIA

Built on the directive of President Sukarno in 1961 and completed in 1975, the Monumen Nasional symbolises Indonesia's struggle for independence.

Photo: Leiden University Libraries, H. C. Beynon, 1977, CC BY-NC-ND 4.0

From a Country on the Move to a Country Under Reconstruction

Moritz Henning

On 17 August 1945, Indonesia declared its independence. However, it took more than four years of fighting, negotiations, and international diplomacy before the Netherlands, which had again occupied parts of Indonesia after the Second World War, finally recognised the sovereignty of the new island state between the Indian and Pacific Oceans on 12 December 1949. Indonesia's first president, Sukarno (1901–1970), now faced the daunting task of uniting a multitude of cultural, economic, religious, political, and even military interests. The years that followed were marred by political unrest and social conflicts arising from the many unresolved problems and difficult compromises that went hand in hand with the negotiation of independence. In a bid to unify his fragmented, multiethnic island country as a single nation-state, Indonesia's president embraced urban planning and architecture as key symbolic elements. Sukarno, who had studied civil engineering with an emphasis on architecture at the Technische Hogeschool te Bandoeng from 1921 to 1926, vigorously pursued the country's architectural development. He frequently voiced his views on the importance of creating a new architecture, for example, in a 1962 speech on the development of Jakarta:

Build Djakarta as beautiful as possible, build it as spectacularly as possible, so that this city, which has become the centre of the struggle of the Indonesian people, will be an inspiration and beacon to the whole of struggling mankind and to all the emerging forces. If Egypt was able to construct Cairo as its capital, Italy its Rome, France its Paris, and Brazil its Brasilia, then Indonesia must also proudly present Djakarta as the portal of the country.[1]

1 Quoted by Lukito, 2016, p. 121.

The building of the former Technische Hogeschool te Bandoeng, designed by Dutch architect Henri Maclaine Pont, opened in 1920.

Photo: Postcard, undated, collection of the author

To make this bold vision a reality, the architectural heritage of colonial rule was to be cast aside to pave the way for a radically modern style that was clean, clear, open, dynamic, and neutral. For Sukarno, these characteristics were an ideal means of symbolically unifying the country and expressing a new national identity.[2]

A Lack of Educational Opportunities in Postcolonial Indonesia

Unfortunately, there were very few opportunities available to budding young students of architecture in Indonesia at that time. As early as 1948, while still under the Dutch, students could again enrol at the former Technische Hogeschool te Bandung (West Java), which had been founded in 1920 and was now operated under the name Nood-Universiteit van Nederlandsch Indië (Emergency University of Dutch East Indies). The education offered, however, corresponded more to a civil engineering degree than an architectural education, and this was to remain the case until the late 1950s.

In 1950, after gaining independence, the former Dutch university was reopened as Indonesia's first technical university under the name Universitas Indonesia Bandung, and a *Bouwkundige Afdeeling* ('Building Section') was opened at the *Fakulteit Teknik* ('Faculty of Engineering'). The curriculum

2 Sopandi, 2014, p. 155.

was based on the course of study offered by the Technische Hogeschool Delft in the Netherlands. Twenty students started in the first year, and the first graduates left the school in 1958. Another option was to study at one of the technical vocational schools in the country. Beyond that, however, studying architecture was only possible abroad. Further educational institutions for architects in Indonesia were only established much later: in 1962 in Yogyakarta and Semarang, in 1963 in Makassar, and in 1965 in Jakarta, Surabaya, and on Bali.[3] Courses of study for urban planners also got off to a late start. In 1959, with the help of the United Nations and Harvard University, the department of Regional and City Planning was established at the Bandung Institute of Technology (Institut Teknologi Bandung).
The situation was hardly any better in many other fields, leaving aspiring Indonesians with little alternative but to pursue their studies abroad. However, this decision was not always motivated by the poor educational system at home. Some Indonesians, for example, initially started their studies in Bandung, but later changed to other universities abroad to further expand their knowledge. Additional factors, such as discriminatory policies that limited access to higher education for ethnic Chinese in Indonesia, also played a role.[4] As a result, more and more young Indonesians went abroad, and over the years, the Federal Republic of Germany in particular became one of the most popular places for Indonesians to study outside their home country.

Federal President Theodor Heuss welcomes Ahmed Sukarno, President of Indonesia, at Cologne-Bonn Airport on 18 June 1956.

Photo: Bundesregierung, Egon Steiner

Diplomatic Relations with Germany

The path to Germany was paved by the political developments at the beginning of the 1950s. Indonesia and West Germany were quick to establish diplomatic relations, in large part because both countries – the newly independent Southeast Asian nation and the postwar Federal Republic of Germany – had to regain their footing on the world stage. After the German military capitulated in May 1945, marking the end of the Second World War in Europe, the victorious powers of France, the UK, the USA, and the USSR assumed responsibility for the administration of the former German Reich. Germany was divided into four occupation zones, and Berlin, which was in the Soviet zone, was subdivided into four sectors. In 1949, the Cold War led to the division into two separate countries. The German Democratic Republic (GDR) emerged as a Soviet-style state in eastern Germany. The three western zones of occupation became the Federal Republic of Germany (FRG) with a parliamentary democracy.

Indonesia was the first Asian country to recognise the Federal Republic of Germany, and diplomatic ties were initiated in 1952 with the opening of a German embassy in Jakarta. In 1953, Indonesia opened an embassy in West Germany. During an extensive 1956 tour that included the USA, Canada,

3 For a more comprehensive account of this period, see Kusno (ed.), 2017, p. 12.
4 See Grimm, 2019, p. 22.

Federal President Heinrich Lübke (left with hat) and President Ahmed Sukarno, 31 October 1963.
Lübke was the first head of state of the Federal Republic of Germany to visit Indonesia

Photo: Bundesregierung, Ludwig Wegmann

Italy, Switzerland, and an audience with Pope Pius XII in the Vatican, Indonesia's President Sukarno also paid a visit to West Germany, where he was considered by many to be an important statesman who embodied a new generation of economic partners.[5]

As for the Indonesians, their approach to West Germany was based on the assumption that this new European country was – at least in the region – untarnished by a colonial past and that, unlike the Netherlands, the USA, and the Eastern Bloc countries, it had no interest in pursuing political ambitions in Indonesia. Moreover, Germany had the potential to become a key economic partner.[6] Sukarno also saw similarities in the histories of both countries. In a speech entitled 'Nothing is Stronger than a United Nation!' and delivered in Heidelberg on 22 June 1956, he made reference to the division of Germany: 'May you, my German friends, also find fulfilment at your side in your struggle for national unity.'[7] Most German politicians, however, were less euphoric, and Indonesia evidently remained a distant country in their eyes. So, despite repeated efforts by the Indonesians, it was not until 1961 that a return visit by a high-ranking German

5 Arens, 2021, p. 2.

6 Ibid, p. 193.

7 Quoted in Tömmel, 2018, p. 101

politician finally took place when Hans-Joachim von Merkatz (1905–1982), the German Minister for Expellees, Refugees, and War Invalids, travelled to the country as part of his trip to Southeast Asia, and it was not until 1963 that German President Heinrich Lübke (1894–1972) visited Indonesia.

Presumably, however, the favourable studying conditions in Germany were of greater importance to most Indonesian students than political niceties. Compared to the rest of Europe, the German higher education system most closely resembled that of the Netherlands, which was already familiar from home, and tuition fees, if they were charged at all, were significantly lower than in countries like the UK and the USA.[8] It is not known when the first students arrived in West Germany, but a few Indonesians were already studying there by the mid-1950s, and their numbers grew steadily after that. In the winter semester of 1958–1959, 336 students from Indonesia were enrolled at West German institutions of higher education. In the mid-1960s their numbers had risen to about 700, and by 1976–1977 there were 3,469. By the end of the 1970s, West Germany had become the leading destination for Indonesians, accounting for 38 per cent of all students abroad.[9]

8 Grimm, 2019, p. 25.
9 Ibid, p. 20 ff.

Left
Berlin, 1958: Reconstruction of the Zoologischer Garten underground station. Kaiser Wilhelm Memorial Church is visible in the background.

Photo: ETH-Bibliothek Zürich, Bildarchiv / Comet Photo AG (Zürich) / Com_L07-0134-0001-0006 / CC BY-SA 4.0

Right
Fallow land, ruins, and new buildings at Strausberger Platz in East Berlin, 1957.

Photo: Manfred Niermann, CC BY-SA 4.0

Arrival in a Country on the Move

In the 1950s, when the first Indonesian students of architecture arrived, Germany was a country still in the midst of reconstruction. In 1945, the country lay in ruins after the destruction of the Second World War. More than half of all homes were destroyed, roads, bridges, and railway lines had been rendered impassable, and industry barely existed. By the mid-1950s, with the support of the Western Allies, the worst ravages of the war, unemployment, hunger, and housing shortages in West Germany had been largely overcome, and the German 'economic miracle' had bestowed the population with prosperity and a new sense of self-confidence. The situation in the GDR had also improved, albeit more slowly and under the political banner of a state ideology shaped by Marxism-Leninism. For the up-and-coming architects, this still 'unfinished' Germany was an ideal environment. Buildings were going up all over the country in an architectural style intended to symbolise a new beginning – much like postcolonial modernism in Indonesia: liberated from the burden of the past, modern, and international.

The German Pavilion at the Brussels World's Fair, Belgium 1958.

Photo: saai | Südwestdeutsches Archiv für Architektur und Ingenieurbau, Karlsruher Institut für Technologie, Eberhard Troeger

Architecture as a Political Statement
Moritz Henning

After the Second World War, the four occupying powers – the United States, the Soviet Union, Great Britain, and France – agreed on common goals for reconstructing Germany. However, they had different ideas about how to implement them. This was also reflected in the differing concepts for rebuilding German cities. In West Germany (Federal Republic of Germany; FRG), reconstruction efforts were based on the Athens Charter – formulated in 1933 by the Congrès International d'Architecture Moderne (CIAM IV) – and its call for the functional separation of dwelling, work, recreation, commercial businesses, and industry, along with the design of cities oriented to the needs of individual motorised transport. In East Germany (German Democratic Republic; GDR), the '16 Principles of Urban Development' – based on the Soviet model of socialist realism – provided a framework in the early 1950s for the development of a spread-out city that was hierarchically structured and centrally organised.[1] With the industrialisation of construction starting in the mid-1950s, this model was replaced by widespread prefabricated construction. In Berlin, the divided city in the middle of the GDR, these different concepts were diametrically opposed to one another.

In many cases, the immediate postwar architecture in West Germany was not obviously different from the architecture of the Third Reich. Many architects, such as Walter Gropius (1883–1969) and Ludwig Mies van der Rohe (1886–1969), had left the country during the Nazi regime, but most of them stayed. After the end of the war, it was their task to rebuild the destroyed country. 'What emerged at first was not something new, but simply *post-fascism*: bare and without ornamentation, shrunken, often asymmetrical, and always with a minimal gesture of hollow representation. This pattern was gradually modernised and brought into line with American standards of materials, construction, and design'.[2] It was not until the 1950s that German architecture made a fresh start.

The destroyed Brandenburg Gate (under reconstruction) with the Reichstag building (l.). The sector border separates West and East Berlin.
Photo: Bundesregierung, Richard Perlia

The German Pavilion at the 1958 World's Fair in Brussels

In aesthetic and political terms, the German pavilion at the 1958 World's Fair in Brussels can be seen as a prototype of West Germany's ambitions at the time. Germany was last represented at a World's Fair in Paris in 1937 with a pavilion designed by Adolf Hitler's state architect Albert Speer (1905–1981). Egon Eiermann (1904–1970) and Sep Ruf (1908–1982) now designed the exact opposite for Brussels: a light, airy, and transparent pavilion where all boundaries seemed to dissolve, allowing visitors to move freely through its open, flowing spaces. It was a sign to the world that Germany had changed. The pavilion also made a clear political statement conveying the FRG's claim as the sole representative of Germany: the word 'Deutschland' was emblazoned on the façade, and a large relief inside the structure depicted Germany in its pre-war borders of 1937.

1 See 'Soviet Models of Architecture', <https://www.stalinbauten.de/karl-marx-allee/#/tafel-10>, accessed 26 September 2022.

2 Hoffmann-Axthelm, 1981, p. 15.

The German Pavilion at the Brussels World's Fair, Belgium, 1958.

Photo: saai | Südwestdeutsches Archiv für Architektur und Ingenieurbau, Karlsruher Institut für Technologie, Eberhard Troeger

The model of the German Pavilion at the 1958 Brussels World's Fair, Belgium, shows the pavilion structure.

Photo: saai | Südwestdeutsches Archiv für Architektur und Ingenieurbau, Karlsruher Institut für Technologie, Rudolf Eimke

Interior of the German Pavilion at the Brussels World's Fair, Belgium, 1958.

Photo: saai | Südwestdeutsches Archiv für Architektur und Ingenieurbau, Karlsruher Institut für Technologie, Eberhard Troeger

The German Pavilion at the World's Fair in Paris, France, 1937.

Photo: BArch, Bild 183-S30757 / Photographer unknown

View over Gendarmenmarkt with the two cathedrals and the Schauspielhaus, East Berlin, 1957.

Photo: Manfred Niermann, CC BY-SA 4.0

Monument to Prussian army General Blücher, Bebelplatz, East Berlin. Second World War damage is still visible in the background, 1961.

Photo: Manfred Niermann, CC BY-SA 4.0

Berlin – the Divided City

Berlin was one of Germany's most bombed and destroyed cities during the Second World War. More than 30 per cent of buildings and roads and about 50 per cent of workplaces were destroyed, and barely 30 per cent of residential buildings were undamaged. Because of its location, the reconstruction of West Berlin was a high priority for the Western powers. The city was seen as a flagship of a free, democratic, and modern Western world in the heart of the Soviet sector and was therefore supported with considerable funding. From 1950 to 1960, the US-initiated European Recovery

Passers-by watch GDR border guards building the Wall in Zimmerstrasse (West Berlin side) on 13 August 1961.

Photo: Bundesregierung, Klaus Lehnartz

Program (ERP), better known as the Marshall Plan,[3] channelled approximately 3.8 billion German marks (the equivalent of about 1.9 billion euros today) into West Berlin in the form of direct payments, loans, and supplies of raw materials, food, and industrial goods. Several important projects were built with Marshall Plan funds, including the Henry Ford Building and the university library at the Freie Universität Berlin (FU; 1952–1954), the FU's Klinikum Steglitz hospital (1959–1969), the America Memorial Library (1952–1954, see p. 47), and the Congress Hall (1956–1957, see p. 37).[4] The West Berlin budget was further subsidised through various measures, such as the Berlin Funding Act (*Berlinförderungsgesetz*) by the western zones participating in the city's reconstruction. From 1949 to 1960, this amounted to around 18 billion Deutschmarks (approx. 9.2 billion euros today).[5]
In contrast, the eastern part of the city had to manage without such benefits. For many years, East Berlin even had to hand over money as part of the GDR's fiscal equalisation scheme. Because of this misguided economic policy, the East German capital struggled economically.[6] It was not until 1957 that East Berlin began receiving subsidies from the East German state budget. The different financial situation in the city's two halves was inevitably reflected in the cityscape and was also perceived by the Indonesian students. One of the architecture students, Mustafa Pamuntjak, for example, remembers West Berlin 'as a West German shop window with a free, prosperous, and glittering life' – in stark contrast to the eastern part of the city with its 'gloomy atmosphere, depressed mood, fear, empty stores, and a down economy.'[7]

While reconstruction plans in the immediate postwar years still assumed a common future for both parts of Berlin, reality soon took a different direction. The increasing division of the civil administration into an Eastern and Western sector was accompanied by diverging structural developments. These soon devolved into a veritable battle of the systems, eliminating any further thoughts of joint development.[8] The divided atmosphere is exemplified on the one hand by the urban ensembles built for the 1957 Interbau international building exhibition in West Berlin and, on the other hand, by the development along Stalinallee (now Karl-Marx-Allee) in East Berlin that began in 1952. On 13 August 1961, the GDR began building the Berlin Wall, which enclosed all three western sectors with an almost impassable barrier measuring several metres in height.

The International Building Exhibition Interbau 1957

In 1953, the West Berlin Senate announced a competition for the reconstruction of the Hansaviertel residential quarter. The term 'reconstruction' is misleading, however, because what was desired was a radical overhaul of the quarter's war-ravished nineteenth-century architecture in favour of the modern principles of a structured, low-density city.[9] First prize, which was revised and served as the basis for the quarter's

3 The Marshall Plan was named after then United States Secretary of State George C. Marshall, who in June 1947 proposed an aid programme for all of the European states.
4 Peters, 1995, p. 195.
5 Ibid.
6 Ibid., 196.
7 Pamuntjak, 2017, p. 66.
8 In 1957, the German federal government and the Berlin Senate announced the 'Capital City Berlin' international urban planning competition, whose planning radius included the territory of East Berlin – without allowing architects living in East Germany to participate. In response, East Berlin launched its own competition for central Berlin shortly thereafter.
9 Göderitz, et al,, 1957.

development, went to Gerhard Jobst (1888–1963)[10], Willy Kreuer (1910–1984; who supervised seven of the nine diploma projects by the Indonesian students in Berlin), and Wilhelm Schliesser. The complex comprised some 1,300 residential units, a library, two churches, a children's day care centre, an elementary school, and a shopping centre built on approximately 25 hectares. Over 50 architects from 14 countries designed the buildings, including Alvar Aalto (1898–1976), Jacob Bakema (1914–1981), Paul Baumgarten (1900–1984), Egon Eiermann, Walter Gropius, Arne Jacobsen (1902–1971), Oscar Niemeyer (1907–2012), Sep Ruf, and Pierre Vago (1910–2002). Not far from the Hansaviertel, Le Corbusier (1887–1965) was able to build his *Unité d'Habitation, type Berlin*. In addition, the exhibition *Die Stadt von Morgen* ('City of Tomorrow') was shown in a large temporary exhibition hall, and numerous country pavilions and accompanying events delved into various aspects of housing, urban development, and modern life.

Interbau opened on 6 July 1957, and although only a third of the buildings had been completed, the show attracted 1.3 million visitors. Among experts, the new Hansaviertel was not without controversy. It was accused of having too many high-rise buildings, overly expensive apartments, and shoddy planning and implementation. It represented 'in its unfinished spatial design, to a certain extent a reflection of our society that has not yet been re-shaped (...)'.[11] The residents, however, were less critical. Despite their complaints about the careless construction work, they were satisfied with their new living situation and proud to live in the Hansaviertel.[12]

A model flat at the International Building Exhibition Berlin Interbau 1957 shows a modern interior design.

Photo: Landesarchiv Berlin, F Rep. 290 Nr. 0056018 / Willi Nitschke

10 From 1921 to 1928, Gerhard Jobst worked as a town planner in the city of Batavia (now Jakarta).

11 Hoffmann, 1957, p. 233.

12 See also Schulz, 2007, p. 31f.

International Building Exhibition Berlin Interbau 1957, aerial view.

Photo: Landesarchiv Berlin, F Rep. 290 Nr. 0083467 / Karl-Heinz Schubert

Apartment building at the International Building Exhibition Berlin Interbau 1957. Architect: Alvar Aalto.

Photo: Landesarchiv Berlin, F Rep. 290 Nr. 0055593 / Horst Siegmann

Apartment building at the International Building Exhibition Berlin Interbau 1957. Architect: Oscar Niemeyer.

Photo: Landesarchiv Berlin, F Rep. 290 Nr. 0059435 / Horst Siegmann

Stalinallee

It was in East Berlin, however, that the first major urban development project of the postwar period was realised. As part of the Nationales Aufbauwerk Berlin, the only significant programme dedicated to East Berlin in the 1950s, more than 2,000 modern equipped apartments were built along Stalinallee in 1952–1953. The construction was not financed by the state but through citizens' bonds, income from the state lottery, and unpaid labour. Further construction phases followed until the end of the 1960s, in which the architectural evolution of Eastern Modernism can still be seen today.[13] Particularly in the early construction phases, this architecture took up classicist elements as a counter-model to the architecture of reconstruction in the West. Its style of 'socialist realism' was intended to appeal to the entire German population, as the then East German prime minister Otto Grotewohl (1894–1964) declared at the cornerstone ceremony in February 1952: 'In its reconstruction work, Berlin should also be a symbol of unity. Berlin is, and shall become, the capital of a united Germany.'[14]

13 Butter, 2005.

14 Quoted in <https://www.stalinbauten.de/karl-marx-allee/#/tafel-27>, accessed 26 September 2022.

The first construction phase of the residential development on Stalinallee in the style of socialist realism, East Berlin, 1953.

Photo: BArch, Bild 183-20145-0016 / Günter Weiß

View of Strausberger Platz and Stalinallee during the first construction phase, East Berlin, 1954.

Photo: BArch, Bild 183-24589-0009 / Heinz Funk

Interested visitors at the model of Stalinallee, East Berlin, 1954.

Photo: Landesarchiv Berlin, F Rep. 290 Nr. 0031241 / Gert Schütz

The appearance of the second construction phase of Stalinallee is characterised by prefabricated construction, 1962.

Photo: Landesarchiv Berlin, F Rep. 209 Nr. 62-1946 / Photographer unknown

The Congress Hall

In addition to the large urban development projects, countless residential buildings, churches, office buildings, factories, and several cultural buildings were also constructed in the Western part of the city. One notable building is the Congress Hall (now the House of World Cultures), completed in 1958 as a gift from the United States to the nascent Federal Republic of Germany. Designed by American architect Hugh Stubbins (1912–2006), the Congress Hall was built in the Tiergarten district, right on the sector border within sight of the opposing East German regime. It was intended to embody Western values such as freedom and modernity and symbolise the German-American friendship. The elegant and futuristic double-curved roof was a daring design for the time, and indeed, the roof partially collapsed in 1980. Indonesian architecture student Soejoedi Wirjoadmodjo seems to have been inspired by this building: the roof of the CONEFO building he designed (1963–1984, see p. 178–181) is strikingly reminiscent of the Congress Hall in Berlin.[15]

Congress Hall, West Berlin, 1957. Architect: Hugh Stubbins.

Photo: Deutsches Historisches Museum, Hans Hartz

15 The Conference of the New Emerging Forces (CONEFO) was an initiative by President Sukarno to establish a new bloc of 'emerging countries' that would be an alternative power centre to the United Nations and the 'old-established forces'. To host CONEFO, Indonesia constructed a new building complex in Jakarta. Since CONEFO never met, the complex – renamed the DPR/MPR Building – now houses the Indonesian national parliament.

Foyer of the Congress Hall, West Berlin, 1959.

Photo: Landesarchiv Berlin, F Rep. 290 Nr. 0064015 / Karl-Heinz Schubert

Congress Hall, West Berlin, 1957 Architect: Hugh Stubbins.

Photo: Deutsches Historisches Museum, Hans Hartz

The new centre of West Berlin, 1957.

Photo: Landesarchiv Berlin, F Rep. 290 Nr. 0053040 / Bert Sass

The New Heart of West Berlin

One of the urban planning and architectural hotspots of the postwar period was within walking distance of the Technische Universität (TU) Berlin, where the Indonesian architecture students were studying. With the division of the city, the area around the Zoologischer Garten (Zoo) train station became the new heart of West Berlin. On the site of the destroyed Haus Gourmenia and the Capitol cinema, the new northern perimeter development of Breitscheidplatz was built from 1955 to 1957 according to plans by Paul Schwebes (1902–1978) and Hans Schoszberger (1907–1997). Stretching from west to east was a row of new buildings: a high-rise office building, the Zoo Palast cinema, the elongated Bikini-Haus (a production facility for women's outerwear – one of the leading industries of the reconstruction years in West Berlin), followed by another high-rise building and a spacious parking garage for 350 cars. From 1961, the Kaiser Wilhelm Memorial Church on Breitscheidplatz, which had been largely destroyed during the Second World War, was supplemented by a new building designed by the architect Egon Eiermann.

A couple looks at the model of the planned new centre of West Berlin, 1958.

Photo: ETH-Bibliothek Zürich, Bildarchiv, Comet Photo AG (Zürich) CC BY-SA 4.0

The new centre of West Berlin with the Zoo Palast cinema, 1957.

Photo: Landesarchiv Berlin, F Rep. 290 Nr. 0054339 / Horst Siegmann

The New Philharmonic Hall

Another important cultural building was erected in the Tiergarten district to replace the Philharmonie (Philharmonic Hall), which had been destroyed during the war, according to plans designed by Hans Scharoun (1893–1972) – probably the best-known representative of organic architecture. Construction began in 1960, and although only Hoemar Tjokrodiatmo, who was in Berlin until 1964, would have been able to see the finished building during his stay in Berlin, the design, which was widely discussed at the time, could hardly have escaped his attention – especially given the fact that Hans Scharoun teaching at the Technische Universität was one of the reasons for the Indonesian students' move from Delft to Berlin. In addition, one of the students, Jan Beng Oei, built the architectural models for the Philharmonie as an intern in Scharoun's office at the time.[16] The building, which is vaguely reminiscent of a circus tent, does not have a classic representative façade; the entrance discretely faces Tiergarten park. One of the Philharmonie's notable features is its unique concert hall: the orchestral stage is located in the centre of the space, with audience seating arranged in tiers all around it.

16 Interview with Jan Beng Oei by Eduard Kögel on 9 July 2022.

The new Philharmonie by Hans Scharoun in West Berlin, 1964.

Photo: Landesarchiv Berlin, F Rep. 290 Nr. 0098709 / Horst Siegmann

Rolf Schwedler, Senator for Building and Housing of West Berlin, at the model of the new Philharmonie, 1961.

Photo: Deutsche Fotothek, Fritz Eschen

Interior of the new Philharmonie in West Berlin, 1992.

Photo: Landesarchiv Berlin, F Rep. 290 Nr. 0340279 / Barbara Esch-Marowski

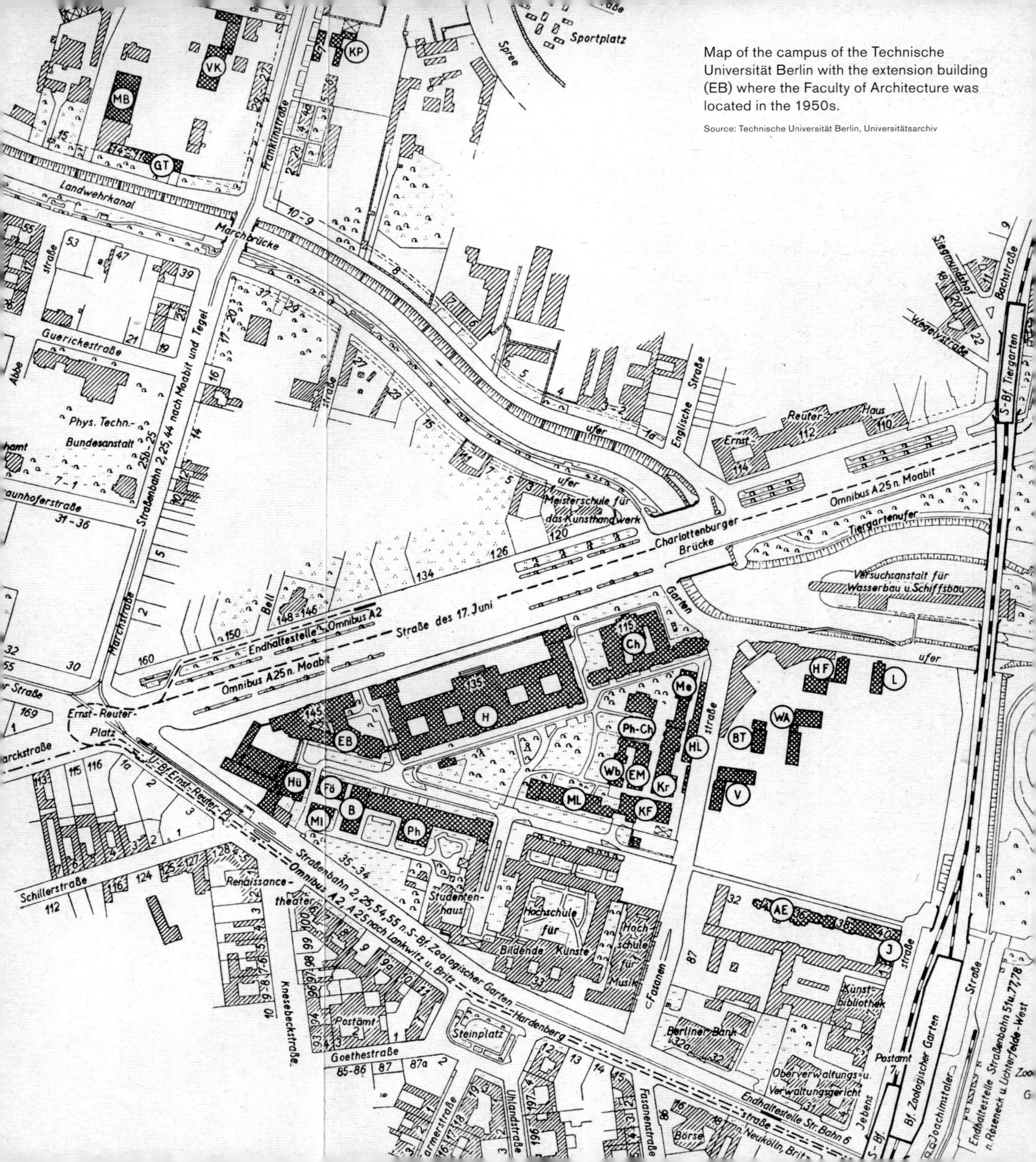

Map of the campus of the Technische Universität Berlin with the extension building (EB) where the Faculty of Architecture was located in the 1950s.

Source: Technische Universität Berlin, Universitätsarchiv

Studying in Postwar Germany
Moritz Henning

Exactly how many students came from Indonesia to study architecture in West Germany during the 1950s is unknown. One of the few available sources of data is a 1959 brochure published by the Indonesian embassy in Germany. In addition to 89 medical students, 44 students of nautical navigation, and 27 students of economics, 17 Indonesians studied architecture during the 1958–1959 winter semester.[1] We have been able to identify the majority of these architecture students: Han Awal (HAN Hoo Tjwan), Eddy Heryadie, Herianto Sulindro (KHO Lin Hek), Jan Beng Oei, King-Han Oei, Mustafa Pamuntjak, Po Hin Thung (THUNG Pohin), Hoemer Tjokrodiatmo, and Soejoedi Wirjoatmodjo studied in Berlin, while Bianpoen (LIEM Bian Poen) and Suwondo Bismo Sutedjo got their diplomas in Hanover. However, other students studied in the Federal Republic of Germany at this time or later, too.[2] For example, Yusuf Bilyarta Mangunwijaya, a well-known figure in Indonesian architectural history, studied architecture in Aachen from 1960 to 1966.

Taking a Roundabout Route to Germany

Some of these students had already studied in Indonesia for a few semesters, e.g., in Bandung, like Eddy Heryadie and Suwondo Bismo Sutedjo, and wanted to extend their knowledge abroad. However, the journey to Germany was not entirely by choice for some of them. Of the 12 architecture students, only Eddy Heryadie and Hoemer Tjokrodiatmo (and later Yusuf Bilyarta Mangunwijaya) seem to have come directly from Indonesia to Berlin. All the others came in a roundabout way. Indeed, although the new opportunities opened up by the country's independence were very appealing, the long-established colonial networks still held considerable sway. Since the 1920s, the Netherlands had been the preferred academic venue for a narrow Indonesian elite, and it remained so until the 1950s. However, what at first seemed like an obvious choice turned out to have grave consequences, as the students soon found themselves caught between the fronts of a protracted conflict. When the Dutch ceded sovereignty to Indonesia in 1949, Papua – now known as Western New Guinea – was omitted because the Netherlands was unwilling to relinquish all of its colonies. To avert a breakdown in negotiations, it was decided that the region, which covered approximately 420,000 square kilometres – more than ten times the size of the Netherlands – would remain under the administration of The Hague after 1949.

However, Indonesia was not prepared to accept this state of affairs indefinitely, and the dispute escalated. In 1954, Sukarno announced his intention to revoke the Netherlands-Indonesia Union,[3] and in 1957 Dutch companies in Indonesia were nationalised and Dutch nationals expelled. Conditions for Indonesian students in the Netherlands deteriorated as a result.[4] Many were subjected to veritable hate campaigns, and some were even expelled from the country.[5] As a result, many Indonesian students left the Netherlands, and among them were all the other architecture students from the 1950s about whom we were able to find information.

A Community Far from Home

Han Awal, Bianpoen, Mustafa Pamuntjak, Suwondo Bismo Sutedjo, and Soejoedi Wirjoatmodjo figure prominently in this group. These five shared similar origins and courses of study that brought them together at the Technische Hogeschool Delft in the Netherlands and then took them to Germany. Above and beyond that, they established ATAP (Indonesian for 'roof'), a loose discussion network of

1 Botschaft der Republik Indonesien (ed.), *Indonesien*, issue VII/11 (1959), p. 11.
2 We know of the following students in German universities at that time: the only woman Oei Giok Lan (1954, Germany), Harisanto (1955, Universität Stuttgart), H. A. Go Kian Dijen (1955, Technische Hochschule Karlsruhe), Lie Eng Hong (1961, Technische Universität Braunschweig), and Burhan Amongpradja (1962, Technische Hochschule Hanover).
3 The Netherlands-Indonesia Union established in 1949 was an attempt by the Netherlands, after independence had been granted, to retain close ties to its former colony, at least within the framework of a confederative union, and was in many ways the Dutch equivalent of the British Commonwealth.
4 West New Guinea was eventually placed under United Nations administration on 1 October 1962 in response to international pressure and transferred to Indonesia on 1 May 1963. In 1969, West New Guinea became part of Indonesia.
5 See Grimm, 2019, p. 24.

Indonesian students on the balcony of Eichkamp International Students' Hostel in Berlin circa 1959/1960. Herianto Sulindro (KHO Lin Hek) is on the far left; Jan Beng Oei is in the doorway at the back.

Photo: Private archive Linda Lochmann

Indonesian architecture and art students from Delft and Amsterdam in 1953, which can only be briefly mentioned here.[6] Its members shared a passion for modern architecture and saw the simplicity of Scandinavian modernism in particular as a model for architectural development in their home country.

ATAP existed until 1957 when most of its members were forced to leave Delft on account of the growing political tensions between Indonesia and the Netherlands. The aspiring Indonesian architects had to abandon their studies in the Netherlands and leave the country, driven by the political fallout from the colonial history of their homeland and the country where they were studying. The students compared the curricula of diverse European universities and decided on West Germany because the programmes were very similar to the one in Delft.[7]

Mustafa Pamuntjak and Soejoedi Wirjoatmodjo went to West Berlin to study at the Technical University (TU Berlin), where they were joined by Han Awal, who did not necessarily have to leave the Netherlands because he was not studying on a government scholarship. He was motivated more by the bonds of friendship – and by the fact that Hans Scharoun and Wilhelm Kreuer were teaching in Berlin.[8]

Other students also left the Netherlands: Po Hin Thung (who took a circuitous route via Rome, where he spent a year), Herianto Sulindro, Jan Beng Oei, and King-Han Oei moved to Berlin, too. A number of them settled in the same part of the city: King-Han Oei, Mustafa Pamuntjak, and Han Awal resided for a while together with their wives in the posh Grunewald district of Berlin, while other Indonesian students lived at Eichkamp International Students' Hostel. Meanwhile, Bianpoen and Suwondo Bismo Sutedjo went to Hanover.

Herianto Sulindro (KHO Lin Hek, with glasses) and Jan Beng Oei (second from right) in the badminton hall in Berlin.

Photo: Newspaper clipping. Private archive Linda Lochmann

6 For a more detailed discussion, see Herlambang, 2007, p. 97–107, and Kusno, 2013, p. 51ff.

7 Pamuntjak, 2017, p. 64.

8 Ibid., p. 64.

THE DIPL.-ING. DEGREE AT THE TECHNICAL UNIVERSITY OF BERLIN

At the time, architectural studies in West Germany concluded with the degree of Diplom-Ingenieur (Dipl.-Ing.), which was introduced in 1899. On 19 October, on the occasion of the centenary of the Royal Technical University of Charlottenburg (today's Technical University of Berlin), the academic degrees of Diplom-Ingenieur (Dipl.-Ing.) and Doktor der Ingenieurwissenschaften (Dr.-Ing.) were introduced at Prussian technical colleges and universities by order of the last German emperor, his Majesty Kaiser Wilhelm II, King of Prussia. In the years that followed, these degrees were subsequently introduced in technical colleges in other regions of the German Empire.

Germany's Diplom-Ingenieur (Dipl.-Ing.) degree is roughly the equivalent of a Master of Science degree or a graduate in engineering and is generally awarded after completing a five-year course of study at a technical college or university. Today, though, as a result of a Europe-wide process of standardisation of study programmes and degrees that culminated in the Bologna declaration in 1999, almost all universities have switched to bachelor's and master's degrees.

When the Indonesian students completed their degrees in Berlin, it was in accordance with the 'Provisional Framework Regulations for the Diploma Examinations of the Technical University of Berlin' (second version), supplemented by the 'Provisional Special Regulations for the Diploma Examinations of the Department of Architecture of the Technical University of Berlin' (second version) of 2 June 1956 and its amendment of 30 August 1960.

Accordingly, architectural studies were divided into five semesters of basic coursework leading up to the preliminary diploma examination (Diplom-Vorprüfung) and four semesters of advanced coursework leading up to the main diploma examination (Diplom-Hauptprüfung). In addition, students were given three months to complete their final projects. When registering for the preliminary diploma examination, students of architecture also had to show that they had completed a six-month internship. The examination consisted of a written exam and an oral exam on structural engineering and introductory design. In addition, oral examinations were given on the subjects of architectural history (ancient and medieval), descriptive geometry, perspective rendering, structural analysis and the strength of materials, installations, art history, building materials, and heating and ventilation. In addition, there was an extra assessment of practice work in the areas of free drawing and painting, sculptural design, construction management and operations, and surveying.

In the second phase of their studies, the compulsory subjects were urban and residential planning, technical structural engineering, design, and surveying of structures. The subject of design usually consisted of four large designs that the student could complete with different professors. Students were required to take at least four electives with a minimum of 16 hours per week in the following areas: special topics in structural analysis, building acoustics, specific areas of architectural history, landscape and garden design, agricultural construction, preservation of historical monuments and, if deemed necessary, specialised areas of architecture, free drawing and painting, sculptural design, and interior design.

The main diploma examination, for which one was allowed to register at the earliest in the fourth semester after the preliminary examination (starting in 1960: after two years), consisted of a final project, a written examination, and oral examinations in compulsory and elective subjects. The key component here was the development of a large-scale architectural design. This assignment was supervised by one of the design professors, whom the student was free to choose. The written exam, which could only be taken after the final project had been accepted, consisted of the completion of three assignments from the fields of design and building theory. Oral examinations were conducted in the compulsory subjects of building theory, urban and residential planning, technical structural engineering, (contemporary) history of architecture, and construction management and operations. In addition, there was a special assessment of practice work in the subject areas of design and surveying of structures, as well as examinations in the elective subject areas. Students were admitted to oral examinations only after passing the written exam.

The overall mark (grade) for the main diploma examination was calculated by combining the marks for the exercises, the oral examinations, and the final project. The final project and the exercises in design were given particular weight. Up to an average of 1.49, the overall score was: excellent, from 1.5 to 2.49: good, from 2.5 to 3.49: satisfactory, and beyond that: adequate.

Studying in Berlin with the Architects of Postwar Modernism

Of the nine students who received their degrees from the TU Berlin and whose work is documented, seven – among them Han Awal, Mustafa Pamuntjak und Soejoedi Wirjoatmodjo – graduated under Professor Wilhelm Kreuer, while two others graduated under Professor Kurt Dübbers (1905–1987), including Jan Beng Oei.

Kreuer and Dübbers had both already been teaching for many years and had distinguished themselves as architects. Kreuer had been at TU Berlin since 1949, first as a research assistant to Professor Gerhard Jobst, who had worked as an urban planner for the Dutch colonial administration in Jakarta between 1921 and 1928. Thanks to the exceptional support of Hans Scharoun, who established the Chair of Urban Planning at TU Berlin and held the position from 1946 to 1958,[9] Kreuer was appointed associate professor in 1951 and full professor one year later.

By the late 1950s, Wilhelm Kreuer had already produced an impressive body of work. The long list of his important contributions to West Berlin postwar modernism includes the America Memorial Library (1953),[10] the Department of Mining and Metallurgy building at TU Berlin (1956), Kreuzberg City Hall (1958), the Church of St. Ansgar (1958), and his urban design for the reconstruction of the war-ravaged Hansa Quarter (1953–1954, realised in a modified form)[11] for the Interbau international architectural exhibition in 1957.

9 Geist, 1993, p. 148.

10 With Prof. Gerhard Jobst, Hartmut Ville, Fritz Bornemann, Francis Keally, and Charles M. Morhardt.

11 With Gerhard Jobst and Wilhelm Schliesser.

Professor Willhelm Kreuer.

Photo: Archive Gerlind Gatza, undated

Technical University of Berlin, Faculty of Mining and Metallurgy, West Berlin. Architect: Wilhelm Kreuer, 1959.

Photo: Landesarchiv Berlin, F Rep. 290 Nr. 0068235 / Bert Sass

The America Memorial Library in West Berlin. Architects: Willhelm Kreuer with Fritz Bornemann, Gerhard Jobst, Hartmut Wille, 1954.

Photo: Landesarchiv Berlin, F Rep. 290 Nr. 0036259 / Horst Siegmann

St. Ansgar, West Berlin. Architect: Wilhelm Kreuer, 1957.

Photo: Postcard, collection of the author, undated

Competition for the Catholic Church Maria Regina Martyrium, West Berlin; perspective of the entrance side. Architect: Wilhelm Kreuer, 1959.

Photo: Staatliche Museen zu Berlin – Preußischer Kulturbesitz/ Kunstbibliothek

Professor Kurt Dübbers.

Photo: Technische Universität Berlin/Universitätsarchiv, Walter Steinbrink

Dübbers, who came from Dusseldorf, worked at TU Berlin from 1946 to 1971, serving as a professor for structural engineering and building design from 1950 onwards. Previously, he had worked as a research assistant and staff member under Paul Bonatz (1877–1956) at the Technical University of Stuttgart. His best-known work in Berlin is the new design for the TU Berlin main building (1960–1965), which had been destroyed during the Second World War.[12] The Schillerhöhe housing estate with 2,000 flats, built from 1953 to 1961 according to a plan by Dübbers,[13] also ranks among the landmark projects of West Berlin's postwar architecture.

12 With Karl-Heinz Schwennicke.
13 With Gerhard Krebs, Alfred Rahn, and Hans Schoszberger.

The new main building of the Technical University of Berlin. Architects: Kurt Dübbers and Karl-Heinz Schwennike, 1965.

Photo: Landesarchiv Berlin, F Rep. 290 Nr. 014 1920 / Karl-Heinz Schubert

In Paul Bonatz's office, Kurz Dübbers worked on the Willi Sachs Stadium in Schweinfurt, Germany, 1936, among other projects.

Image: Postcard, undated, Kunstanstalt Straub u. Fischer, photographer unknown

The Hahn-Meitner Institute for Nuclear Research. Architect: Kurt Dübbers, 1956–1965.

Photo: Collection of the author, photographer unknown

The Schillerhöhe housing estate, West Berlin, 1955 to 1961. Architects: Kurt Dübbers with Gerhard Krebs, Alfred Rahn, Hans Schoszberger.

Photo: Postcard, undated, Kunst und Bild, photographer unknown

Rational Functionalism and Free-form Architecture

The study of architecture in West Germany in the 1950s and 1960s was influenced by the legacy of the *Neues Bauen* movement (part of New Objectivity) from the 1920s and the notions of organic architecture developed by Hans Scharoun's circle in Berlin. This approach, embracing rational functionalism and a free-form architecture that engaged with landscapes and complexity, was also reflected in the teaching at TU Berlin and in the final theses and subsequent works of the students. Little is known about Professor Dübbers' teaching, but the classes under Professor Kreuer's Chair of Urban Planning were a 'haven for Scharoun admirers'.[14] The hub of this intense activity was the 'Kreuer Seminar', as the two department drawing rooms in the 1902 extension of the TU Berlin, where the Faculty of Architecture was located at the time, were called.

There, the students would design, draft, discuss, argue, and socialise. Student competitions were an important element

14 Redaktionsgruppe Kreuer 100, 2012, p. 219, p. 287.

The extension building (EB) of the Technical University from 1902, which housed the Faculty of Architecture in the 1950s.

Photo: Technische Universität Berlin, Universitätsarchiv, photographer unknown

of Kreuer's approach. During one-day, weekend, and end-of-semester contests, students honed their decision-making skills and prepared themselves for the world of professional competitions. The challenge of integrating the buildings into the urban environment played an essential role in the design, with the 'free floor plan' as the guiding principle.[15] Models of inspiration included Scharoun's spatial fantasies, Frank Lloyd Wright's freely flowing spaces, Le Corbusier, Dutch modernism, and Scandinavian architects like Alvar Aalto.[16] The 1957 Interbau international architectural exhibition in Berlin served as a direct source of ideas with structures by Pierre Vago, Oscar Niemeyer, Paul Baumgarten, Walter Gropius and The Architects' Collaborative (TAC), van den Broek and Bakema, Alvar Aalto, and many other architects from Germany and abroad. Field trips were another essential teaching element. In 1958, for example, they travelled to Rotterdam and to Brussels for the World's Fair. They travelled to Finland, as well as Britain, the USSR, and Poland in 1959 and 1966. Herianto Sulindro and King-Han Oei travelled with Herta Hammerbacher (1900–1985), the professor for landscape architecture and the first female professor at the architecture faculty, to visit the Bundesgartenschau (Federal Horticultural Show) in Cologne and Dortmund in 1959.

Unfortunately, we do not know which courses and in particular which design exercises beyond the diploma thesis the students attended. Nor do we know anything about the content of the lectures and exercises at the Faculty of Architecture at that time. Corresponding records neither exist at the TU Berlin nor could they be identified in the archives and inheritances of the architects. Only in the case of Soejoedi Wirjoatmodjo and Jan Beng Oei do we know that they also attended the seminars of Hans Scharoun, who taught urban planning and housing until the summer semester of 1959. However, the Indonesian students felt right at home at TU Berlin: 'The system and the way of studying in a friendly atmosphere transformed our anxiety when we arrived in Berlin into a sense of confidence that we could indeed complete our studies,' recalls Mustafa Pamuntjak.[17] Han Awal sums up the importance of German training in an interview in 2007: 'In the

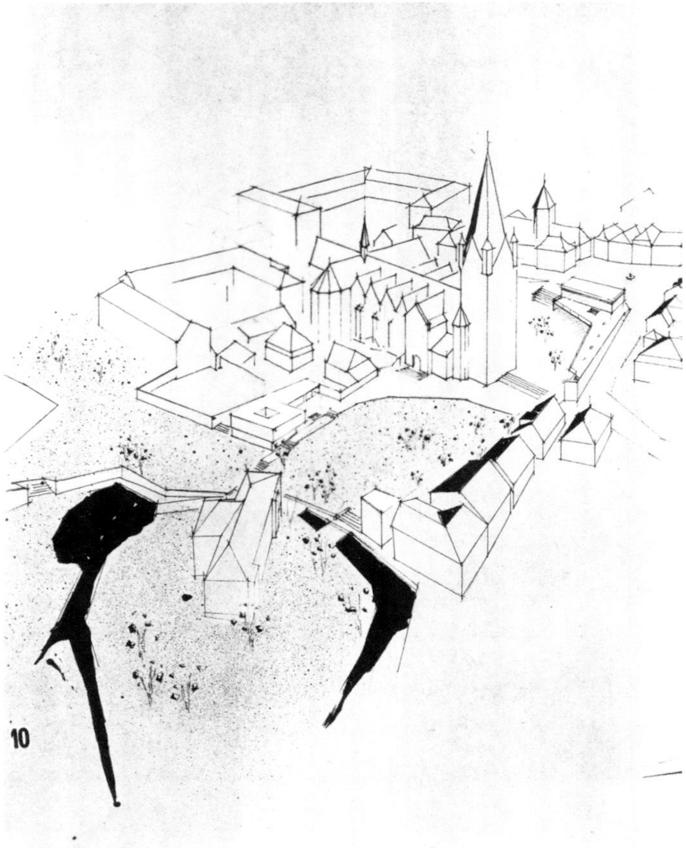
10

Netherlands, I learned a lot about architecture from a technical point of view. Perhaps because the country is so small, Dutch architects put great emphasis on precision. Even a centimetre difference in size is discussed. It was only in Germany that I learned about the big concepts of architecture.'[18]

Practical Experience in Berlin and Elsewhere

Besides their studies, the students learned on a practical level, too. As is the case today, it was common for students to complete internships in architectural firms or distinguish themselves in other ways. From Mustafa Pamuntjak, for example, we know that he worked in the office of West Berlin architect Herbert Noth (1907–1967) in 1959–1960. Soejoedi Wirjoatmodjo went to Freiburg in 1958 to work in

15 Ibid., p. 173.
16 Ibid., p. 172.
17 Pamuntjak, 2017, p. 67.
18 <http://tokohindonesia.com/ensiklopedi/h/han-awal/index.shtml> accessed 1 September 2022.

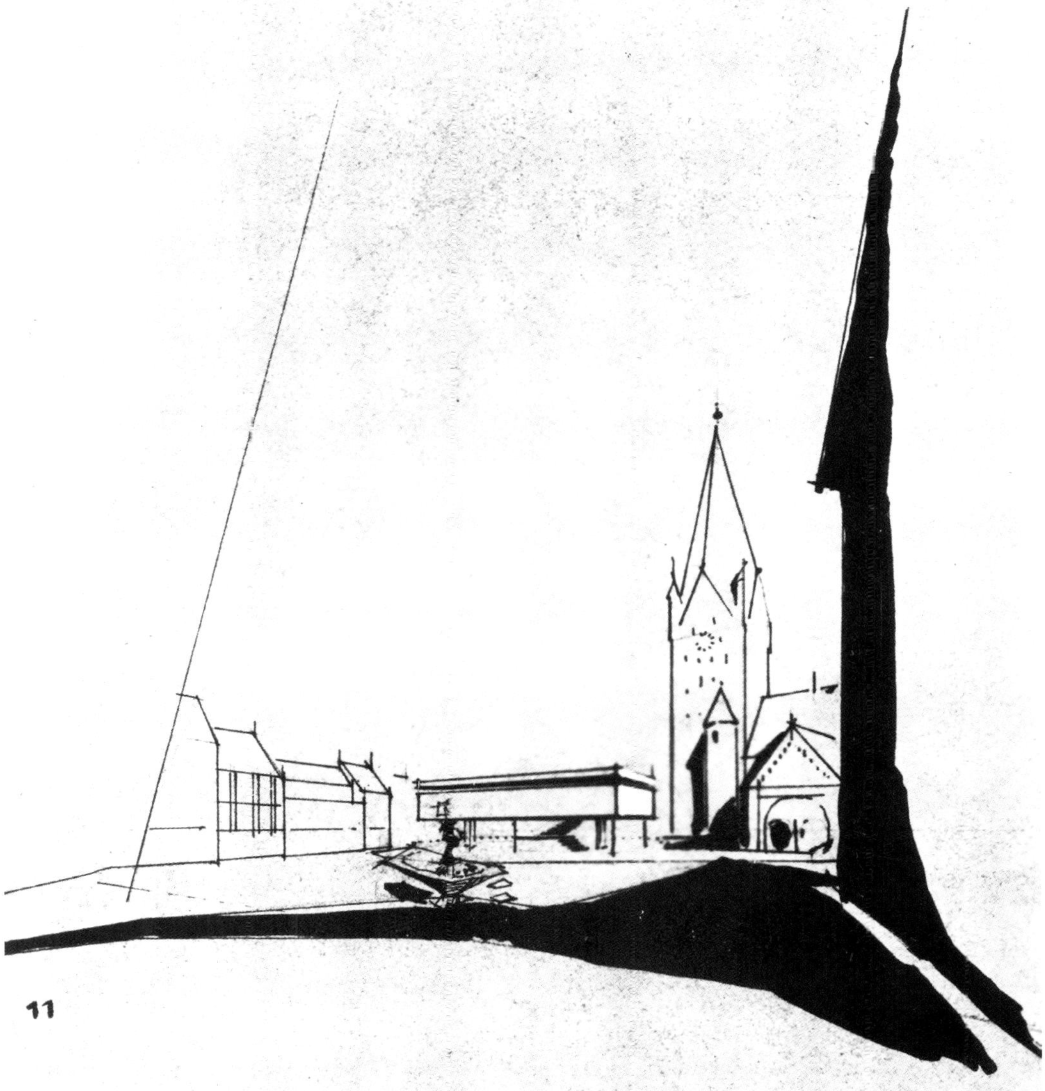

Mustafa Pamuntjak and King-Han Oei: Redesign of the surrounding area of the cathedral in Paderborn, competition entry, 1959.

Source: Stadt- und Kreisarchiv Paderborn, S – Fotosammlung

The huge new hospital in Berlin-Steglitz was planned in the office of Berlin architect Franz Mocken when Hoemar Tjokrodiatmo worked there after graduating.

Photo: Institut für Geschichte der Medizin und Ethik in der Medizin – Universitätsmedizin Charité

Herbert F. Kasper's architectural firm. Hoemar Tjokrodiatmo won third prize in a Germany-wide student competition for building products manufacturer Eternit in 1959,[19] and Mustafa Pamuntjak collaborated with King-Han Oei in a competition to redesign the surroundings of the cathedral in Paderborn. In addition, some of the students gained further practical experience in Germany after completing their studies. For instance, Hoemar Tjokrodiatmo spent some time working with Berlin architect Franz Mocken on hospital, office, and housing projects, while Mustafa Pamuntjak worked with his former teacher Wilhelm Kreuer until 1961.[20] Soejoedi Wirjoatmodjo went to Dusseldorf to work for Hentrich & Petschnigg, one of the most successful architectural firms in West Germany at the time. Bianpoen, who studied in Hanover, gained experience there in the urban planning office after graduation and before returning to Indonesia.

Some of the Indonesian architects later returned to Germany, at least temporarily. Tjokrodiatmo, for example, stayed in Berlin again between 1968 and 1974[21] and Eddy Heryadie,

19 Student competition 'Eternit am Bau', Baumeister 3, 1959, p. 214.

20 Following his CV, Pamuntjak worked on a project for the Departments of Physics and Chemistry at the University of Cologne and a NATO Operational Building.

21 Trisnawati, 1990, p. 6–7.

who became the head of the Bandung Urban Planning Office after returning to Indonesia, travelled to Braunschweig in December 1964 at the invitation of the German Academic Exchange Service. The first town twinning between an Indonesian and a German city was initiated in 1960 with Bandung twinned with Braunschweig. Heryadie worked with the Braunschweig city planning department in December 1964, the Berlin planning department in January 1965, and then spent another month at the one in Dusseldorf.[22]

Four of the 12 young Indonesian architects discussed here did not return to Indonesia for their professional careers. After graduation, Jan Beng Oei worked first with Hans Scharoun and then with Chen Kuen Lee (1915–2003) before successfully establishing his own firm. King-Han Oei became a partner in the Cologne architectural firm of Heier Monse and Partner. Herianto Sulindro worked in Hamburg until end of 1963. In 1964, he went to Zurich in Switzerland and worked as a civil servant in the city administration until he retired in 1993. Meanwhile, he also worked freelance and designed a number of houses in Locarno and Ascona. Po Hin Thung worked in various positions and functions from the Netherlands in development aid in Asia, Africa, and South America. The others went on to start a new chapter in their lives back in Indonesia.

22 Letters, 8 Dec. 1964, 22 Dec. 1964, 25 Jan 1965, Braunschweig City Archives, Files of the Office for Council Affairs (E 15: 162.1, 238).

The Dreischeibenhaus by Düsseldorf architects Hentrich and Petschnigg was completed in 1960, when Soejoedi Wirjoatmodjo joined the office.

Image: hpp, AERO Foto A. Schwarzer, Mönchengladbach, undated

A model of the Dreischeibenhaus by the Düsseldorf architects Hentrich and Petschnigg was presented at the International Building Exhibition in Berlin in 1957.

Photo: Manfred Niermann, CC BY 4.0

Po Hin Thung's PhD (1993) was published by the Technische Universiteit Eindhoven.

Image: Technische Universiteit Eindhoven

12. Sep. 1962
Professor Rudolf Hillebrecht
41 247
41 248
41 249
41 250
41 251
41 252
41 253
41 254
41 255

Reconstruction in Hanover
Eduard Kögel

Reconstruction in Hanover

In the 1950s, Hanover was considered a model city for post-war reconstruction. About 90 per cent of the city centre had been destroyed in October 1943. Many German cities lay in ruins after the Second World War, yet no other West German city was so rigorous in setting new standards in the redevelopment of transport infrastructure, parks, and public spaces, outlining a new land policy that prioritised public over private concerns.

As part of the political reorganisation of western Germany, Hanover became the capital of the newly created state of Lower Saxony. Accompanying this new role was a desire to transform the design of the city, which in 1947 had about 380,000 inhabitants. By 1961, the population had grown to 574,000; since then, this number has stagnated as residents have moved to the surrounding areas.[1] The Exportmesse trade fair was launched in 1947 to boost the economy and compete with the trade fair in Leipzig. Located in the Soviet sector of divided Germany, Leipzig became a hub for trade between the Eastern and Western Blocs.

Rudolf Hillebrecht (1910–1999) was the driving force behind Hanover's development. As the city's planning director from 1948, Hillebrecht implemented the details of the urban redevelopment concept for Hanover with passion, winning over citizens and politicians alike. As early as 1951, Hanover staged the Constructa building exhibition to present new solutions for urban development and housing construction. That same year, the city hosted the first edition of the Federal Garden Show (*Bundesgartenschau*), putting on a public showcase of the first concepts for a new urban landscape.

1 In 2020, the city had 534,000 inhabitants. See <https://www.macrotrends.net/cities/204343/hannover/population> accessed 23 September 2022.

Hanover inner city after the war in 1945.

Photo: Margaret Bourke-White (USAAF)

Hanover railway station after the air raids, 1945.

Photo: Margaret Bourke-White (USAAF)

Portrait series Rudolf Hillebrecht, 12 September 1962.

Photo: SLUB Dresden, Deutsche Fotothek, Fritz Eschen

The new, modern Hanover was also proudly presented at the Constructa building exhibition in 1951.

Source: Cruses Buchhandlung Hannover, photographer unknown

'The Miracle of Hanover': Rudolf Hillebrecht on the cover of the magazine.

Source: DER SPIEGEL 23/1959

In 1956, the Swiss architecture journal *Bauen + Wohnen* dedicated a special issue to Hanover's reconstruction. According to the editors: 'We chose Hanover because, in our opinion, in no other German city has it been possible to carry out such a positive and large-scale reconstruction from the structurally horrible state in which it was at the end of the war. Nowhere else have such far-reaching planning ideas become effectuated. It may be a case of luck but we are more inclined to believe that it is the personal achievement of an energetic and often consciously rigorous man, the spiritus rector of the entire building activity in Hanover in the years after 1945.'[2] The 'guiding spirit' was planning director Rudolf Hillebrecht, to whom the weekly magazine *Der Spiegel* devoted a major article in 1959, titled 'The Miracle of Hanover'.[3] In more than 400 meetings held with local citizens, the city's planning director convinced numerous Hanoverians to sell or trade in their properties so the city could implement its transport plan. The historic street layout, which radiated from the city centre, was overhauled and transformed into a grid.

2 'Hannover', Editorial, Bauen + Wohnen, Special Cities Issue Hanover/Basle, 10/1956, German version p. 325, English version no page number, translator unknown.
3 'Das Wunder von Hannover', Der Spiegel, 23/1959, p. 61–63, 66, 68.

A Swiss critic wrote about the traffic plan for Hanover: 'What does the current development plan entail? 1. All federal highways will be routed tangentially past the city centre, preventing passenger vehicles and especially heavy vehicles that do not have their destination directly in the city centre from driving through the city centre. 2. A very wide inner-city ring will encircle the city centre. 3. High-capacity radial (feeder) roads will connect the tangents with the city ring.'[4]
Hanover was to become a 'transit-friendly city', creating ideal conditions for both public and individual traffic. According to Hillebrecht: 'Cars can be used for recreation if people enjoy driving them'.[5] From today's perspective, however, he has been criticised for taking a 'one-sided, motorist's point of view', creating only a car-friendly city instead of a transit-friendly city.[6]

Architects as Co-designers of a New City

A number of architects contributed significantly to the city's reconstruction. After opening his architectural practice in 1951, Friedrich Lindau (1915–2007) designed several landmark administrative buildings. He later also wrote about architecture and urban development.[7] As head of the Hanover State Building Department, Paul Wolters (1913–1998) was responsible for several outstanding public buildings, including the Chamber of Agriculture and the Le Corbusier-inspired Church of St. Adalbert. Dieter Oesterlen (1911–1994) gained widespread attention for his design of a new nave for St. Martin's Church in 1957, which had been entirely destroyed in the war except for the church tower.[8] He also designed a modern extension for the war-damaged Leineschloss palace, built from 1956 to 1962. The building still serves as the state parliament building today. Oesterlen later wrote: 'It was a good idea on the part of the state parliament and the city to take on the ruins of the Leineschloss, saving the architectural monument from certain decay (see the demolition of the castle in Brunswick in 1960), filling it with new life, and connecting the past with the present.'[9]

New Beginnings at the Technische Hochschule

The Technische Hochschule (TH) in Hanover (now Leibniz University) also had to be rebuilt in the 1950s. In 1960, the makeshift repaired building of the architecture department, a former industrial printing plant from the late-nineteenth century, had to accommodate 532 students, and the space was tight.[10] In 1961, newly appointed Professor Friedrich Spengelin (1925–2016) and his assistant Horst Wunderlich were commissioned to design an additional floor and a new roof for the building – located across the street from the Continental high-rise (1956) designed by Ernst Zinsser (1904–1985), which became part of the university in 1995.

The architecture faculty was composed of architects and planners who also ran their practices on campus until the late 1950s, and their work shaped the new cityscape.[11] Ernst Zinsser, the brother-in-law of West Germany's first chancellor, Konrad Adenauer (1876–1967), taught design and building science there starting in 1947, and realised many notable projects in the following years.[12] In 1956, Zinsser redesigned the atrium of the former Welfenschloss palace, which served as the university's main building and had suffered considerable damage during the war. It became one of the university's main event venues and is still in use as such today.[13] Wilhelm Wortmann (1897–1995) joined the university in 1956 as a professor of urban planning, housing, and regional planning. He developed the city's land-use plan in 1950–1951 and subsequently dealt with the concept of the regional city, which became a central aspect of Hanover's development.[14] City planning director Rudolf Hillebrecht was named an honorary professor in 1951, and it can be assumed that he addressed urban planning issues from the city in his teaching. Ernst Zietzschmann (1907–1991), the Swiss architect and editor-in-chief of the Zurich magazine *Bauen + Wohnen*, became the director of the Werkkunstschule (School of Applied Arts) in Hanover in 1958 and designed its new main building. Zietzschmann was also active at

4 Zietzschmann, 1962, p. 61–65.
5 Dorn, 2017, p. 286f.
6 Zalewski, 2006, p. 92.
7 Lindau, 1998; Lindau, 2001.
8 Oesterlen, 1958, p. 378.
9 Oesterlen, 1964, p. 79.

10 Spengelin, 2003, p. 251.
11 Haas, 2000, p. 41.
12 Ibid.
13 Ibid., p. 115.
14 Gerken (ed.), 2006, p. 569.

the TH Hanover, where he lectured on modernism. His topics included architectural developments in Switzerland, Japan, and England, and the work of Le Corbusier.[15] The sociologist Hans Paul Bahrdt (1918–1994) was an associate professor of urban and regional sociology from 1959 to 1962. In his seminal book from 1961, *Die moderne Großstadt* ('The Modern City'), he argued that social and societal considerations should be integrated into the development of new cities and settlements.[16]

15 Ibid., p. 580.
16 Bahrdt, 1961.

Top
The former printing plant of J. C. Koenig and Ebhard Company was used by the Faculty of Architecture of the University Hanover. In 1961, an additional floor and a new roof for the building were added.

Photo: Christian Schroeder CC BY-SA 3.0

Bottom
The new atrium in the former Welfenschloss palace designed by Ernst Zinsser in 1956.

Photo: Christian A. Schröder CC BY-SA 4.0

Welfenschloss Hanover between 1890 and 1900.

Source: CC

The former Welfenschloss palace as the main building of the university in Hanover in 1957.

Photo: Gerd Breternitz (1927–2001), source Annika Breternitz CC BY-SA 4.0

The Continental Hochhaus in Hanover, built in 1953, was the tallest high-rise in West Germany at the time. Architect: Ernst Zinsser.

Source: Postcard, photographer unknown, undated

The new, car-friendly Hanover around Königsworther Platz, with the Continental Hochhaus, 1960.

Photo: Bildarchiv Region Hannover, Heinz Koberg. Signatur: ARH NL Koberg 147

The new city centre of Hanover in 1961.

Photo: Bildarchiv Region Hannover, ARH NL Koberg 164, Heinz Koberg

Bianpoen in Hanover.

Photo: Suwondo Family Archive

Bianpoen (left), Carla (his wife), and friends in Hanover.

Photo: Suwondo Family Archive

Suwondo in Hanover.

Photo: Suwondo Family Archive

Bianpoen (centre) in the newly designed atrium at TH Hanover.

Photo: Suwondo Family Archive

Indonesian Students in Lower Saxony

While most of the Indonesian students chose to study at the Technical University (TU) in West Berlin after leaving Delft, Suwondo Bismo Sutedjo[17] and Bianpoen[18] went to the TH Hanover, graduating in 1961. Bianpoen chose Hanover because it was considered the most devasted city after the war, but also the city that recovered the fastest in terms of urban development. Another reason for him to choose Hanover was its proximity to his fiancée in Münster.

Bianpoen commenced his studies at the Technische Hogeschool in Delft in 1951. His class included Han Awal and Herman Hertzberger (b. 1932), who later became a leading exponent of structuralism.[19] Bianpoen graduated with a degree in architecture (Dipl.-Ing.) from Hanover in March 1961 and worked at the city's planning department under Rudolf Hillebrecht until 1962 when he returned to Indonesia. Upon returning to Indonesia, Bianpoen and Suwondo were heavily involved in teaching. They also worked as planning consultants and penned articles about architectural and urban development, and designed several buildings. Bianpoen received his PhD in economics from Erasmus University in Rotterdam in 1983. His dissertation focused on the economic foundations of Jakarta's urban development and the living conditions of the poor in the city's informal *kampung* settlements.[20]

17 Roeder, 1980, p. 336f.
18 Setyautama (ed.), 2008), p. 193–194.
19 Jaarboek van de Technische Hogeschool te Delft, 1951, p. 65.
20 Bianpoen, 1983.

The Concept of the Regional City

In Hanover in the early 1960s, city planning director Hillebrecht coordinated a 'team of 100 to 120 planners, engineers, and architects from the city planning department, the civil engineering department, and the department for drainage, horticulture, and surveying' who, in addition to overhauling the traffic infrastructure, were increasingly interested in the idea of the polycentric regional city.[21] During these years, Bianpoen worked in the Hanover administration and was undoubtedly exposed to those ideas. Starting around 1960, the structural change in the region became clearly visible, as residents moved to the surrounding villages and small towns and commuted to their jobs by car. The planners sought new tools to guide urban and regional development in response – an experience that may have influenced Bianpoen's later ideas for the development of Jakarta.[22]

21 Zietzschmann, 1962, p. 65.
22 Dorn, 2017, p. 268.

If the students from Hanover wanted to visit their friends in Berlin, they had to cross the Soviet sector.

Photo: Bundesregierung, Gert Schütz

Jalan Thamrin, Jakarta, was developed as a major thoroughfare from the 1950s on. Buildings along the street were required to be minimum of five stories high.

Photo: Nationaal Museum van Wereldculturen, Boy Lawson, 1971, CC BY 4.0

Interweavings – 77 Years of Architecture, Politics, and Economy in Indonesia

Setiadi Sopandi

A Steep, Long, and Winding Road

With the proclamation of independence on 17 August 1945, Indonesia embarked on a turbulent journey that did not end until the resignation of Indonesia's second president, Soeharto (1921–2008), in May 1998. The rollercoaster ride started right after the end of the Second World War with a direct confrontation with the British-led Allied forces and the Dutch military. Immediately after the proclamation of independence, Jakarta fell to the Allied forces and was occupied by the Dutch civil administration, forcing the Indonesian Republican leaders to move to Yogyakarta. Following two military offensives by the Dutch (in 1947 and 1948), the Netherlands and Indonesia undertook lengthy mediated negotiations that led to the transfer of sovereignty to Indonesia by the end of 1949.

The price of sovereignty was high, while the path to independence was steep. Indonesia had to sustain a chaotic monetary and economic situation. In the bitter agreement of 1949, Indonesia was declared responsible for the costs of the two offensives launched by the Dutch. In addition, the country had to return all Dutch pre-war production assets and therefore had to work hard to endure a lengthy nationalisation process. Dutch private firms returned and continued their operations under the new circumstances.

The monetary disorder was eliminated by a 'cut' to end the circulation of various banknotes. In 1950, the government issued a programme for citizens to surrender half of their old banknotes in exchange for the new legal currency. Indonesia also went through a process of nationalising De Javasche Bank – the colonial central bank for the Dutch East Indies – into the Bank of Indonesia in 1953 and established state-owned banks to kickstart the economy.

Succumbing to Authoritarianism

The country held the first liberal and democratic general election in 1955. Despite its apparent democratic success, the election failed to form solid political coalitions. With no apparent dominant political coalition, the fractured parliament was unable to form a constitution and a stable government. Amid this overwhelming crisis, Indonesia also faced intensifying tensions with the Netherlands over the unresolved territory of Papua. To make the situation even more complicated, the rising separatist movements were often supported by foreign intervention, especially by contesting Cold War powers.

Official portrait of President Sukarno, 1949.

Photo: wikimedia commons

This situation led to a fundamental political shift towards the end of the 1950s, which gave birth in 1957 to the idea of 'guided democracy' – a quasi-democratic authoritarian government shaped by President Sukarno (1901–1970). This had a snowballing effect of national disintegration, intensified friction among ideological factions, and sparked division among the armed forces. In this seemingly problematic situation, Sukarno took the opportunity to overhaul the political system. He turned the tide to his advantage by riding on the growing wave of nationalism and anti-Dutch sentiment. The call for continuing revolution and mass mobilisation in his fiery speeches garnered support for his vision.

By the end of the 1950s, Indonesian political factions were divided into several unbridged strongholds: the nationalists, the Islamists, the communists, and the military. President Sukarno dismissed all members of parliament on 5 July 1959 and appointed a new body that favoured his policies. He formed a non-party entity in the parliament filled with his supporters, bypassing the opposing factions. He gave the military the legitimacy to crush separatist movements and launch radical anti-Dutch demonstrations and offensives, which the communists highly endorsed. In doing so, President Sukarno established a fragile triumvirate – Sukarno, the military, and the communists – which paved his way to authoritarianism. He established a socialist-style administration and launched a centralised system of 'guided economy', enabling him to exercise almost absolute power.

In late 1957, as tensions over the status of Papua increased, mass demonstrations took place in Jakarta fuelled by President Sukarno's rhetoric. The angry mobs took to the streets, occupying and seizing Dutch-owned firms and production facilities. This escalated to the expulsion of 46,000 Dutch nationals from the country, followed by Indonesia's offensives against the Dutch occupation force in Papua in the following years. The late 1950s was also the culmination of long-standing armed conflicts between the Indonesian government and regional separatist rebellious forces. The USA-backed Revolutionary Government in Sumatra and Sulawesi were defeated in 1958. The Islamic states in West Java and Aceh were dissolved in 1962. This momentum solidified the military and helped to put it in an advantageous political position.

On the other hand, closer ties between President Sukarno and the communists irritated the military. Sukarno supported the communists' anti-Western agenda by condemning Western pop music, praising the Soviet one-party system, and allowing radical propaganda by communist organisations. The communists condemned liberal artistic expression in fine arts and literature and did not hesitate to persecute artists and authors who were not considered 'revolutionaries'.

Building the Capital

President Sukarno had been deeply fascinated with the idea of using architecture and urban planning to elevate the country's morale. The re-establishment of Jakarta as the capital after independence and the creation of new governmental institutions inspired him to initiate architectural design competitions in the 1950s. Fuelled by nationalism and anti-colonial sentiment, he launched competitions for the design of the central bank, national monument, and national mosque – all located in the precinct of the former colonial civic centre, renamed Medan Merdeka, literally 'freedom square'. All three buildings were designed by the architect Friedrich Silaban (1912–1984), who eventually became Sukarno's most trusted hand for architectural considerations. Sukarno also requested several other plots of land surrounding the square and ordered the construction of a highway leading to the satellite town of Kebayoran Baru, which was to be developed as a modern business district. Silaban became a leading figure on the architectural scene and was personally commissioned by Sukarno to design dozens of institutional buildings in Jakarta and other major cities.

In addition to the three award-winning projects above, Silaban was commissioned to revise the appearance of the Medan Merdeka through several other unrealised projects, like the National Theatre and the Ministry of Foreign Affairs. In addition, he was commissioned to design the West Papua Liberation Monument (1962), Banteng Hotel (1962, unfinished), the Gedung Pola (1965), the air force headquarters (1961), Bank Nasional Indonesia (1963), and several other projects throughout the capital.

The massive construction activity aligned with Jakarta's preparations to host the 4th Asian Games in 1962. By 1958, a series of major architectural infrastructure projects had been

Bank Indonesia, Jakarta.
Architect: Friedrich Silaban.

Photo: F. Silaban Archive, arsitekturindonesia.org, undated

Bank National Indonesia.
Architect: Friedrich Silaban.

Photo: F. Silaban Archive, arsitekturindonesia.org, undated

Gelora Bung Karno, main stadium. Stamp issued by the Government of the Republic of Indonesia in 1962.

Source: wikimedia commons

initiated to support the grand event. The Soviet Union provided architectural and engineering services as well as loans for building the project, effectively strengthening its influence over Indonesia.

The heart of the project was the multisport event complex Gelora Bung Karno (GBK), occupying a trapezoidal area of 350 hectares. The crown jewel in the middle of the complex is the main stadium, with a monumental, sheltered capacity of 110,000 spectators. There are also various other sports facilities, such as an indoor stadium, aquatic stadium, open-air hockey pitch and athletics court, the main tennis stadium, a basketball stadium, three open-air tennis courts, and an open practice court. The first Indonesian radio and television station (supported by Japanese expertise), an international athlete village, and a parking area were also built.

Hotel Indonesia, Jakarta, 1971.

Source: naar fotocollectie, Joost Evers, CC0 1.0

Regarded as more than a cherry on top, President Sukarno invited the Danish-American architect Abel Sørensen (1915–1982) and his wife Wendy Becker to design the country's first tall building, the Hotel Indonesia, right in the middle of the new highway between Jakarta and the Asian Games complex. In front of the hotel, a roundabout and a monumental sculpture were erected to welcome the 1962 Asian Games delegates. Serving as landmarks, several similarly styled sculptures were erected in nodes along the new major roads. Hotel Indonesia was among several large architectural projects fully funded by Japanese war reparations.[1]

At the same time, with help from the USA, Indonesia built a flyover intersection and a section of Jakarta's first ring road. The Semanggi intersection – right at the northern corner of the GBK – forms a node on the city's north-south axis with the new east-west ring road. The east ring road provides access to Tanjung Priok, Jakarta's harbour. The construction of the ring road offered new opportunities for expansion, and new residential, commercial, and industrial districts with a water treatment plant were developed.

Until 1965, dozens of large-scale architectural commissions throughout Jakarta were initiated by President Sukarno. The interplay between architectural spectacles and politics surprised global spectators as well as Indonesians, not only because of their sheer monumentality and scale but also because of their presence amid the country's alarming economic situation.

Semanggi interchange.

Source: Department of Information, Indonesian Police, Jakarta, 1976

A Need for Architects and Engineers

Due to the rising demand for engineers and architects, Indonesia urgently needed engineering schools throughout the country. Until 1959, there was only one engineering (and architecture) school – the former Universitas Indonesia, now Institut Teknologi Bandung – for the whole country. Engineers (and architects) belonged to a highly regarded profession essential to nation-building. Roosseno Soerjohadikoesoemo (1908–1996) – nicknamed 'Indonesia's father of concrete' – and Soetami (1928–1980) were highly decorated figures, both serving as ministers and in other important roles in several institutions. Most architectural services were still offered by a handful of architects and engineers trained in Bandung or abroad – or by graduates of technical vocational schools. The second architecture school was established in 1960 as part of Universitas Katolik Parahyangan in Bandung. By 1962, Universitas Gajah Mada in Yogyakarta and Universitas Tarumanagara in Jakarta were established. Universitas Indonesia began offering an architectural programme in 1964. The architectural courses were modelled after the tradition set in Bandung and the Technische Hogeschool Delft in the Netherlands, which put architectural studies under the faculty of engineering. Despite the relative autonomy in the profession – the Indonesian Institute of Architects was established in 1959 – many aspects of architects' work were closely related to engineering issues. This meant that the group of young architects that returned from Germany in the early 1960s – Soejoedi Wirjoatmodjo (1928–1981), Han Awal (1930–2016), Bianpoen (1930–2020), Suwondo Bismo Soetedjo (1928–2019), Hoemar Tjokrodiatmo (1931–2019), Mustafa Pamuntjak (1932–2020), Eddy Heryacie (b. 1931), and Yusuf Bilyarta Mangunwijaya (1929–1999) – arrived just in time to satisfy the growing demand for architectural projects and educational institutions.

1 The Japanese military invaded the British and Dutch colonies in Southeast Asia during the Second World War and set up a military government in Indonesia from 1942 to 1945.

Global Politics

President Sukarno made Indonesia a very active player in global politics. After successfully establishing the Asian-African Conference in Bandung in 1955, Indonesia became a vocal advocate of the anti-imperialist cause. However, Indonesia was developing an ambivalent attitude towards the global superpowers of the USA, the Soviet Union, and the People's Republic of China. This stance put Indonesia in the hot seat on several occasions.
During the 4th Asian Games in Jakarta, the authorities refused to issue visas for Israeli and Taiwanese delegations following pressure from Arab countries and China. This act prompted the International Olympic Committee to sanction Indonesia and deny its participation in the 1964 Olympic Games in Tokyo.
Indonesia put up an armed confrontation in response to the formation of the Federation of Malaya between 1963 and 1966. Indonesian leaders considered the British involvement in its establishment as a new form of imperialism, and China and the Soviet Union supported this confrontative attitude. When the United Nations welcomed Malaysia as a non-permanent member of the UN Security Council, Sukarno took this as an insult to Indonesia. The state immediately resigned from the UN and formed a counter-body called the Conference of New Emerging Forces (CONEFO).
In the heat of the moment and with funding support from CONEFO member countries China and the United Arab Emirates, Indonesia planned to construct the CONEFO assembly hall in the precinct of the GBK in Jakarta. In 1964, an architecture competition was announced, and in a relatively short time, a proposal by Soejoedi Wirjoatmodjo in collaboration with civil engineer Sutami (1928–1980) was selected. Sukarno appointed the Minister of Public Works and Energy, Soeprajogi, to manage the CONEFO building project, and he ran the project like a military operation.
The CONEFO building was to be inaugurated on 17 August 1966 – a short timeline for a project that was not only large in scale but also the first of its kind in Indonesia. All available architects and engineers, as well as students from the Institut Teknologi Bandung were brought together to work on the project. The labour-intensive construction showed its first results one year before the deadline. However, the unstable political situation in 1965 erupted into a coup in October, creating uncertainty in many plans, including this project.

Economic Catastrophe

The chaotic political situation in the 1950s already had severe consequences for the national economic situation. Despite modest growth until 1959, Indonesia experienced a dramatic crisis in the first half of the 1960s. Poor rainfall in Java in the early 1960s resulted in low rice production. The military and communist factions had poorly managed the seized former Dutch companies, which led to a sharp decline in output in the manufacturing and service sectors. This was worsened by deteriorating infrastructure and the decline of the Indonesian currency, leaving industry unable to import raw materials and equipment. The government made a further mistake by granting the elite exclusive import rights, which led to widespread corruption and even higher import costs. The poor governance directly resulted in declining investment and a deep deficit. By 1966, the government printed 800 times more bank notes than in 1955, and inflation rates had risen to 600 per cent. Finally, the government had to accept that the Indonesian currency could no longer be maintained and had to be devaluated.

Official portrait of President Soeharto, 1978.

Photo: wikimedia commons

The economic catastrophe culminated in the alleged coup, which remains a murky mystery until now. The assassination of seven high army officials on the eve of 1 October 1965 led to a widespread anti-communist purge and terror throughout the country over the next several months. It was probably the bloodiest event in Indonesia's recent history. Students took to the streets in mass demonstrations, demanding that the government persecute the Indonesian Communist Party and take action to lower the skyrocketing inflation. The chaos also produced collateral damage to the Chinese communities seen as the culprit for the economic disaster. President Sukarno was quickly losing legitimacy, and his communist supporters were persecuted by the military, who took full advantage of the turn of events. Soeharto, a high-ranking army general, acted swiftly to restore order in Jakarta, taking a pivotal role in the crisis and coming out as the acting-President after March 1966 and establishing the New Order government (1966–1998).

New Order

By 1966, Indonesia had embarked on a massive economic restoration programme. The country faced a foreign debt of 530 million USD. Amid declining export earnings, it had to reschedule its debt payments. In addition, it needed a massive financial injection in the form of grants and loans. This required strategies to lower inflation, accelerate economic growth and reduce government spending. The anti-communist New Order government, firmly led by Soeharto, turned to Western countries for aid and investment. The administration dismissed the old generation of economists and installed US-trained staff. They proposed a monetary and production policy approach. The government was to enforce its fiscal and monetary policies and consult continually with international organisations like the International Monetary Fund and the World Bank. The bitter pill eventually led to a modest improvement in the country in the following years. However, in order to strictly level the inflation rate, the government had to curb economic growth and money supply. These measures caused banks to limit loans and effectively held back productivity in the private sector. There were also significant drawbacks due to the chaotic conditions in ports and railways. Frustration among the populace led to sporadic protests and violent attacks against the Chinese minority.

Soeharto was designated acting president in 1968. By then, the new government had gained firm control of the political situation, and after a decade of declining living standards, economic improvements were being felt. The gross national product grew rapidly and persistently, with the agricultural sector contributing the most, closely followed by the trade sector.

The transition period ended in 1969 and was immediately followed by the first five-year development plan (Rencana Pembangunan Lima Tahun), which was fully funded by foreign loans. One of the most significant economic moves by the New Order government was the nationalisation of the oil and gas extraction industry. The merger of two national oil companies in 1968 created Perusahaan Pertambangan Minyak dan Gas Bumi Negara (Pertamina) – the national oil and gas industry that holds a monopoly on the trade.

Indonesia, through Pertamina, benefited from the global oil boom of the 1970s, which boosted the national economy dramatically. During the early 1970s, Pertamina grew to become the wealthiest and most powerful company in the country. By 1981, Indonesia became the world's largest liquid petroleum gas producer. Apart from oil and gas-related companies, Pertamina owned various other businesses in the health, housing, telecommunication, agriculture, steel, and cement sectors.

During the years of the oil boom, the Indonesian economy grew miraculously. In Jakarta and other big cities, there was a building boom: tall office buildings, hotels, residential development, and commercial establishments mushroomed.

Between 1976 and 1988, Indonesia also achieved immense success in agriculture, education, and healthcare. In the early 1980s, it succeeded in reducing rice imports to almost zero and became self-sufficient in rice. Literacy among the population increased despite the rural-urban divide. Indonesian family planning was one of the best population control programmes in the world. Despite the success, the authoritarian government became even stronger and allowed no opposition or criticism. The media and political opponents were silenced and persecuted, while elections were generally rigged in Soeharto's favour. Corruption was deeply instilled in every vein of the bureaucratic system. Several major bloody incidents in 1975, 1982, 1984, and 1985 reflected the New Order's repressive approach.

Construction Boom

In 1971, in anticipation of the new surge in construction, Indonesia released new regulations and standards for reinforced concrete buildings. Until the early 1970s, there were only two cement plants in the entire country: Indarung, West Sumatera; and Gresik, East Java. By 1971, a third plant opened in Tonasa, Makassar, followed in 1974 by the fourth in Baturaja, Palembang, and the fifth in Cibinong in 1975. The first locally produced steel product was made at the Krakatau Steel plant in Cilegon in 1971.

Many large-scale projects initiated during the previous regime continued in the 1970s. The Wisma Nusantara skyscraper project resumed in 1971 and was completed in 1973 after standing like a rusty skeleton for several years. The CONEFO project continued and was completed in 1983 as the house and assembly hall for the Indonesian parliament. The national monument project was completed in 1975, and the national mosque, Istiqlal, followed in 1978.

Wisma Nusantara building at Jalan Thamrin, Jakarta, 1971.

Photo: Nationaal Museum van Wereldculturen, Boy Lawson, CC BY 4.0

The national or Istiqlal Mosque, Jakarta, 1973. Architect: Friedrich Silaban.

Photo: F. Silaban Archive, arsitekturindonesia.org

The Pembangunan Jaya corporation initiated the Proyek Senen commercial district in Jakarta in 1961 by engaging the provincial government. The project set a precedent of public-private partnership in developing new urban infrastructures. Proyek Senen aimed to redevelop informal market activities into modernist, orderly, multi-storey infrastructures. The first block was built in 1966, soon followed by the second and third blocks, and the fourth block was completed in 1978.

Some oil-related establishments contributed to the new modernist skyline of Jakarta: the Oil Centre building (1966–1971), the Pertamina headquarters (1971–1972), the Landmark building (1986), and Jakarta Hilton International (1974–1985), with the latter built in several phases. The first part, the Hilton Executive Club (1974), was designed by Yuswadi Saliya (b. 1938) from Atelier Enam Arsitek as the first brutalist building in Indonesia.

The 1970s saw the construction of modern luxury hotels in Jakarta: the President Hotel (1972; as an annexe to the Wisma Nusantara skyscraper), Sahid Jaya Hotel (1971–1973), Hotel Borobudur (1974), Mandarin Oriental Hotel (1976–1979), and Aryaduta Hotel (1983). Notable buildings in the capital also include Bina Graha (1970: the President's office), the Veteran building (1974), the National Television headquarters (1976), the French embassy (1975), the Wisma Hayam Wuruk (1976), the S. Widjojo Centre (1978–1981), the ASEAN Secretariat (1978–1981), and Bank Dagang Negara (1981). The Pembangunan Jaya headquarters (1972–1974) and the Wisma Kosgoro (1971–1976) were the first glass-curtain high-rise buildings in the country. From the late 1960s, several social and cultural infrastructure programmes were also initiated in Jakarta: the Jakarta Arts Centre (Taman Ismail Marzuki; 1968), the Kampung Improvement Programme (1974), and the Youth and Sports Complex (1977).

Culture on Display

Taman Mini Indonesia Indah ('Beautiful Indonesia in Miniatures') was initiated in 1970 by the first lady, Tien Soeharto. The open-air architectural theme park covers 150 hectares in a southern suburb of Jakarta. The idea was to bring together the multifaceted aspects of Indonesian culture and display dozens of traditional house types and religious buildings representing 26 provinces and five recognised religions. The

President Sukarno accompanied by Governor Soemarno receiving an explanation of the mock-up of the Senen Project in the context of the II Pola Pembangunan Exhibition held at the Pola Building in 1962.

Photo: Government of the Special Capital Region of Jakarta, 1977

Hilton Executive Club, Jakarta. Architect: Yuswadi Saliya/Enam Arsitek.

Photo: Aga Khan Trust for Culture, photographer unknown, 1975 project was an example of the state's aspirations to advance national cultural expression through architecture.

The New Order administration focused on the literal expression of regional culture in public facilities. In the mid-1970s, regional parliaments and administrative buildings were adorned with modern interpretations of vernacular architectural roof forms. In the late 1970s, regionalism began to gain a foothold on the Indonesian architectural scene. The firm Atelier Enam completed several commendable projects that used regional architectural forms for hospitality, such as Nusa Dua Beach Hotel (1980–1983), and religion, such as

Philippine President Ferdinand Marcos' wife Imelda Marcos accompanied by Mrs Tien Soeharto visits Taman Mini Indonesia Indah (TMII), Jakarta, 1974.

Photo: TEMPO/Syahrir Wahab; 015/062/1974; 01506210

Government building in Padang, West Sumatra. The roof is reminiscent of traditional Minangkabau architecture.

Photo: Leiden University Libraries Digital Collections, H.C. Beynon, 1971

Said Naum Mosque was designed in the Indonesian Hindu-Javanese architectural tradition yet is well adapted to the Muslim form of worship. Architect: Atelier Enam Architects and Planners / Adhi Moersid, 1977.

Photo: Aga Khan Development Network, Kamran Adle

Said Naum Mosque.

Photo: Aga Khan Development Network, Kamran Adle

Said Naum Mosque (1976). With the rise of the tourism industry, especially in Bali, there was a demand for new hotels to be culturally and climatically appropriate to the local conditions and the industry.

The overwhelming construction boom in the 1970s brought Indonesian architects into direct contact with global architectural trends and practices. The advent of postmodernism and regionalism in Indonesian architectural discourse was a liberating moment that challenged cultural identity amid a rapidly globalising world. Stimulated by insights from cultural studies and anthropology, architects began to seek inspiration beyond technical and engineering aspects, developing a growing sensibility for local traditions, customs, crafts, materials, history, and landscapes.

In 1982, the Indonesian Institute of Architects held a congress to reflect on an 'Indonesian architecture'. The concern was what kind of approach, attitude, and sensibility Indonesian architects should have. The congress was attended by leading architects and professors from different disciplines, who shared their unique views. Friedrich Silaban, who belonged to the first generation of Indonesian architects, considered the quest for a national architectural style futile. Instead, he proposed a technical, textbook approach for architects to (passively) deal with the climate and address local and national sensibilities.

In contrast to Silaban, most of the other speakers – mainly from the younger generation – addressed the importance of acknowledging local cultures and traditions and the need for Indonesian architects to properly understand them philosophically and contextually, taking a critical approach. Academics encouraged architects and students to learn more about vernacular building and landscaping traditions, their meanings, forms, and construction techniques. In the absence of their actual manifestation in contemporary architectural projects, they turned to few successful examples. The most celebrated of these was the Wisma Dharmala Sakti in Jakarta (1983–1986), designed by the American architect Paul Rudolph (1918–1997).

The strongest voice to the 'cultural' (or 'regionalist') approach was Yusuf B. Mangunwijaya. His works were inspired by the view that architecture should liberate people, especially the underprivileged. His non-profit works are good examples of

Perspective rendering of the Dharmala Headquarters Building, Jakarta, Indonesia, ca. 1982. Architect: Paul Rudolph.

Source: Library of Congress, 2019647270

Yusuf B. Mangunwijaya published *Wastu Citra* in 1988.

this view and an effective means of broadening the scope and relevance of the so-called architectural services to the vast Indonesian territory. His seminal publication, *Wastu Citra* (1988), was widely accepted as a philosophical basis for the ethical practice of Indonesian architecture.

A New Dawn

By the early 1980s, the golden years of the oil industry were over. Indonesian oil revenue declined, and growth dropped considerably. The imposition of a quota by the Organisation of the Petroleum Exporting Countries (OPEC) reduced oil production, leading to a deterioration in the country's terms of trade. The global economy was also affected, impacting non-oil exports and investments. In 1986, the government imposed a restriction on fiscal spending and had to devalue the currency. This measure was taken to help non-oil exporters, especially in the manufacturing sector. It helped accelerate growth after 1987 and sustained it until the early 1990s. By the mid-1990s, however, Indonesia's economic miracle was over.

In the early 1990s, a group of self-proclaimed 'Indonesian Young Architects' took a central role on the architectural scene. Still at the beginning of their professional careers, these recent graduates held regular gatherings filled with discussions, presentations, and visits to recently finished works. The group, led by Yori Antar Awal (b. 1962) and Irianto Purnomo Hadi (b. 1961), both graduates of Universitas Indonesia, attracted architecture students and the media with their fresh and exciting approach to architectural commissions, which was in stark contrast to the attitude of the older generation. The seemingly reckless young architects began a fun, tireless campaign, irritating their seniors in the printed media, which published their works. Their colourful, personal, attractive, and carefree formal explorations contrasted with the meticulous, anonymous, humble, and careful architectural works of their elders.

Working in a different social and (geo-)political climate, these young architects developed a new awareness about their role in the industry, especially amid the increasing competition and growing economic crisis. They demonstrated a stronger sense of identity and professionalism in competing with foreign practices. They showed concern for the unruly built development in Indonesia's big cities, lax building regulations, low public acknowledgement of architecture, and – what irritated them the most – the indifference of the wider Indonesian architectural community to these problems.

The friction and indeed the exciting exchange between the younger and older generations was exemplified by the personal and professional relationships between Yori Antar and his father, Han Awal. Yori Antar is often seen as the icon of the motivated, carefree, explosive, rebellious architects of his generation. Han Awal, in contrast, is associated with deep, sensitive, soft-spoken authority and the intellectual seniors. Although Yori Antar and Han Awal seldom worked on the same projects, they shared a studio and a warm, deep care for the profession. The two also hosted and developed discussions, activism, and ideas in their office and home in Tulodong, Jakarta. The creative and intellectual forces between the two radiated to Yori Antar's circle of colleagues – especially among fellow students and graduates from Universitas Indonesia – which soon spread to other cities, especially to Institut Teknologi Bandung and Universitas Katolik Parahyangan. Although their activities were never formalised, they set a new tradition for younger Indonesian architects in showcasing their works to the public and being expressive in their professional presence as well as their architectural works.

Sugiharto Steel House, Jakarta, 2002. Architect: Ahmad Djuhara.
Photo: Aga Khan Developxment Network

The 1990s proved to be a very challenging decade for Indonesian architects. Despite constant favourable economic growth prior to 1998, Indonesian inflation rates soared, which was proof of a poor economic foundation.

In 1997, the country was hit by a devastating financial crisis that swept across Asia and brought down many countries formerly hailed as Asian economic miracles. The Indonesian currency again took a downturn in the face of the ever-stronger US dollar. In July 1997, one US dollar was valued at 2,500 Indonesian rupiahs. By October 1997, it had nearly doubled to 4,000 Indonesian rupiahs. By January 1998, the rupiah hit rock bottom at 17,000 rupiahs per US dollar. Unable to pay overdue loans and imports, the Indonesian government and industries – especially the construction and property sectors – came to a halt, and they were followed by many other sectors. The years 1997 and 1998 were also particularly bad for rice production due to the drought. The multidimensional crisis ignited calls for regime change. Soeharto's government, which had been in power since 1966, was no longer popular due to his autocratic rule and military oppression. In May 1998, major demonstrations – mainly initiated by students – were held in major cities demanding the government take extreme measures to help the collapsing economy. One of their main points was to halt the massive corruption within and structural damage to the Indonesian economy and bureaucracy.

The demonstrations escalated to violent riots, and the death of four student protesters made the situation worse. Angry protesters demanded that President Soeharto step down and disband the parliament. Riots broke out in the streets of major cities, and Chinese quarters and businesses were looted and burned. Mobs occupied the streets. Public areas and facilities were shut down for days. It was an ongoing nightmare for many Indonesians. The student protests continued and resulted in their occupation of the Parliament building (DPR-MPR, formerly CONEFO Project).

After several days of mass protests and violence, the chain of events culminated in the resignation of President Soeharto on 21 May 1998. This ended the 32-year reign of the New Order government and opened a path to a new liberal democratic era in Indonesia.

For Indonesian architects, the 1998 crisis was a great reset. Established design and engineering firms took a harsh blow to their business, significantly downsizing their activities or closing their practices altogether. Architects were laid off and had to find freelance commissions for several years to stay afloat. Fresh graduate architects entered the industry with few options; many had to establish their own freelance practices with minimal experience and made the best of whatever commissions they could get. The crisis introduced a new sensibility to the younger generation of Indonesian architects both in terms of their design approach and practice. The young generation of architects developed an attentiveness towards details and economy, which included reviving the modernist vocabulary to emphasise efficiency as an aesthetic gesture. With the lack of large-scale projects in the early 2000s, small, efficient private houses were considered a fitting architectural statement for the era. Architecture was practised in small design studios rather than big engineering consulting firms. Many started as collaborative practices and kept their small business units even if they received sizeable commissions. Many of today's renowned Indonesian architecture practices were established during and after this period. They have often retained the narrow scope of their services and limited the scale of their studio without compromising the possibility of opportunities they could have.

The new policies of democratisation and decentralisation also significantly improved professional associations and governmental bodies. From the mid-2000s, architects began taking an active role in the design of public buildings and facilities thanks to competitions held by municipal and provincial governments. The endorsement of the Indonesian Institute of Architects (IAI) also opened up access to government commissions to smaller firms and creative ideas – an area previously reserved for those with good connections. Decentralisation has enabled local governments and state-owned companies to take initiatives to upgrade urban public facilities, including revitalising urban areas and rehabilitating heritage assets.

The involvement of Indonesian architects in the public space and infrastructure accelerated after 2012 when the government prioritised developing physical infrastructure throughout the country's vast territory, especially the eastern provinces. Over the last decade, Indonesian architectural studios have been immersed in fast-paced, large-scale development projects. They have been entrusted with the design of urban open spaces, airports, seaports, public monuments, museums, parks, transportation facilities, and tourism destinations; with the restoration of vernacular and religious buildings; and – last but not least – a brand new capital on the island of Kalimantan.

Bibliography

van Zanden, Jan Luiten, Daan Marks, *An Economic History of Indonesia 1800–2012* (London: Routledge, 2012).

Booth, Anne, *The Indonesian Economy in the Nineteenth and Twentieth Century: A History of Missed Opportunities* (London: Palgrave Macmillan, 1998).

Al Rahab, Amiruddin, *Ekonomi Berdikari Sukarno* (Depok: Komunitas Bambu, 2014).

Ricklefs, Merle Calvin, *A History of Modern Indonesia since c. 1200*, 4th edition (New York: Palgrave Macmillan, 2008).

DIPLOMAS

Final Projects by the Indonesian Architecture Students

Eduard Kögel

Nine final projects by Indonesian architecture students are preserved in the archive of the Architekturmuseum of the TU Berlin; these documents were the starting point for our research and exhibition project 'Dipl.-Ing. Arsitek'. Bianpoen's final diploma project and diploma certificate from the TH Hanover were preserved in his personal family archive. All of the students' final projects are architectural tasks situated in Indonesia, and nearly all of them involve buildings for the community. Interestingly, nearly all the graduates proposed a pavilion system with individual buildings often connected by covered walkways for protection from the natural elements. Featuring modular building elements for natural ventilation or the roof structure, they reflect ideas that have been adapted for a modernity in the tropics. All the works show consideration for local climatic conditions and reinterpret traditional solutions with modern functional design.

The Indonesian students' architectural concepts were undoubtedly influenced by various discourses at that time. For example, discussions about architecture in the tropics had been conducted at the Architectural Association in London since the early 1950s in the context of British colonial architecture.[1] Structuralist ideas in the Netherlands found expression in Aldo van Eyck's (1918–1999) orphanage in Amsterdam, completed in 1960; the Dutch architect Herman Hertzberger (b. 1932) – a fellow student of Han Awal and Bianpoen in Delft – worked in the same direction.[2] In Germany, the architects Sep Ruf and Egon Eiermann presented a new perspective on postwar modernism with their German pavilion for the 1958 World's Fair in Brussels, which was widely discussed in architectural journals at the time. All these ideas of light, transparent pavilions, and parasols can be found in the students' final projects. Obviously, these themes were discussed in the seminars and influenced the conceptual attitude in the search for a new architecture as an expression of a modern Indonesian society.

1 Drew, 1956.
2 van Eyck, 1962, p. 16–23.

TRANSCRIPTION OF NAMES AND NAME CHANGES

While examining the documents of the featured architects, it became apparent that some of them were active under different names at different stages of their lives. This reflects some of the challenges faced by ethnic Chinese in Indonesia at the time. Six of the 12 architects covered in this project belonged to this minority.[1]

For ethnic minorities in Indonesia, gaining access to higher education after independence was already difficult and it was often a reason for going abroad to study.[2] When General Soeharto came to power in the mid-1960s, the situation worsened as his militias perpetrated massacres among members and sympathisers of the Indonesian Communist Party and the Chinese minority. As a result, Indonesian citizens of 'foreign descent' (meaning mainly ethnic Chinese) were strongly urged to assimilate and 'encouraged' to adopt Indonesian-sounding names from around 1966 to 1968.[3]

The architects returning from Germany were also affected. After gaining his diploma from the Technische Hochschule (TH) in Hanover with his Chinese name LIEM Bian Poen, he later called himself simply Bianpoen, the name under which he defended his doctoral thesis in 1983 in Rotterdam.[4] The other five architects of Chinese origin studied at the TU Berlin: King-Han Oei, Jan Beng Oei, THUNG Pohin (later Po Hin Thung), HAN Hoo Twjan (later Han Awal), and KHO Lin Hek (also Lien and later Herianto Sulindro).[5]

Jan Beng Oei and King-Han Oei remained in Germany after their education and continued to use their names, adapting to the German custom by placing the surname Oei at the end. Although both architects shared the same surname (a common name in Indonesia); they were not related. The architect now known as Han Awal enrolled for studies at the Technische Hogeschool in Delft in 1951 under his Chinese name, HAN Hoo Twjan.[6] On the index card of his final project in Berlin, his name is listed as HAN Hoo Tjv. Meanwhile, his diploma certificate correctly states his name as HAN Hoo Twjan.[7] He changed his name to Han Awal after his return to Indonesia; after that, only his immediate family continued to use his original name. Kho Lin Hek changed his name to Herianto Sulindro in 1968, despite not returning to his native country and spending his working life in Switzerland from 1963. Po Hin Thung kept his name and later worked in the field of development aid in the Netherlands.

There are also variations in the spellings and transcriptions of the other architects' names. Only Mustafa Pamuntjak kept his original name,[8] while Eddy Heryadie later used Harjadi or Haryadi. Soejoedi Wirjoatmodjo signed his name on his final project in Berlin as Sujudi and also in Javanese script, which would be transcribed today as Suyudi Wiryatmaja, after the last change to transcription conventions in 1975. The name Soejoedi was sometimes also transcribed as Sujudi, although according to modern transcription, the 'oe' should become 'u' and the 'j' should become 'y'. Soewondo Bismo Soetdjo's first name is written as Suwondo today, and Hoemar Tjokorodiatmo's first name is sometimes written as Humar.

The priest, architect, and poet Yusuf Bilyarta Mangunwijaya, who did not belong to the group mentioned above, studied at the RWTH Aachen between 1960 and 1966. He is often referred to as Romo (Father) Mangun. As both a man of letters and an architect, he followed his own unique path to contemporary architectural expression.

1 Today, 3.6 per cent of the population is of Chinese origin.
2 Grimm, 2019, p. 22.
3 Beittinger, 2004, p. 55.
4 Bianpoen, 1983.
5 For clarity, the family names are written here in all capital letters; during their studies, some of the students adapted to the German name-writing convention of placing the family name at the end, after the given name.

6 Jaarboek, Technische Hogeschool te Delft, 1951, p. 61.
7 'Auszeichnung', in Technische Universität Berlin, Akademische Reden 9, 15 November 1960, p. 63.
8 The last name of Mustafa Pamuntjak is spelled Pammuntjak on the index cards of his final project at the TU Berlin.

Eddy Heryadie
b. 1931

Eddy Heryadie submitted his final project for the 'Bandung Youth Centre' under Professor Wilhelm Kreuer in May 1961. The influence of Hans Scharoun is evident in the design of the modern complex, situated outside the city of Bandung on a gentle slope and built around a polygonal courtyard. The U-shaped facility is accessed on the ground floor, with a banquet hall and cafeteria with a viewing terrace on the lower level. Public functions, such as exhibition spaces, the auditorium, and the restaurant, are grouped on the ground floor in the same wing. Another wing holds workrooms and two-storey guest dwellings. Covered open spaces provide space for informal interactions; the design of these and other architecturally staged transition zones between indoors and outdoors demonstrate the consideration given to local climate conditions. Residential courtyards and the community garden provide public zones with expansive views of the city. Folded concrete roof elements are used on several of the smaller pavilions in the complex.

One photo of the model and seven architectural drawings are available in the TU Berlin architectural archive (site plan, basement floor plan, ground floor plan, upper floor plan, general view, auditorium section view, and a perspective view).

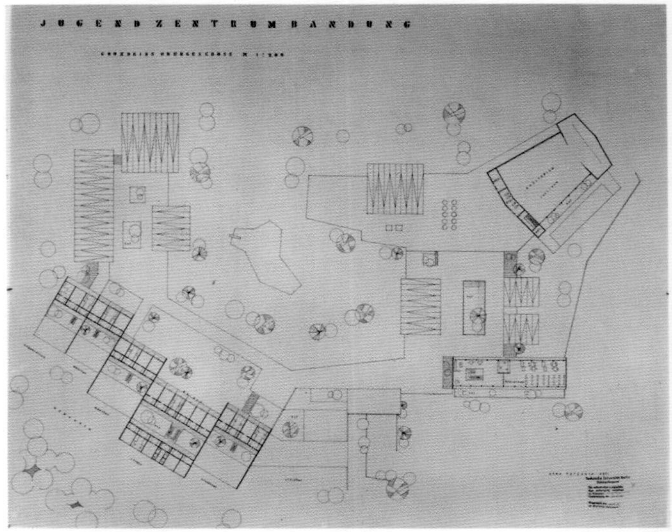

Source: Technische Universität Berlin, Architekturmuseum, Inv. Nr. 66220

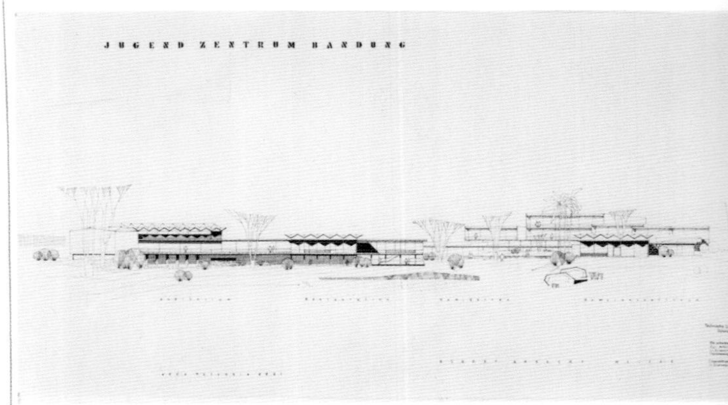

Source: Technische Universität Berlin, Architekturmuseum, Inv. Nr. 66223

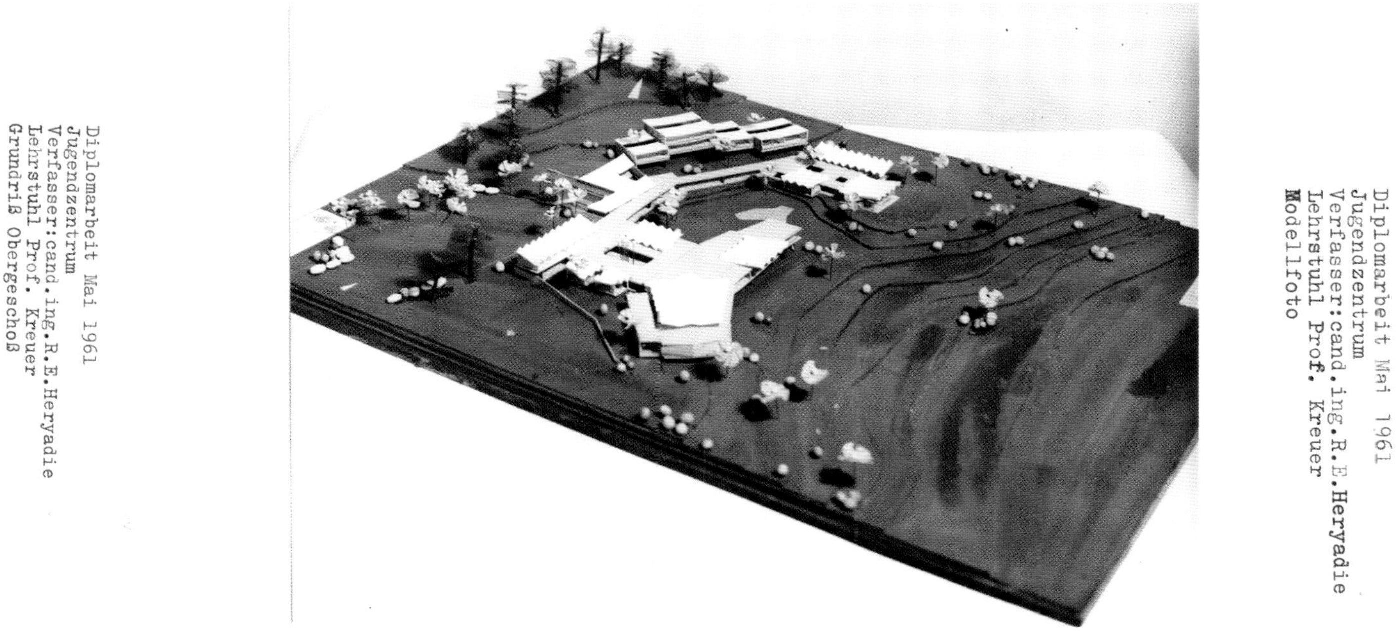

Source: Technische Universität Berlin, Architekturmuseum, Inv. Nr. 66216

Source: Technische Universität Berlin, Architekturmuseum, Inv. Nr. 66223

Han Awal
HAN Hoo Twjan/ HAN Hoo Tjv, 1930–2016

In May 1960, Han Hoo Twjan completed his architecture degree under Professor Wilhelm Kreuer at the TU Berlin with his final project for a 'Community Centre in Indonesia'. The proposed complex is situated on a palm tree-lined pedestrian mall along an east-west axis. To the west are a two-storey pavilion serving as a neighbourhood centre, single-storey pavilions holding youth facilities, as well as a library, health centre, and an administrative office. To the east, further pavilions house the police and fire departments, the bank, and the post office, along with retail shops, service providers, and eateries (referred to as *warungs,* Indonesian for 'small businesses'). The individually designed pavilions are protected from the elements by a grid of square folded screens, each supported by a pole, while allowing for natural ventilation. The screens can be placed individually or in groups and later expanded by adding additional screens.

Only four photos of the drawings have been preserved in the TU Berlin archive (ground floor plan, upper floor plan, sections, and elevations). The work was awarded a bronze plaque for remarkable achievement.[1]

1 'Auszeichnung', in Technische Universität Berlin, Akademische Reden 9, 15 November 1960, p. 63.

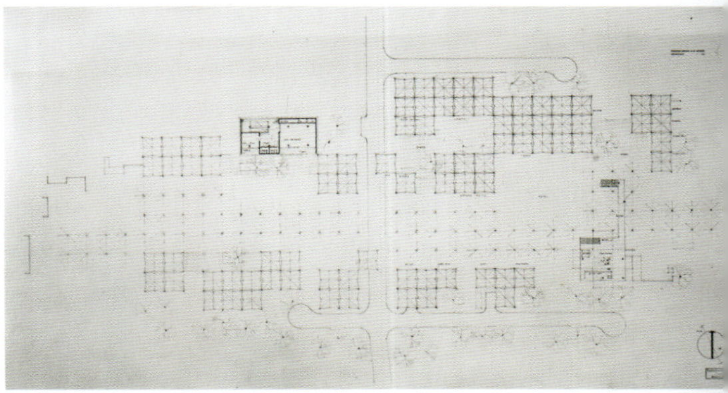

Source: Technische Universität Berlin, Architekturmuseum, Inv. Nr. 70009

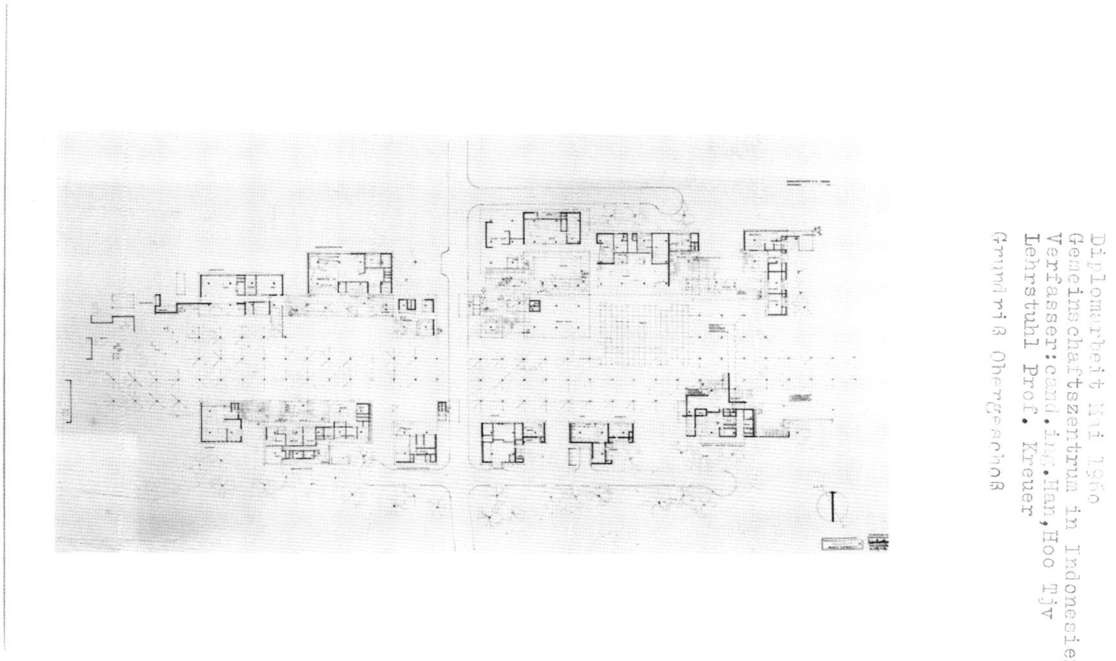

Source: Technische Universität Berlin, Architekturmuseum, Inv. Nr. 70010

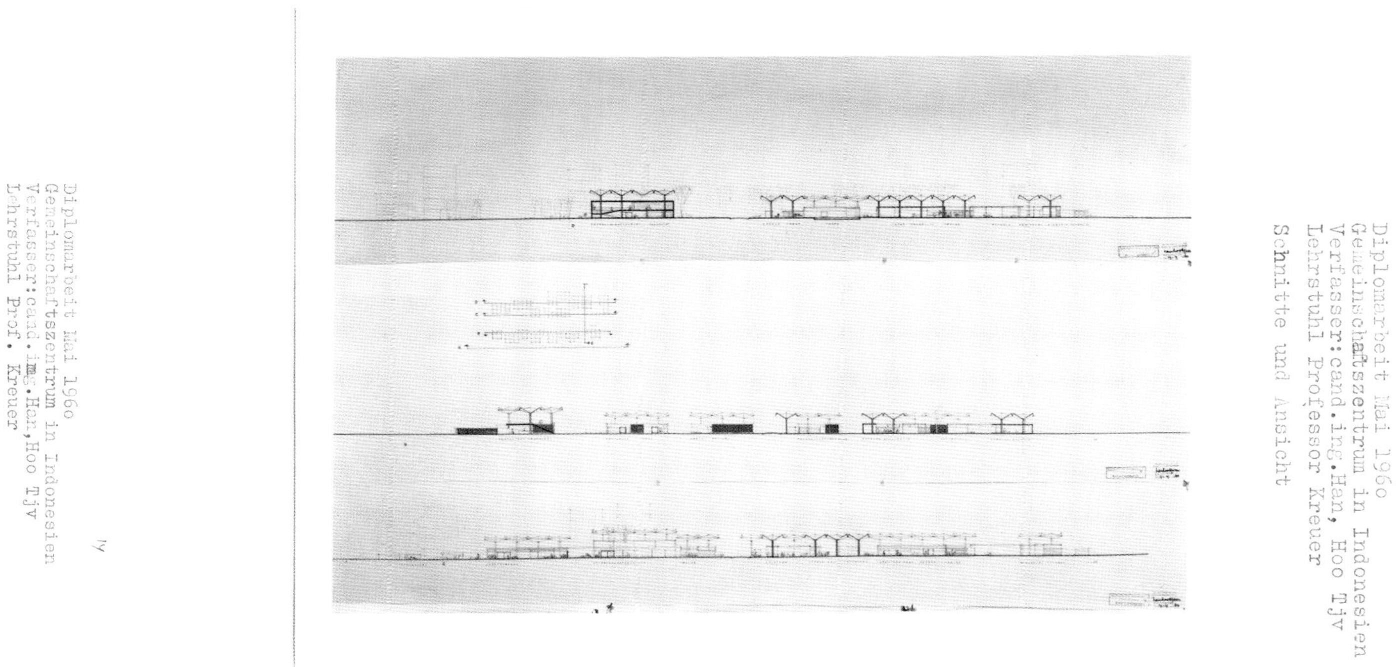

Source: Technische Universität Berlin, Architekturmuseum, Inv. Nr. 70012

Herianto Sulindro
until 1968; KHO Lin Hek, b. 1928

Herianto Sulindro (KHO Lin Hek) submitted his final project for an 'Upper Secondary School and Boarding School in Bandung' under Professor Kurt Dübbers in May 1960. For the layout of the complex, he decided to separate the two areas of the secondary school and the boarding school by a central axis on which the gymnasium, assembly hall, and refectory are arranged. Four villas for the school administrators and instructors are set somewhat apart from the rest of the buildings. The day school and the boarding school are each organised in units of equal size and grouped in clusters of three pavilions around a garden courtyard. The complex is designed for roughly 100 boys (three buildings) and 70 girls (two buildings). All buildings are single-storey and raised off the ground like traditional wooden structures. They are connected by a network of covered walkways that provide protection from the sun and rain. The striking roof design consists of four sloping elements that combine to form a series of tent-like roofs. The strict spatial organisation creates well-defined green outdoor spaces in a design that could be applied to pavilions on other sites.

Three photos of the model have been preserved in the TU archive, along with seven photos of architectural drawings (site plan, floor plan of the entire complex, floor plan of the flats, two sheets with elevations, and two perspective views).

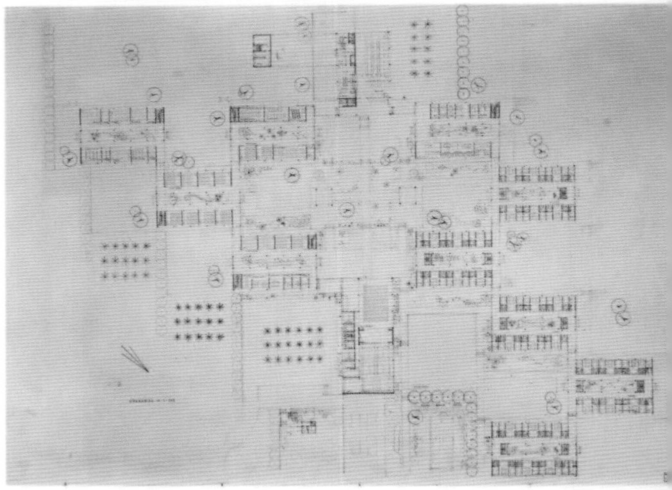

Source: Technische Universität Berlin, Architekturmuseum, Inv. Nr. 67241

Source: Technische Universität Berlin, Architekturmuseum, Inv. Nr. 67243

Source: Technische Universität Berlin, Architekturmuseum, Inv. Nr. 67238

Source: Technische Universität Berlin, Architekturmuseum, Inv. Nr. 67246

Hoemar Tjokrodiatmo
1931–2019

Hoemar Tjokrodiatmo submitted his final project for the 'Bandung Technical Training Centre' under Professor Wilhelm Kreuer in May 1960. Tjokrodiatmo solved the design challenge by placing the public functions on a raised platform, with five three-storey student housing pavilions linked by covered walkways. The height of the various academic buildings depends on their function. Laboratories, a drawing room, administrative offices, an exhibition space, and workshops are housed in separate pavilions connected by a spacious covered communication zone. The cafeteria/lounge area on the ground floor opens onto a landscaped atrium; classrooms are grouped around that on the first floor. At the centre of the campus, the tallest building houses rooms for recreation, a cafeteria, and a library on the ground floor and first floor. The second floor holds a large auditorium with a foyer and stage. The design responds to the local climatic conditions by dividing the building mass into pavilions joined across a green landscape.

Two photos of the model and five photos of the architectural drawings are available in the TU Berlin archive (ground floor plan, first floor plan, second floor plan, section, elevation, and perspective views).

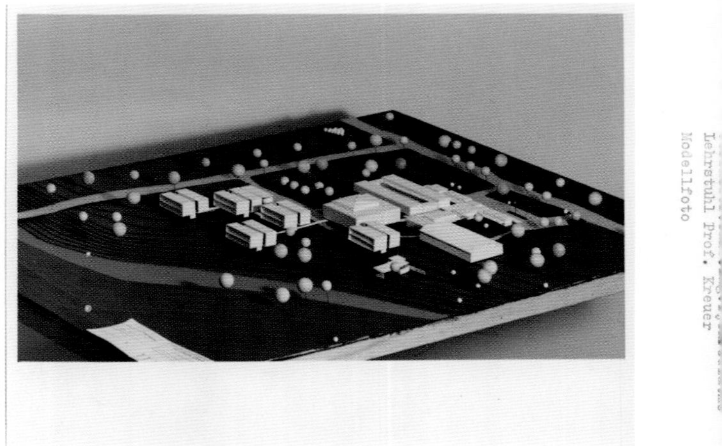

Source: Technische Universität Berlin, Architekturmuseum, Inv. Nr. 68263

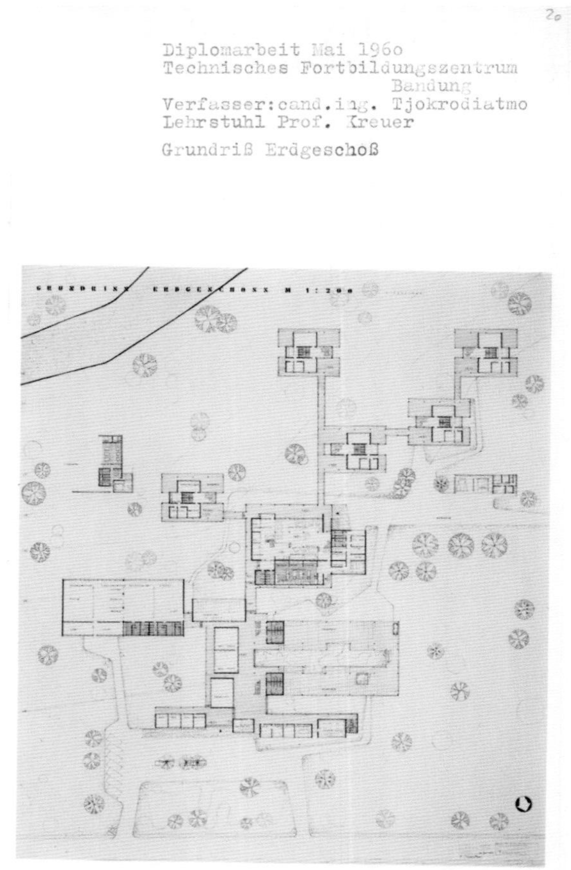

Source: Technische Universität Berlin, Architekturmuseum, Inv. Nr. 68264

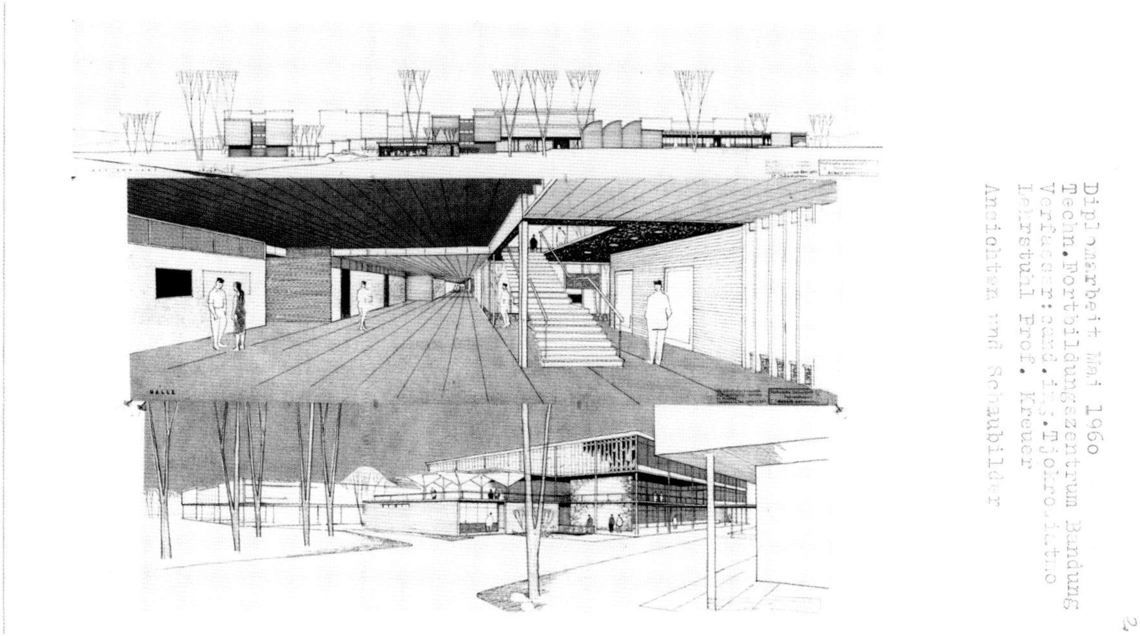

Source: Technische Universität Berlin, Architekturmuseum, Inv. Nr. 68268

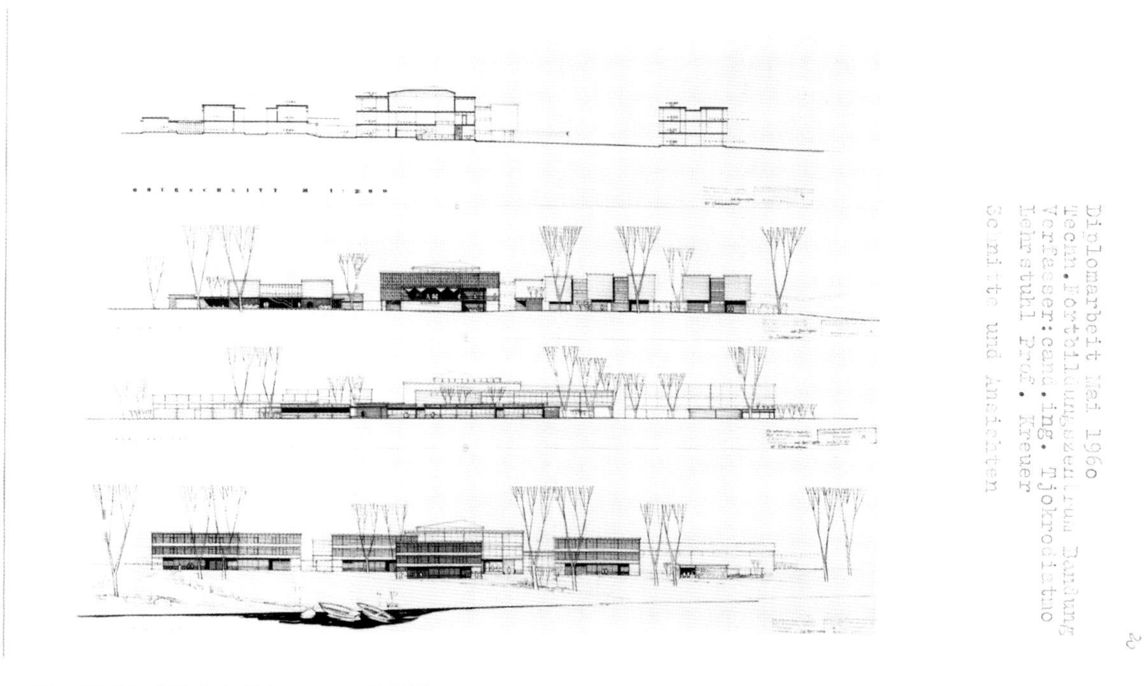

Source: Technische Universität Berlin, Architekturmuseum, Inv. Nr. 68267

Jan Beng Oei
b. 1933

Jan Beng Oei submitted his final project for the 'Filmstudio Indonesia' under Professor Kurt Dübbers in May 1960. Located by the sea, the film studio is broken up into several individual pavilions that enclose larger and smaller courtyards in a linear arrangement. The two-storey pavilions and halls are arranged along an axis terminated by a six-storey administrative building with a canteen at the base. From there, a covered walkway leads to the studio halls with buildings for costumes and makeup opposite it. Linearly arranged workshop wings form an inner courtyard bordered by the warehouse building. Oei's design conveys an organic, open space that mediates between the natural and the built environments. The roof shape differs depending on the building's function. Flat roofs, folded concrete elements, and forms divided into airy segments create variety and lend each pavilion a unique character.

Two photos of the model and seven additional photos of drawings are preserved in the TU Berlin archive (site plan, ground floor plan, first floor plan, elevations, sections, and two perspectives).

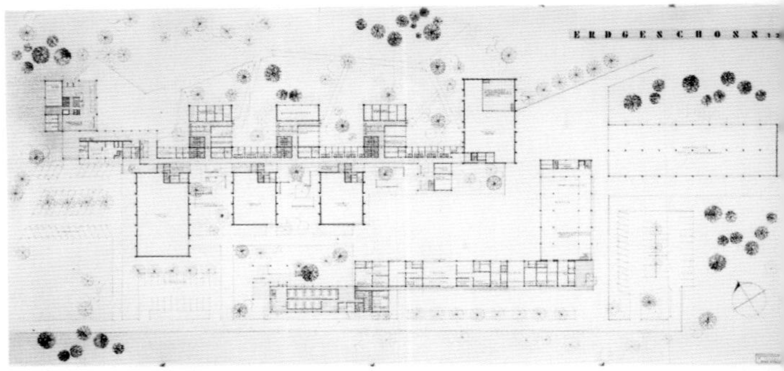

Source: Technische Universität Berlin, Architekturmuseum, Inv. Nr. 68886

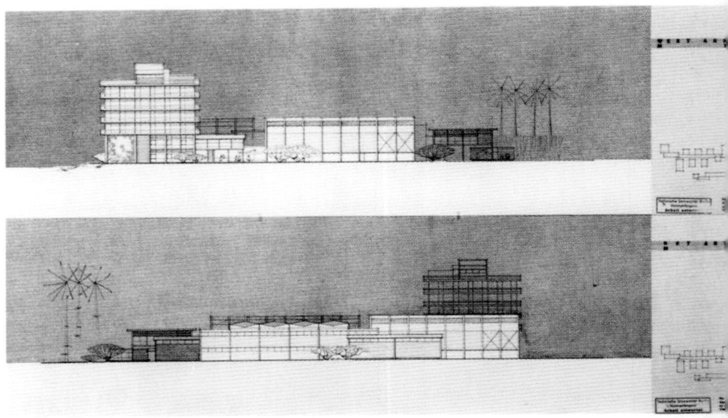

Source: Technische Universität Berlin, Architekturmuseum, Inv. Nr. 68888

Source: Technische Universität Berlin, Architekturmuseum, Inv. Nr. 68884

Source: Technische Universität Berlin, Architekturmuseum, Inv. Nr. 68890

King-Han Oei
1931 – 2021

King-Han Oei submitted his final project for a 'Conference Centre on the Java Sea, Indonesia' under Professor Wilhelm Kreuer in November 1960. The degree candidate arranged the buildings of this seaside venue in a linear manner. Their various functions, including the conference hall, refectory, administration, two pavilions with conference rooms, library and – somewhat detached from the rest of the complex – a hotel, are housed in separate structures (one to three storeys) and are accessible along a central covered walkway. The pavilions are designed with a modular, variable system of pillars and are integrated individually into the topography of the site. The conference hall, designed for 1,380 visitors, is crowned by four large concrete arches serving as the signature element of the complex. In front of the entrance, the hall features a reflecting pool that showcases the façade. Viewed from a distance, the buildings appear as a cluster of cubic pavilions that contrasts with the curved shape of the conference hall.

Seven architectural drawings have been preserved in the TU Berlin archive (site plan, floor plans, ground floor plans, elevations, two sheets of sections, and one perspective view).

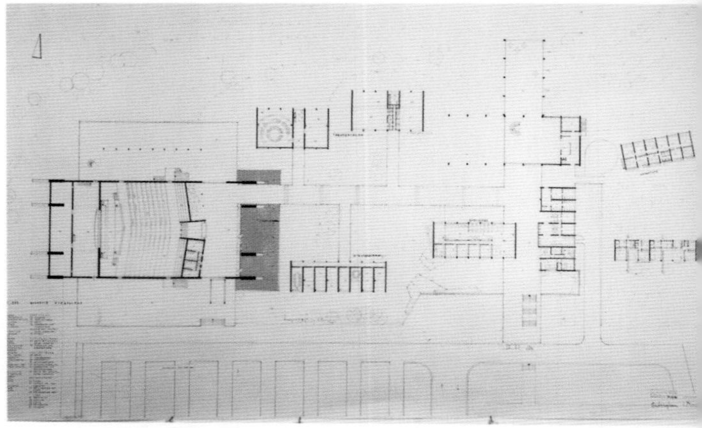

Source: Technische Universität Berlin, Architekturmuseum, Inv. Nr. 69809

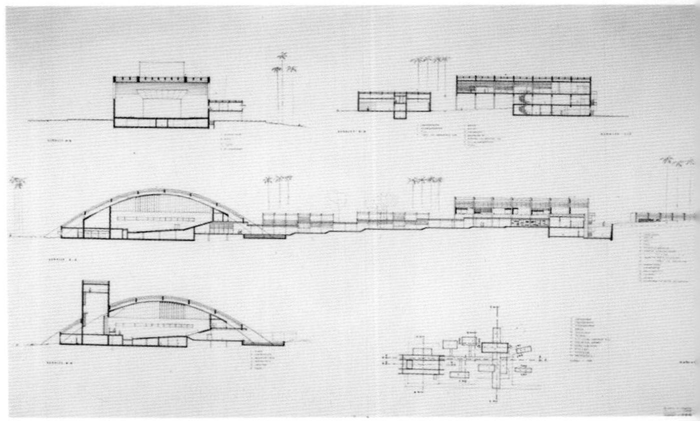

Source: Technische Universität Berlin, Architekturmuseum, Inv. Nr. 69811

Source: Technische Universität Berlin, Architekturmuseum, Inv. Nr. 69804

Source: Technische Universität Berlin, Architekturmuseum, Inv. Nr. 69813

Mustafa Pamuntjak
1932–2020

Mustafa Pamuntjak submitted his final project for a 'Broadcasting Building' under Professor Wilhelm Kreuer in 1960. Pamuntjak prepared the urban planning concept together with his fellow student, Po Hin Thung. The design comprises a broadcasting building (Pamuntjak) and a cultural centre (Thung), separated by an access road. Seven one- to two-storey pavilions are grouped around a garden courtyard and are complemented by a 13-storey, square high-rise building. Covered walkways connect the individual pavilions. These spacious buildings are characterised by a regularly spaced grid of columns that support the barrel roofs. On the ground floor, only small areas are spatially enclosed, while the open areas connect fluidly with the garden landscape. It is not clear from the surviving documents what functions the high-rise building performs. As the perspective shows, the barrel roofs are broken up by garden courtyards that allow for natural lighting and ventilation.

Six photos of the architectural drawings have been preserved in the TU Berlin archive (site plan, ground floor plan, upper floor plan, two sheets with elevations and sections, and a perspective view).

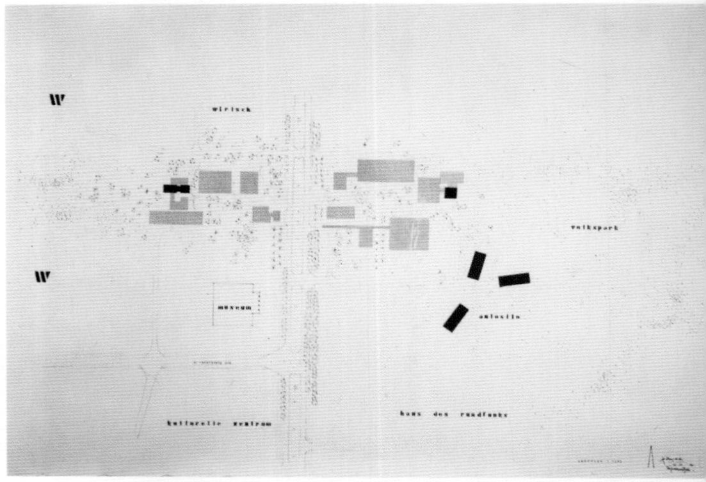

Source: Technische Universität Berlin, Architekturmuseum, Inv. Nr. 68913

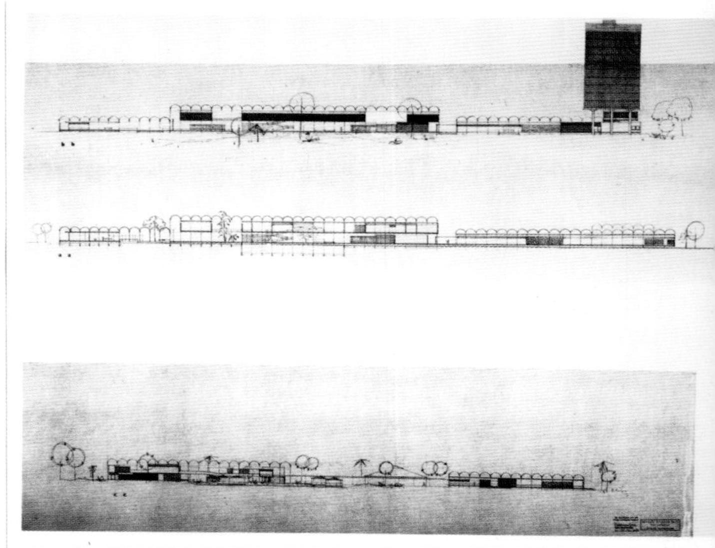

Source: Technische Universität Berlin, Architekturmuseum, Inv. Nr. 68917

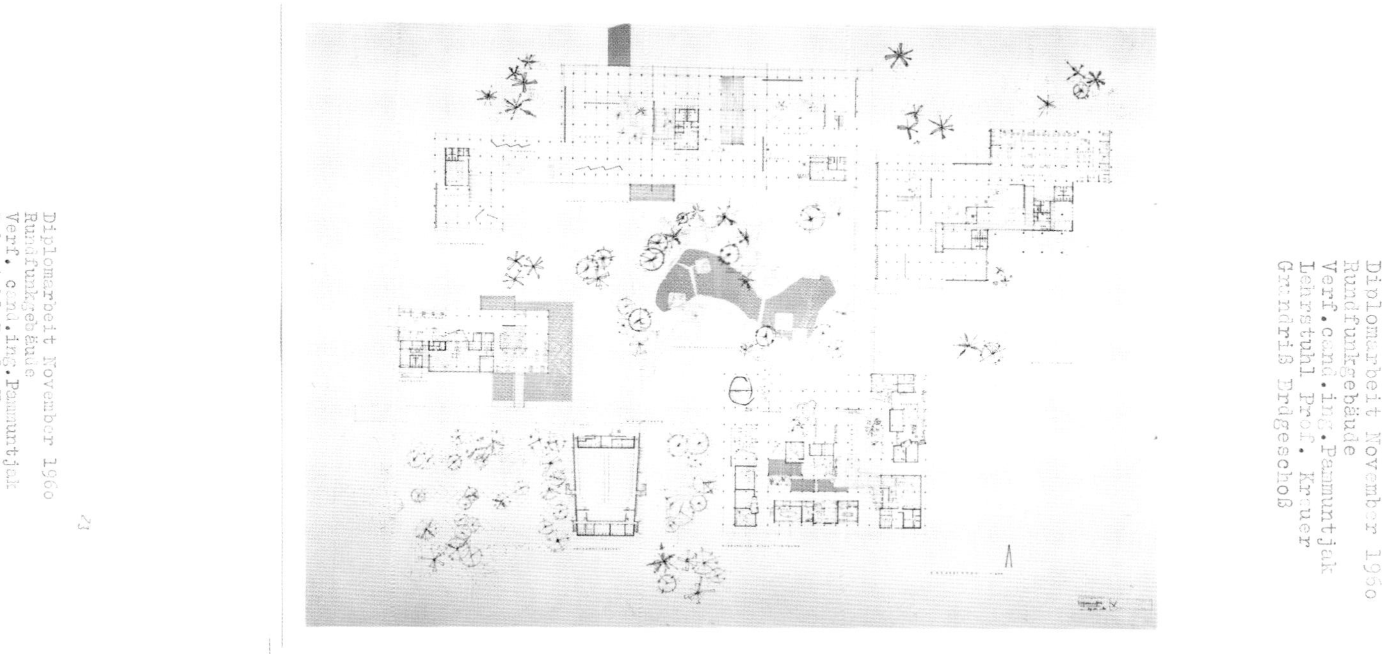

Source: Technische Universität Berlin, Architekturmuseum, Inv. Nr. 68914

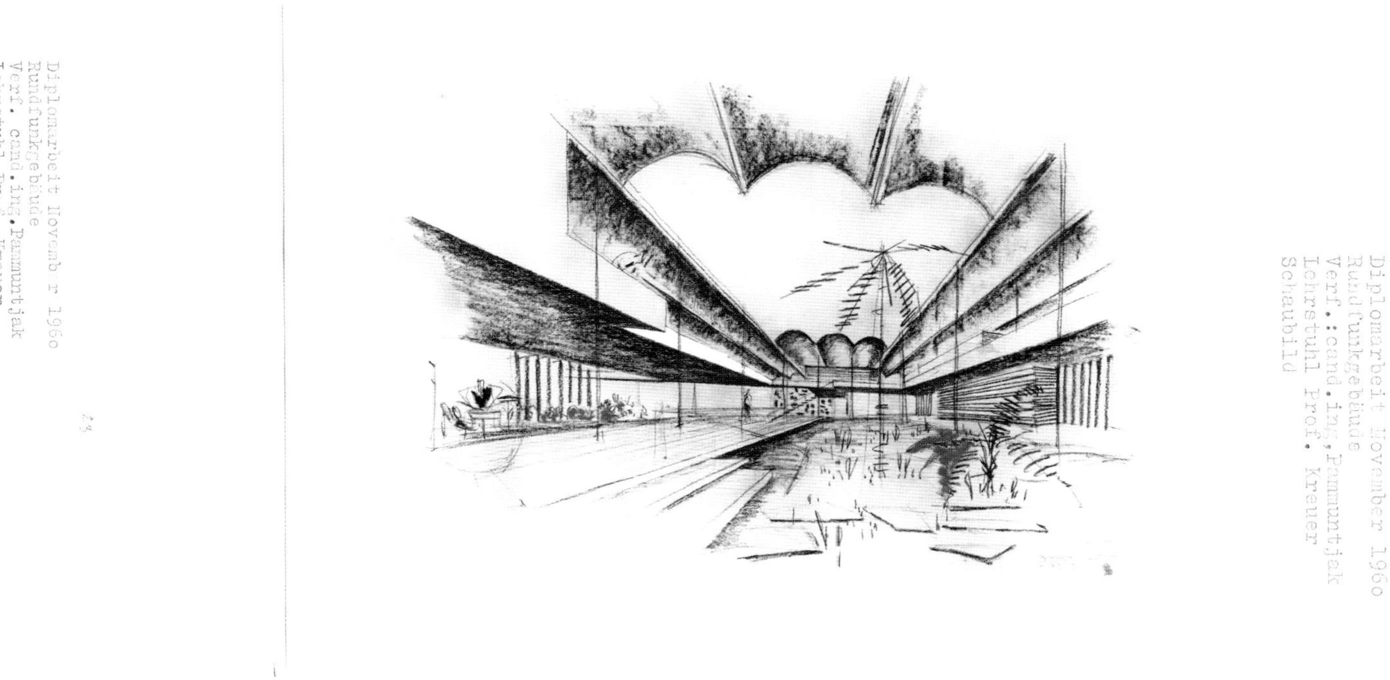

Source: Technische Universität Berlin, Architekturmuseum, Inv. Nr. 68918

Po Hin Thung
THUNG Pohin, b. 1933

Po Hin Thung submitted his final project for a 'Cultural Centre' under Professor Wilhelm Kreuer in November 1960. Thung developed the planning concept for the site together with Mustafa Pamuntjak, to whom the site plan is attributed. Thung's group of buildings consists of five two-storey pavilions complemented by an eight-storey high-rise building. The pavilion roofs are comprised of barrel vaults with small spans, covering various open areas on the ground floor. The cultural centre consists mainly of studios and classrooms for children and teens. At the base pavilion of the high-rise building, two polygonal spaces jut out from the grid-like layout: the 'smoking salon' and an area for 'spiritual education'. The high-rise is asymmetrically bisected by the entrance area, and the façade is structured with lamellas and an abstract stone finish. The first two floors are not enclosed but form a covered open space that directly adjoins the base pavilion with its two polygonal structures.

Four photos of architectural drawings have been preserved in the TU archive (floor plans, ground floor plans, upper floor plan, and elevations).

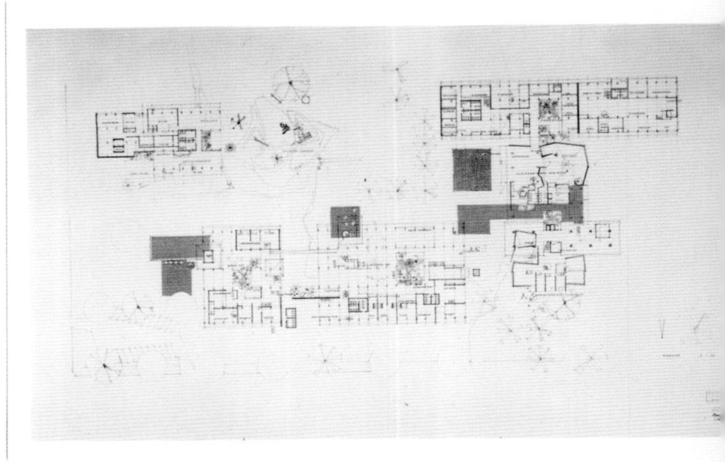

Source: Technische Universität Berlin, Architekturmuseum, Inv. Nr. 70038

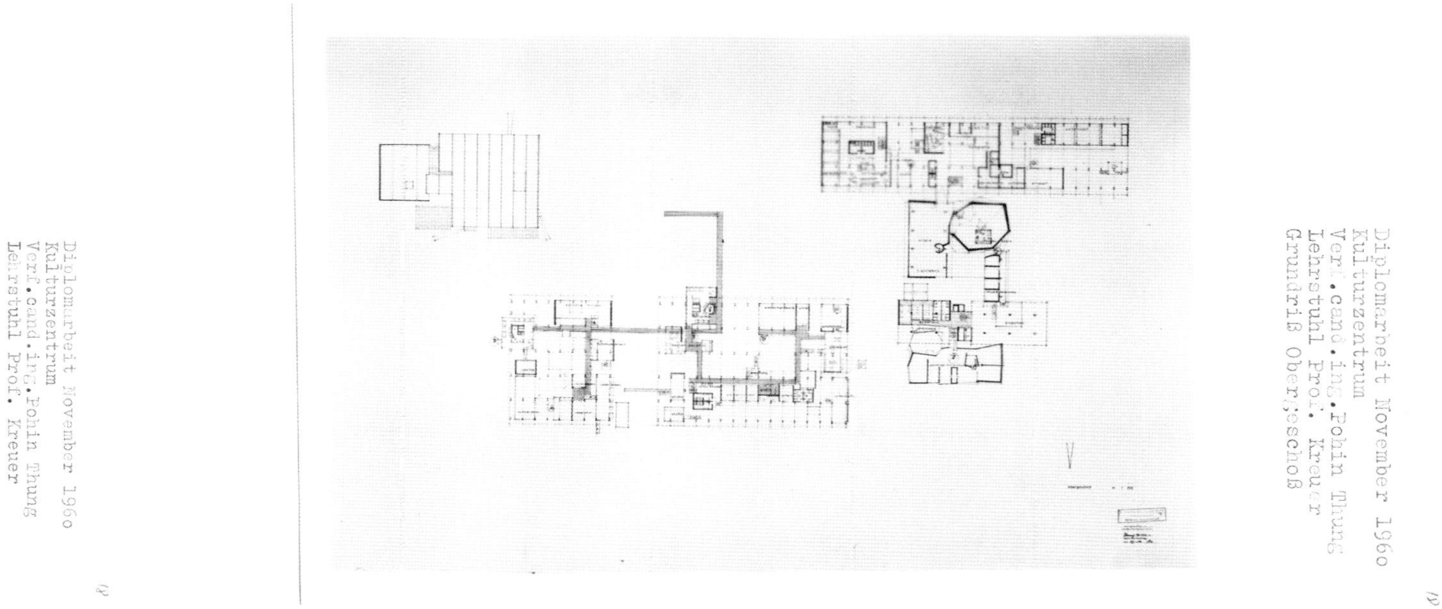

Source: Technische Universität Berlin, Architekturmuseum, Inv. Nr. 70039

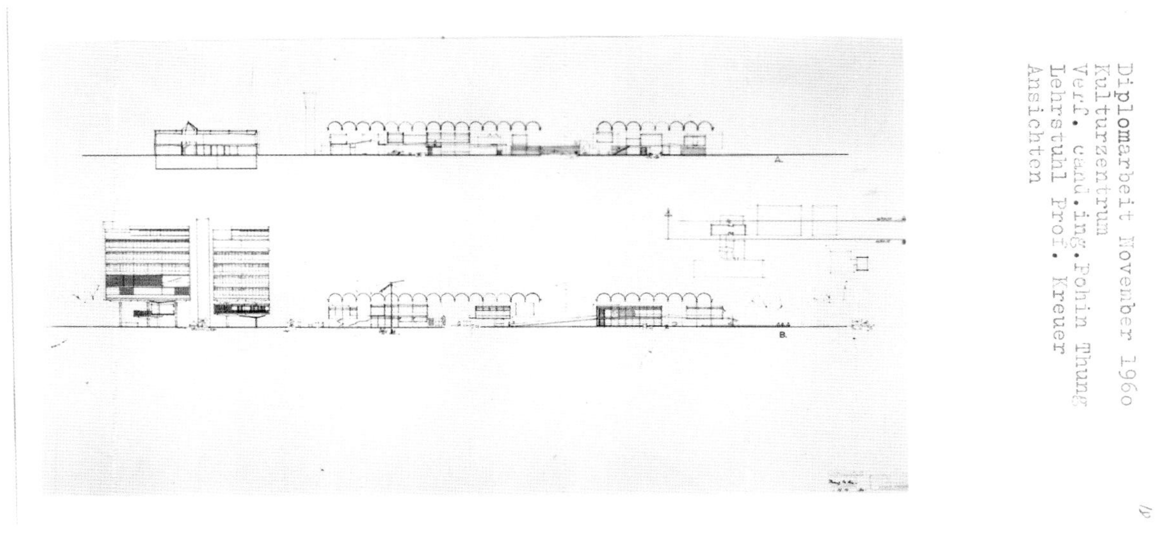

Source: Technische Universität Berlin, Architekturmuseum, Inv. Nr. 70040

Soejoedi Wirjoatmodjo 1928–1981

Soejoedi Wirjoatmodjo submitted his final project for an 'Islamic Sanctuary' to Professor Wilhelm Kreuer in November 1960. As an Islamic retreat, an Indonesian *pesantren* is a boarding school similar to the *madrasa* of the Arab world and mainly consists of a school, a mosque, and residence halls. Since the floor plan and site plan are missing from the archive today, the spatial composition can only be deduced from photos of the model. The communal rooms are grouped around a round courtyard at ground level, while the residents' single rooms are tiered upwards on eight storeys over the steep topography. The drawings are on grey paper, and the lettering and the trunks of the palm trees are in white. Black cardboard was chosen as a strong contrast for the spatial depictions of the perspective drawings; with this minimalist approach, Wirjoatmodjo created a powerful artistic effect.

Two photos of the model have been preserved in the TU Berlin archive, along with five photos of the plans (section and elevation, elevation, sectional views, and two perspective collages). In recognition of his outstanding achievements, Wirjoatmodjo was one of two graduates to receive a bronze plaque for his final project.

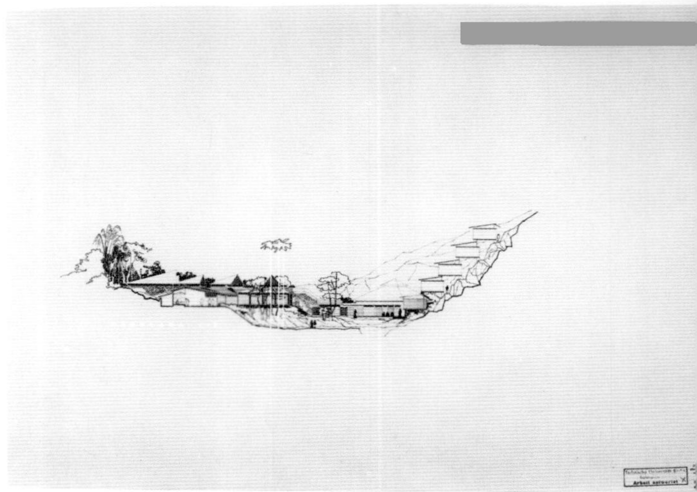

Source: Technische Universität Berlin, Architekturmuseum, Inv. Nr. 72560

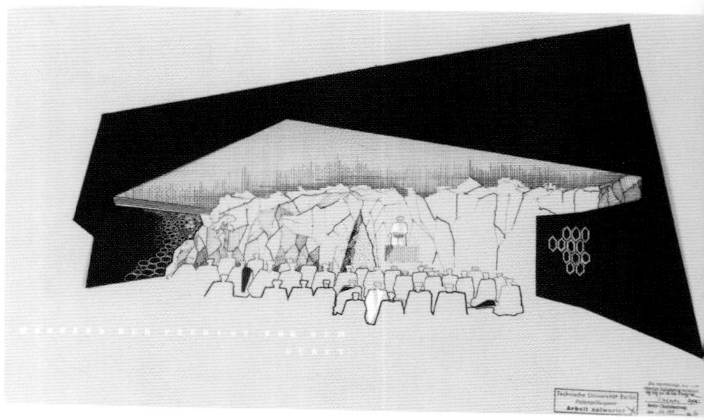

Source: Technische Universität Berlin, Architekturmuseum, Inv. Nr. 72563

Source: Technische Universität Berlin, Architekturmuseum, Inv. Nr. 72558

Source: Technische Universität Berlin, Architekturmuseum, Inv. Nr. 72562

Bianpoen
LIEM Bian Poen,
1930–2020

Bianpoen received his diploma from the Technische Hochschule (TH) in Hanover in March 1961. It was not possible to identify his supervising professor. The mention of a palm forest, the depiction of palm trees, and the pavilion concept for a Catholic Church facility suggest that Bianpoen designed his final project with Indonesia in mind.
The proposed building site is located across the street from an existing church. The project comprises a single-storey complex that is elevated on columns, grouped around a series of courtyards and connected by covered walkways. A chapel, consecration hall, mortuary, cemetery, retreat house, employee apartments, and dormitories separated by gender are recognisable. The roof consists of hyperbolic paraboloid shells mounted on supports. Exterior walls are partially louvred for better lighting and ventilation. The architectural concept of a pavilion structure with an additive umbrella roof and a climate-friendly design is similar to the final projects produced by the Indonesian students in Berlin.

The plans on tracing paper are only labelled rudimentarily. They have been kept in the family archive. Eight drawings have survived: floor plans, elevations, sections, a detail sheet, and a perspective view.

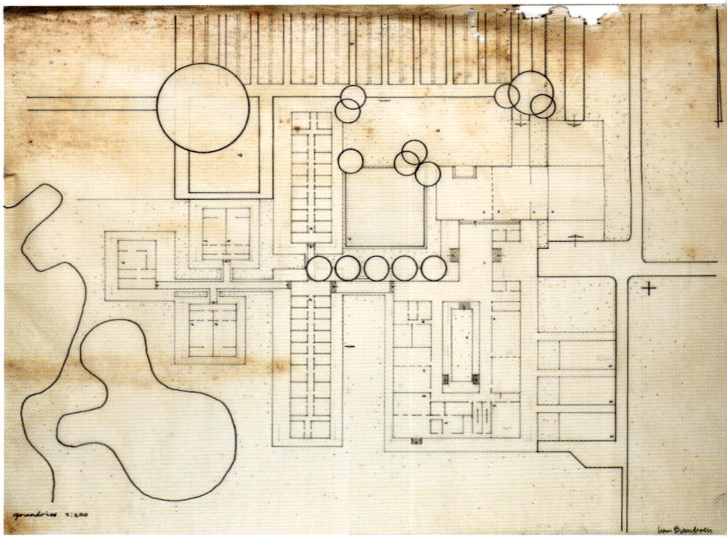

Source: Private archive Bianpoen family

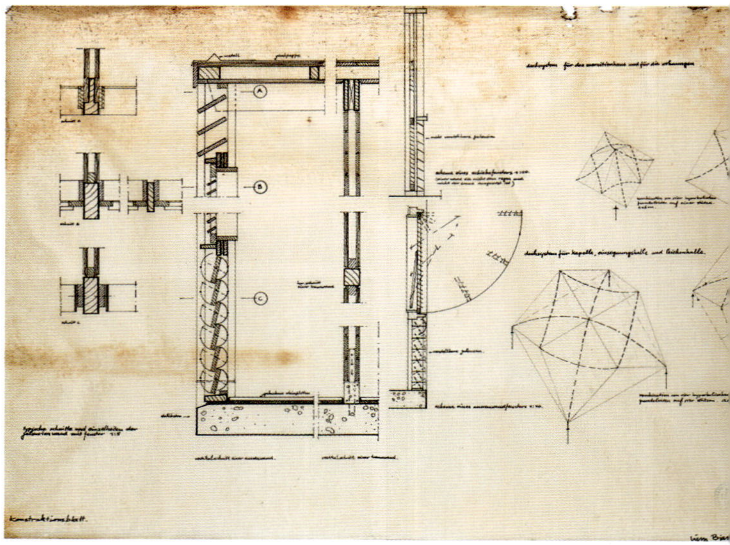

Source: Private archive Bianpoen family

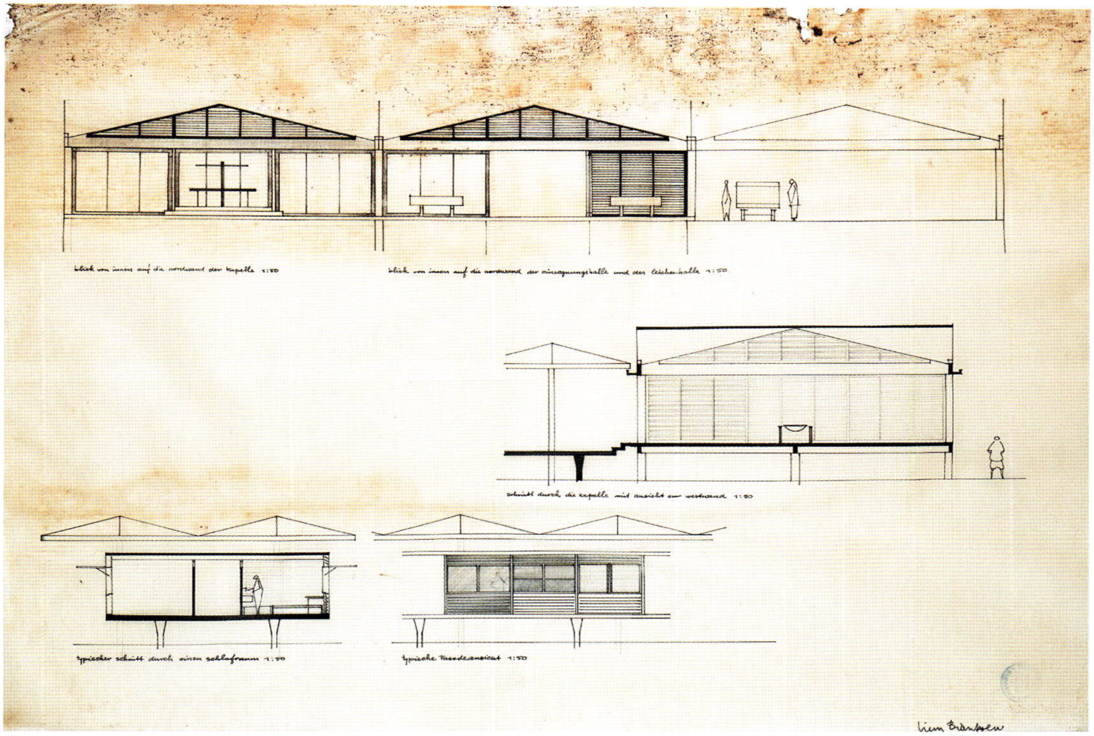

Source: Private archive Bianpoen family

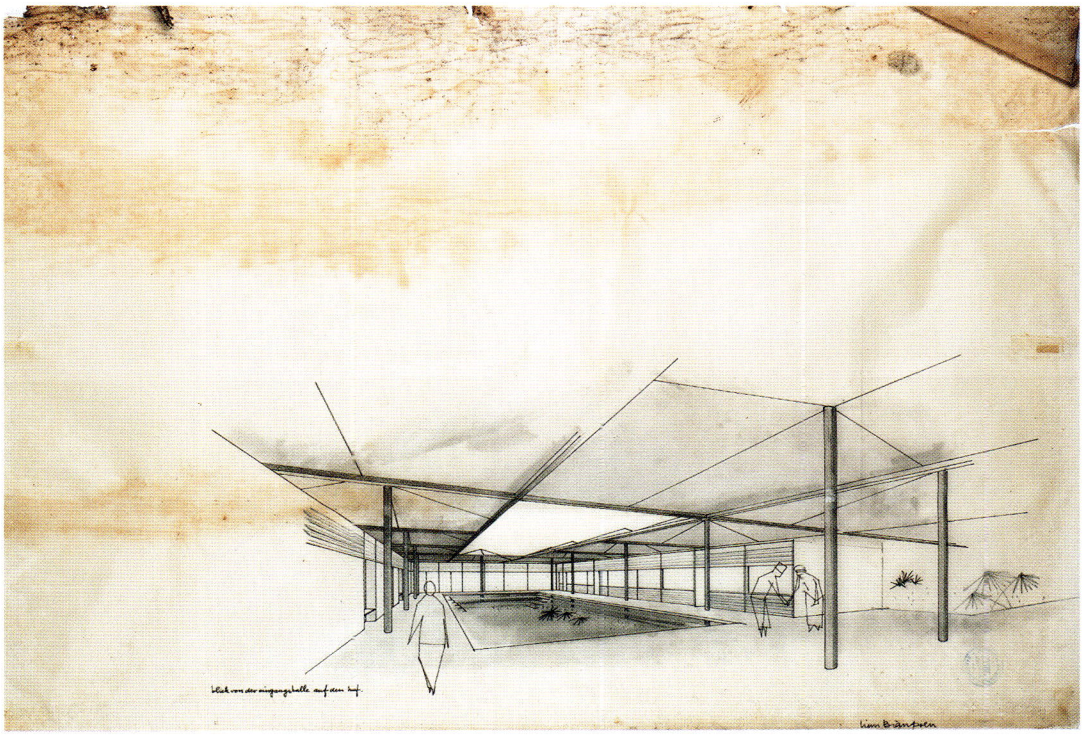

Source: Private archive Bianpoen family

HAN AWAL DLM
SERAGAM WAMILDA
SEBAGAI SAKSI 1961
SEBAGAI PENGANTEN JAWA
WANCIN MEMPERKENAL
KAN SALAH SEORANG
TEMAN KEPADA AYAH-
NYA DI PRINSENHOF
DI BALKON RUMAH
KOS WANCIN DI DELFT
PIDATO SEBAGAI
KETUA JURUSAN
DI ITB 1966-1969
MAHASISWA DI DELFT
1949 - 1951
1954 - 1957
ANAK PERTAMA 1928
SOEMINI DAN SOETEDJO
TECHNISCHE HOCHSCHULE HANNOVER
ZEUGNIS
Diplom-Hauptprüfung
TEILNEHMERAUSWEIS
NAME SOETEDJO, SOEKONDO
LAND INDONESIEN
HOCHSCHULE TH HANNOVER
Fahrberechtigungsausweis für Studenten
30.4.1962

BIOGRAPHIES

Han Awal in front of a model of his unrealised design for the expansion of Bank Indonesia, ca. 1980s.

Photo: Han Awal & Partners

Prarentjana Teaching Hospital St. Carolus Salemba Jakarta. Architects: Bianpoen / Han Awal.

Source: Han Awal & Partners

Han Awal
1930–2016
Adelia Andani Djarot

Han Awal was born HAN Hoo Tjwan in Malang on 16 September 1930. His father, Han Kang Hoen, was a respected and influential figure and his mother, Kwee Liam Nio, was a housewife and seamstress. In 1951, Hoo Tjwan moved to Delft, where he studied architecture at the Technische Hogeschool on a scholarship from the Diocese of Malang. Together with fellow Indonesian architecture and art students, he formed ATAP, a study group dedicated to discussing contemporary architecture and organising events and excursions. He also joined several student associations, such as the Indonesian Ikatan Mahasiswa Katolik Indonesia (Catholic Student Association) and the Perhimpunan Pelajar Indonesia (Indonesian Student Association). When the Indonesian government closed its embassy in the Netherlands in 1957 due to the dispute over Papua, Hoo Tjwan was not forced to leave the country because he could have graduated within the following year. However, out of loyalty to his fellow Indonesian students, he, too, left the Netherlands. After almost eight years in Delft, he moved to West Germany to complete his degree at the Technische Universität in Berlin.

In 1960, right after obtaining his Diplom-Ingenieur degree, he returned to Indonesia and started his career as a practising architect, landing his first major project with Universitas Katolik Atma Jaya Indonesia (Atma Jaya Catholic University Indonesia) in Jakarta. In the same year, he joined the Ikatan Arsitektur Indonesia IAI (Indonesian Architecture Association) and worked for the architecture consultancy firm Estetika. During his time there he was involved in the design development of the Press House in Jakarta for the 4th Asian Games in 1962. In 1962, Hoo Tjwan enlisted in the military service, joining the Directorate of Army Engineers in Bogor until 1964. In the following year, he continued to work for the army as a civil servant, where he handled a new building complex for the Conference of New Emerging Forces (CONEFO) as an operational advisor and then as the first assistant of architect Soejoedi Wirjoatmodjo. Hoo Tjwan's career in architecture education started not long after. He began working at the Universitas Indonesia (University of Indonesia) as an adjunct lecturer in 1965, a year after the opening of the architecture department. He later became assistant chancellor at the Akademie Arsitektur Pertamanan AKAP (Academy of Landscape Architecture) in Jakarta (1969–1971) as well as a distinguished lecturer at the Universitas Katolik Soegijapranata in Semarang (1990–2003) and Universitas Merdeka in Malang (1997–2004). In 1968, Hoo Tjwan started an architecture consultant firm with his friend Mustafa Pamuntjak and three draughtsmen. Their practice was located in the garage of Hoo Tjwan's family house in South Jakarta, built in 1962. During this time, the New Order government issued a directive for Chinese citizens to change their names to Indonesian ones. When their firm was registered in 1971, it bore Hoo Tjwan's new name, Han Awal, and operated as Han Awal & Partners (HAP). After establishing HAP, the projects expanded in number and variety. The office designed hospitals such as Rumah Sakit Akademik Atma Jaya (1973–1995) and Siloam Hospitals Lippo Cikarang (1995) in Jakarta; Catholic churches such as Gereja Katolik Bunda Hati Kudus (1964) and Gereja Katolik Santo Yakobus (1985) in Jakarta, and Protestant churches such as GPIB (Gereja Protestan Indonesia bagian Barat) in Jakarta (1993) and GPIB Bandung (1994); schools such as SMA Pangudi Luhur (1963) and SMP Pangudi Luhur (1976); offices and factories such as Pabrik PT Schering Indonesia (1973), Pusat Penelitian Ilmu Pengetahuan dan Teknologi scientists' dormitory (1980), and Kantor dan Percetakan Gramedia (1982); as well as hundreds of private houses. In the late 1980s, HAP expanded its services to include project administration, management, and coordination.

In 1982, Han experienced a turning point in his career with the Jakarta Cathedral restoration project, which marked his entry into the conservation of historic buildings. In 1995, together with Cor Passchier (b. 1945) and Budi Lim (b. 1953), he restored the Gedung Arsip Nasional (National Archive Building) in Jakarta, an eighteenth-century Indies Style house initially owned by Governor-General Reynier de Klerk (1710–1780). In 2002, Han established Pusat Dokumentasi Arsitektur (PDA, Architecture Documentation Centre) as part of an agreement between IAI and the Royal Institute of Dutch Architects (BNA). He also co-founded the Jakarta Old Town Revitalisation Corporation (JOTRC) in 2014, where he became a member of the advisory board.

Han has received several national and international awards, such as the IAI Award (1979, 1999, 2009), the Award for Excellence from UNESCO Asia Pacific Heritage Awards (2001), and the Professor Teeuw Award for contributing to Indonesian-Dutch cultural exchanges through collaborations between IAI and BNA (2007). For his lifetime contribution to architecture and conservation, he received the Medal for Service in National Culture (Satya Lencana Kebudayaan) from the Indonesian government in 2012. Han Awal passed away on a peaceful afternoon on 14 May 2016.

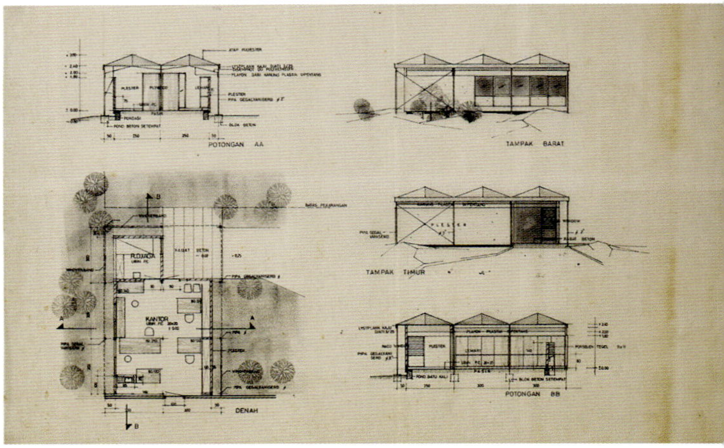

First Office of Han Awal, Jakarta, 1970. Architect: Han Awal.

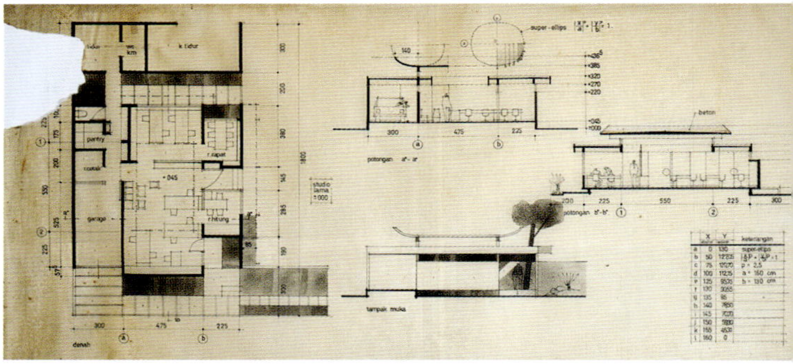

Expansion of the Han Awal studio, Jakarta, 1972. Architect: Han Awal.

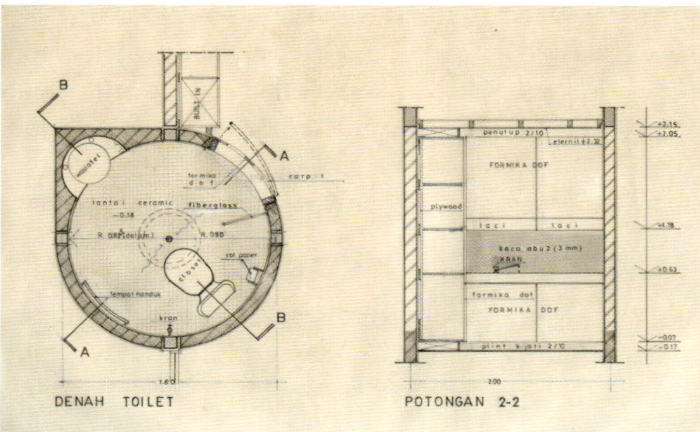

Detail planning for the toilet, 1976.
Architect: Han Awal.

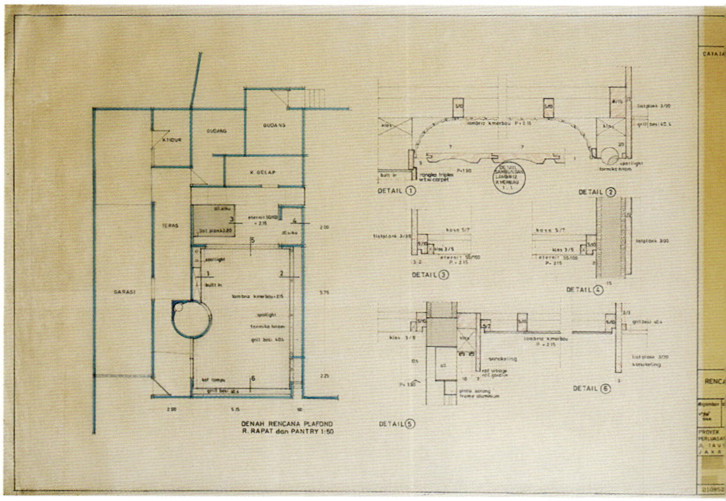

Second office extension and study, ceiling plan for meeting and pantry, Jakarta, 1976. Architect: Han Awal.

Source: Han Awal & Partners

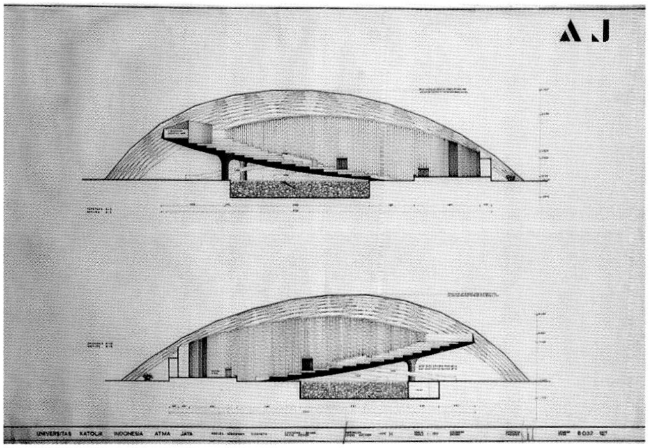

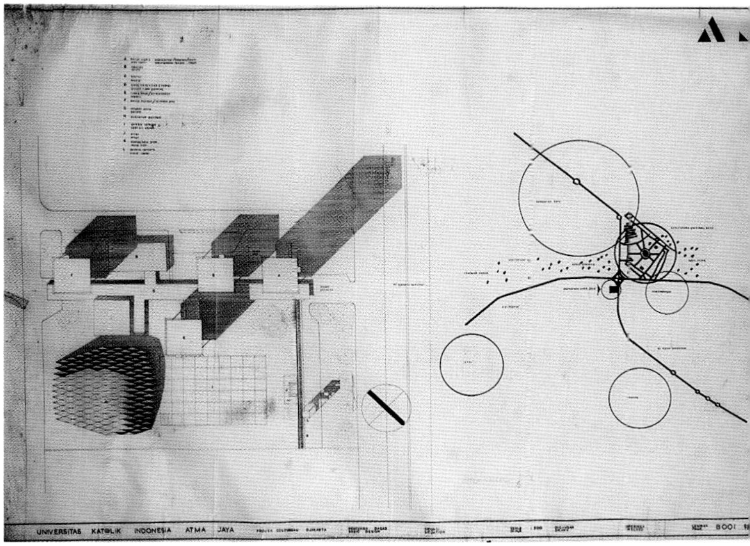

Atma Jaya Catholic University of Indonesia, Jakarta, 1960 Architect: Han Awal.

Source: Han Awal & Partners

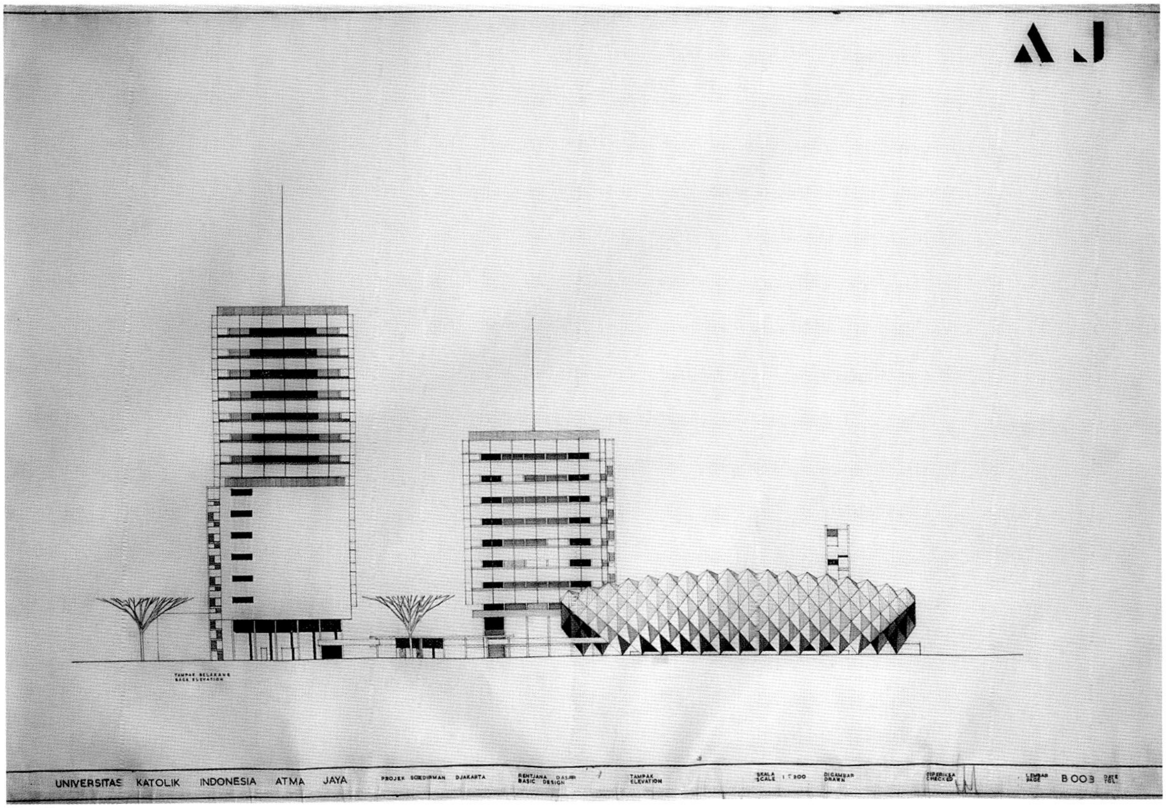

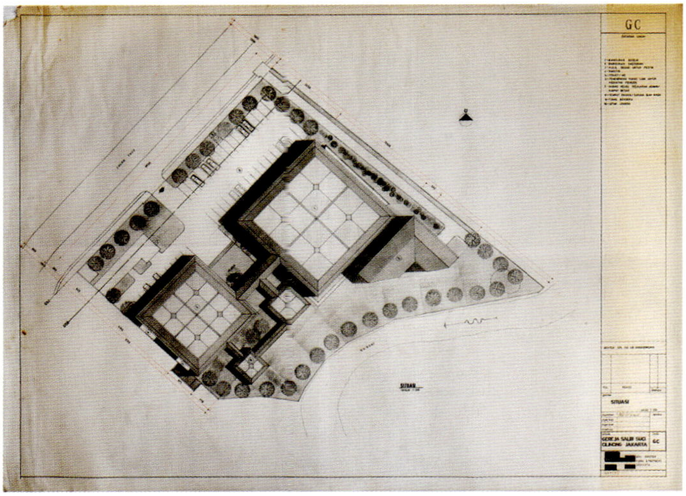

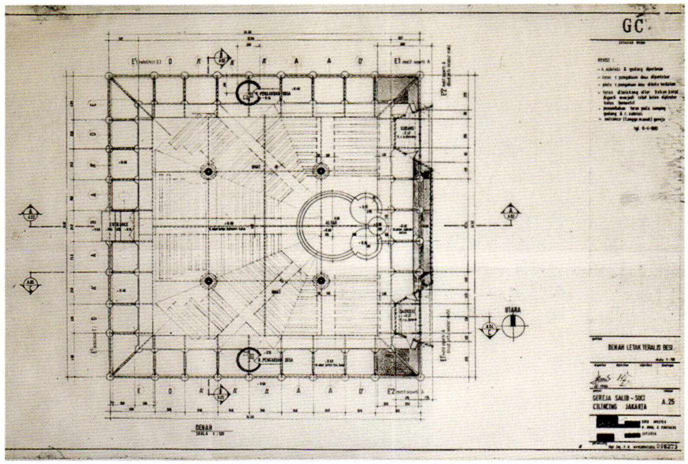

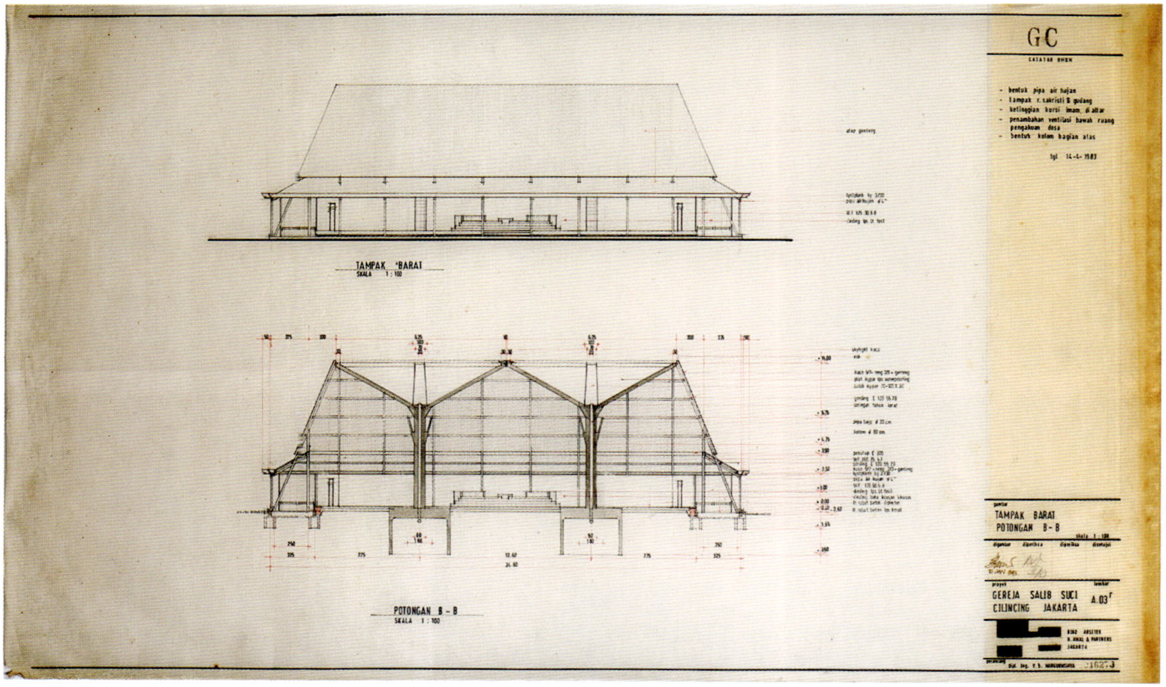

Gereja Katolik Salib Suci Paroki Cilincing (Holy Cross Catholic Church, C lincing), Jakarta, 1982–1984. Architect: Yusuf Bilyarta Mangunwijaya / Han Awal & Partners. (See p. 210–211.)

Source: Han Awal & Partners

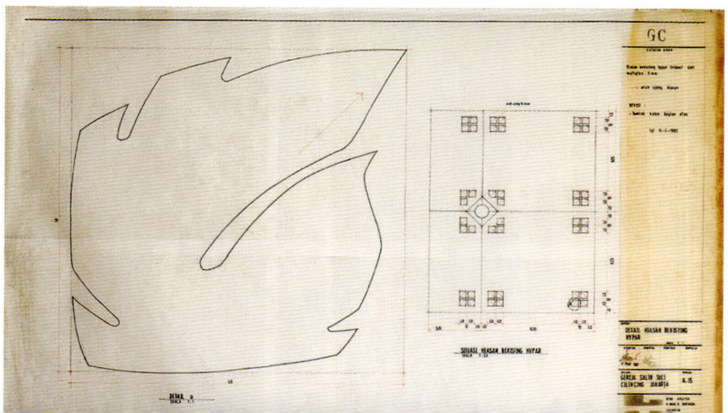

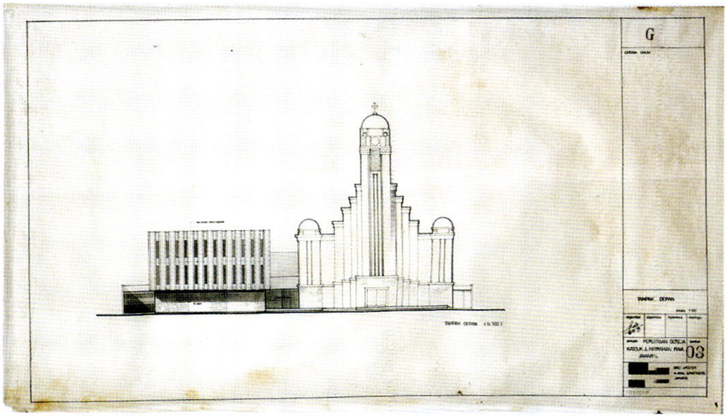

Extension Catholic Church. Jl. Matraman Raya, Jakarta, 1979.
Architect: Han Awal & Partners.

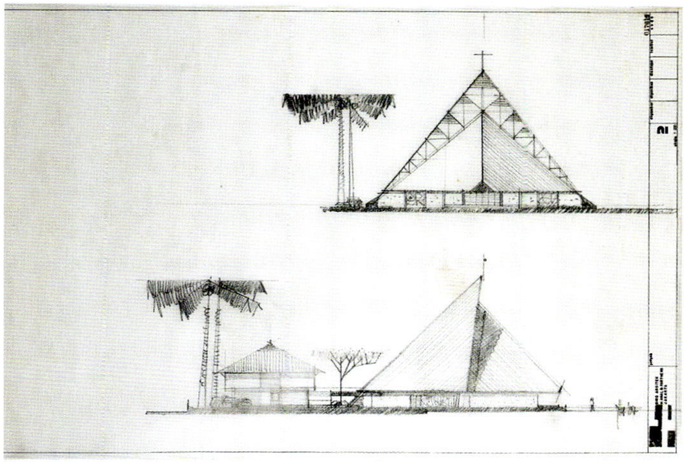

Gereja Katolik Santo Yakobus Jakarta, 1988.
Architect: Han Awal & Partners.

Holy Family Catholic Church, Rawamangun Jakarta, 1985.
Architect: Han Awal & Partners.

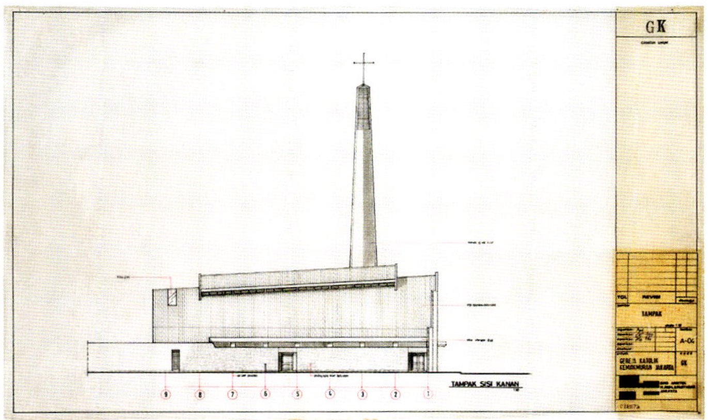

Gereja Katolik Bunda Hati Kudus Kemakmuran (Sacred Heart's Lady Catholic Church, Kemakmuran) Jakarta, 1988.
Architect: Han Awal & Partners.

Source: Han Awal & Partners

Renovation of the neo-gothic Gereja Santa Maria Pelindung Diangkat ke Surga (St. Mary of the Assumption Cathedral), Jakarta, 1982–1984. Architect: Han Awal & Partners.

Source: Han Awal & Partners

KAT
CATATAN UMUM
gambar
PENGUKURAN POTONGAN MEMANJANG &
SISTEM POTONGAN ATAP
SKALA 1:100
digambar
diperiksa
disetujui
proyek
lembar
PEMUGARAN
GEREJA KATHEDRAL
AJ/41
BIRO ARSITEK
H.AWAL & PARTNERS
JAKARTA

KAT
PENGUKURAN
TAMPAK SELATAN
PEMUGARAN
GEREJA KATHEDRAL

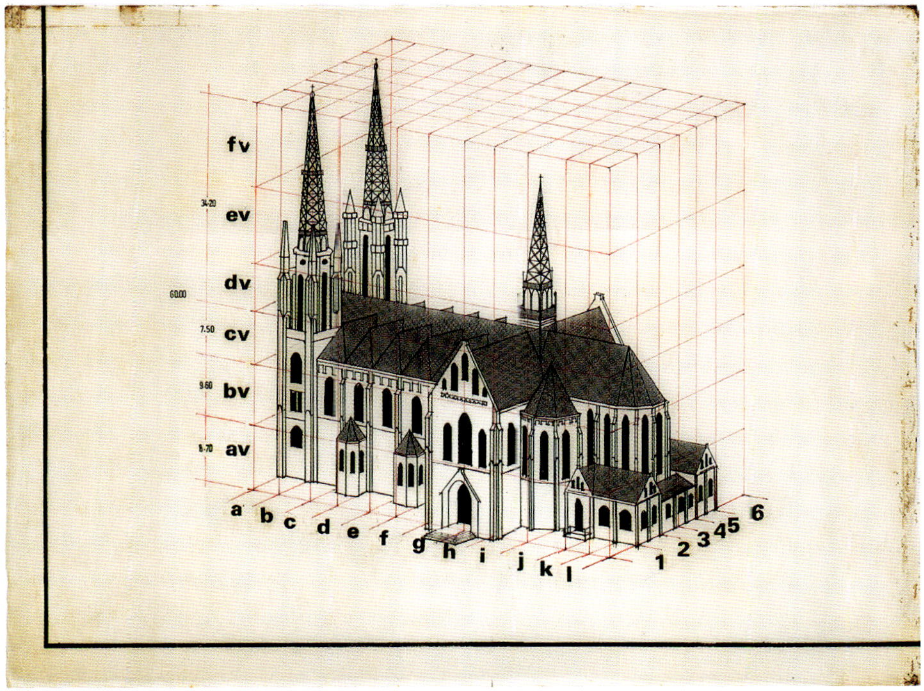
fv
ev
dv
cv
bv
av
a b c d e f g h i j k l
1 2 3 4 5 6

Herianto Sulindro (KHO Lin Hek), 1957.

Photo: Private archive Linda Lochmann

Diploma certificate of Herianto Sulindro (KHO Lin Hek), 1960.

Source: Private archive Linda Lochmann

DIE
TECHNISCHE
UNIVERSITÄT
BERLIN

VERLEIHT MIT DIESER URKUNDE

Herrn Lin Hek Kho
geboren am 15. Dezember 1928 in Sukaradja/Java

DEN GRAD

DIPLOM-INGENIEUR

NACHDEM ER IM ORDNUNGSMÄSSIGEN VERFAHREN DIE DIPLOMPRÜFUNG IN DER FAKULTÄT FÜR ARCHITEKTUR ABGELEGT HAT

BERLIN-CHARLOTTENBURG, DEN 1. Juni 1960

DER REKTOR

DER DEKAN

Herianto Sulindro
b. 1928
Eduard Kögel

Herianto Sulindro was born on 15 December 1928 in Sokaraja, Java. In 1952, he began studying architecture in Bandung. In November 1957 he moved to the Netherlands, where he studied in Delft for a few months under his original name KHO Lin Hek. He soon transferred to the TU Berlin in January 1958, receiving his diploma two years later. Together with Jan Beng Oei and King-Han Oei, he played badminton on both the university team and in the club Helios. A newspaper article dubbed the skilled player the 'badminton professor' due to his 'incredible tricks'. During his studies, he lived in the Eichkamp International Student Residence designed by Hans Christian Müller.

In mid-1960, he applied for architecture jobs throughout Germany and was hired by the firm of Adolf Böhringer in Hamburg, where he designed the Parkhotel Thordsen in Husum, completed in 1962. In mid-1962, Herianto Sulindro moved to the Hamburg Building Authority, where he was involved in major urban planning projects under the direction of Werner Hebebrand (1899–1966). In early 1963, he applied for a job in Switzerland and was hired in November as an *Aushilfsarchitekt* ('assistant architect') at the Urban Planning Department in Zurich, where he remained until his retirement in 1993. His work there during the 1960s addressed population development, a new centre and local transportation infrastructure for the district of Seefeld, a new centre for the district of Höngg, and the design of parks and public spaces.

He married in 1967 in a civil ceremony in Jakarta and then three months later in the Catholic Church in Zurich-Albisrieden. It was not until 1968 when he had already been living in Switzerland for several years that he changed his Chinese name to the Indonesian-sounding name Herianto Sulindro. Around 1969, Sulindro, who used both names interchangeably that year, considered emigrating to the United States but ultimately remained in Zurich. In the 1980s, he was promoted to the position of senior officer (Adjunkt). In the 1970s and 1980s, alongside his work at the planning department, he designed multifamily homes for friends in Lufingen, Locarno, and Ascona. Herianto Sulindro retained his Indonesian citizenship and returned to his homeland in 2017, where he now lives in a retirement home.[1]

1 The presentation of Herianto Sulindro's professional career was possible thanks to the support of his daughter, Linda Lochmann, who generously granted us insight into the family's private archive.

Student work in Bandung: interior design for a student flat, 1955. Student: Herianto Sulindro (KHO Lin Hek).

Source: Private archive Linda Lochmann

Student work in Bandung: Design for the home of a dentist, 1956. Student: Herianto Sulindro (KHO Lin Hek).

Source: Private archive Linda Lochmann

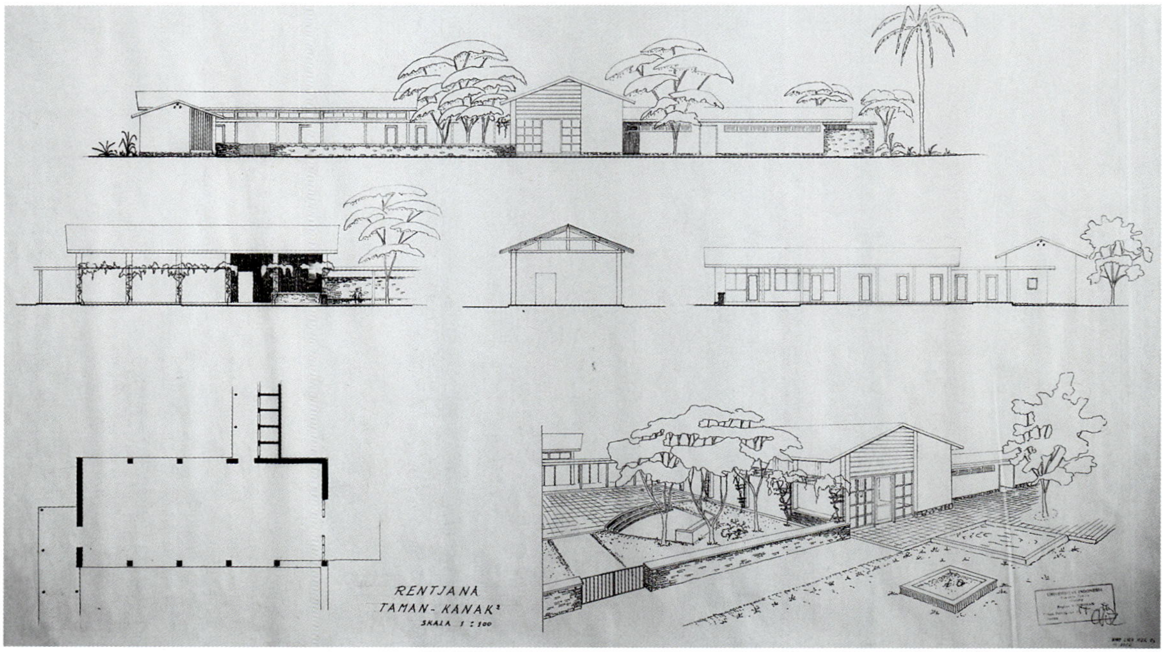

Student work in Bandung: Kindergarten. Student: Herianto Sulindro (KHO Lin Hek), 1955 / 1956.

Source: Private archive Linda Lochmann

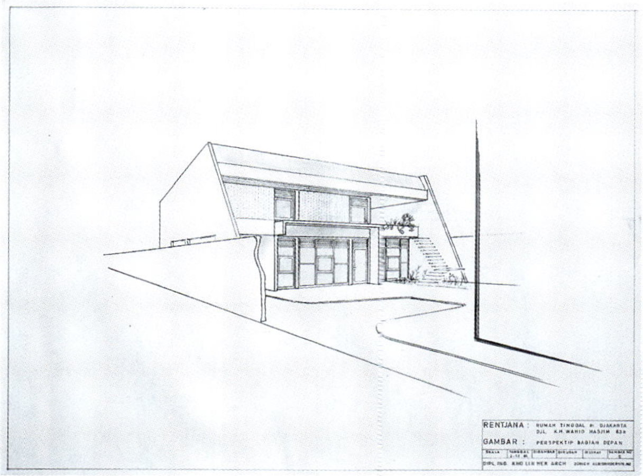

Design for a family home, Jakarta, 1964.
Architect: Herianto Sulindro (KHO Lin Hek).

Source: Private archive Linda Lochmann

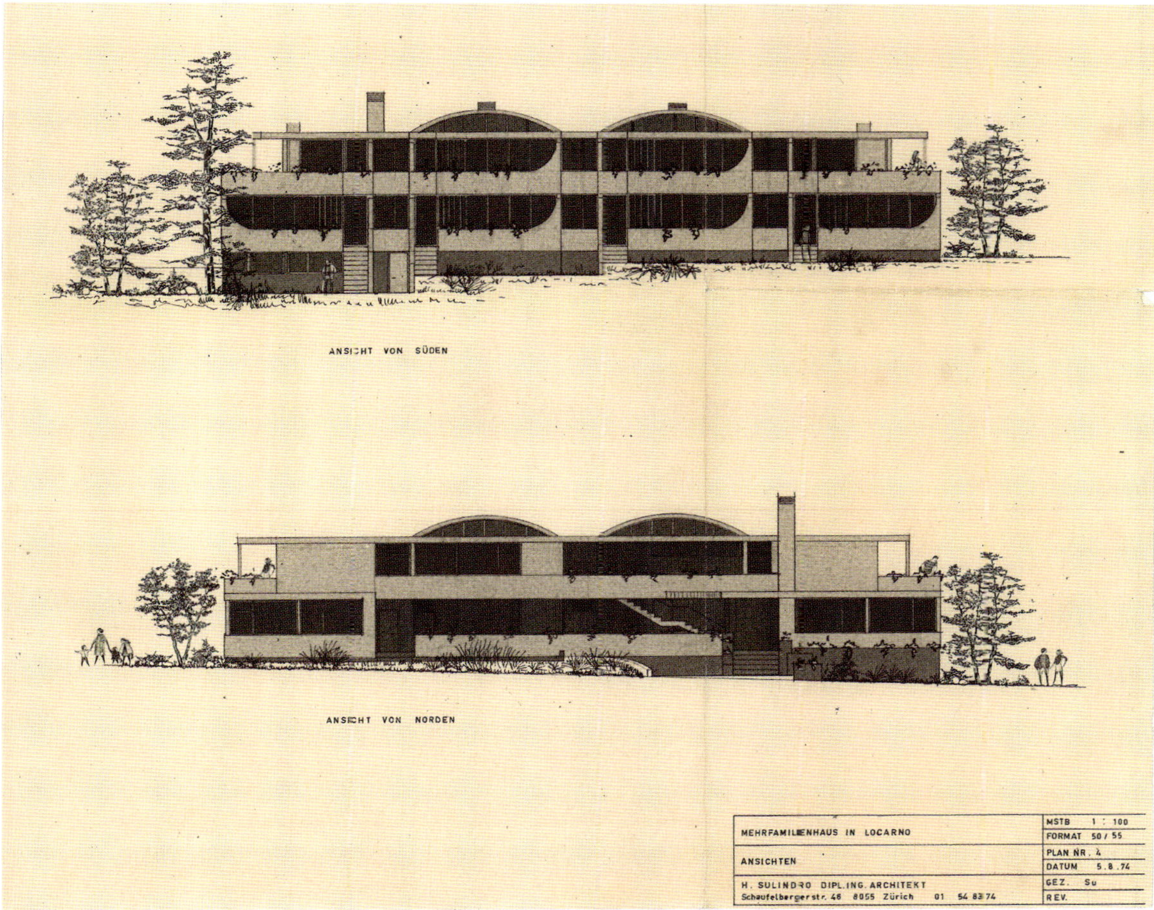

Apartment house, Locarno, 1974.
Architect: Herianto Sulindro.

Source: Private archive Linda Lochmann

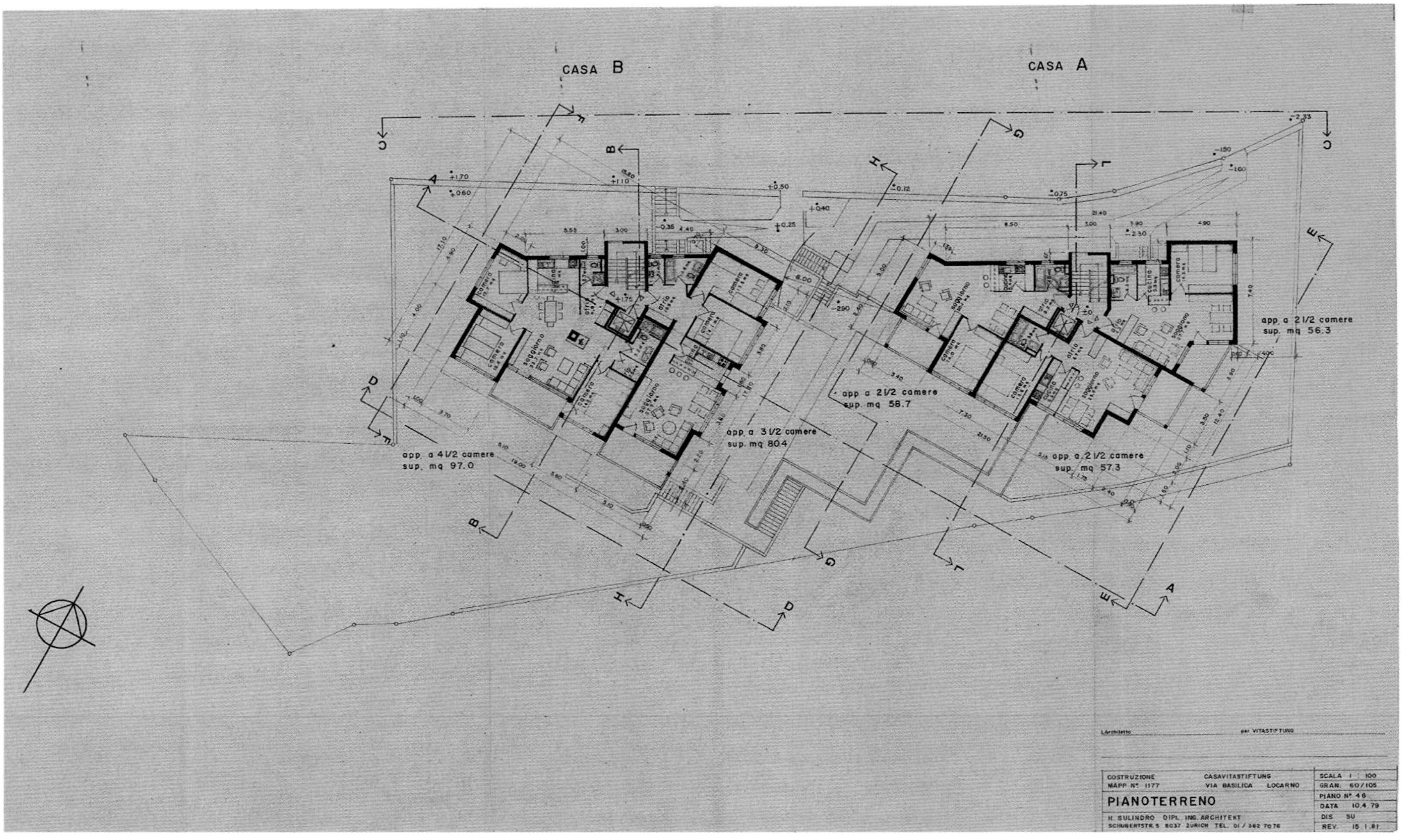

Floor plan for two apartment bui dings (Casa A and Casa B), Locarno, 1981. Architect: Herianto Sulindro.

Source: Private archive Linda Lochmann

Open fireplace on the ground floor and on the first floor of Casa A, 1984. Architect: Herianto Sulindro.

Source: Private archive Linda Lochmann

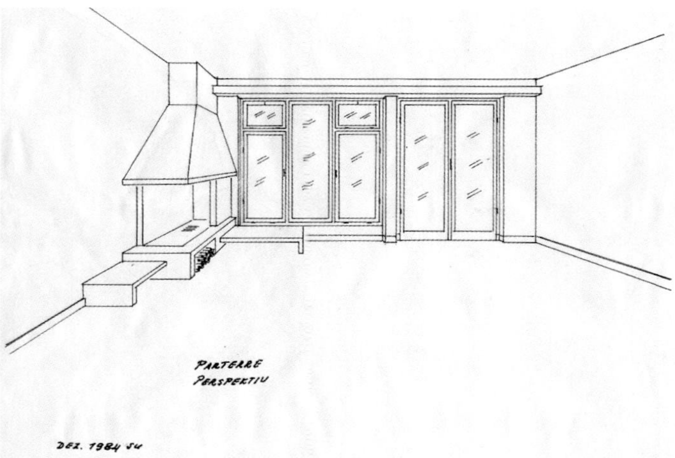

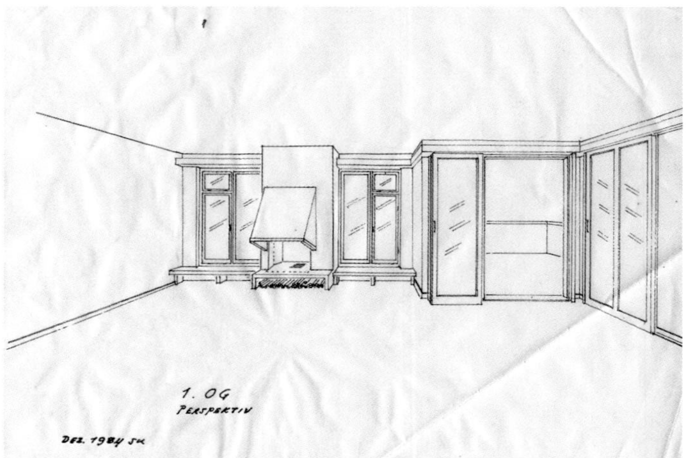

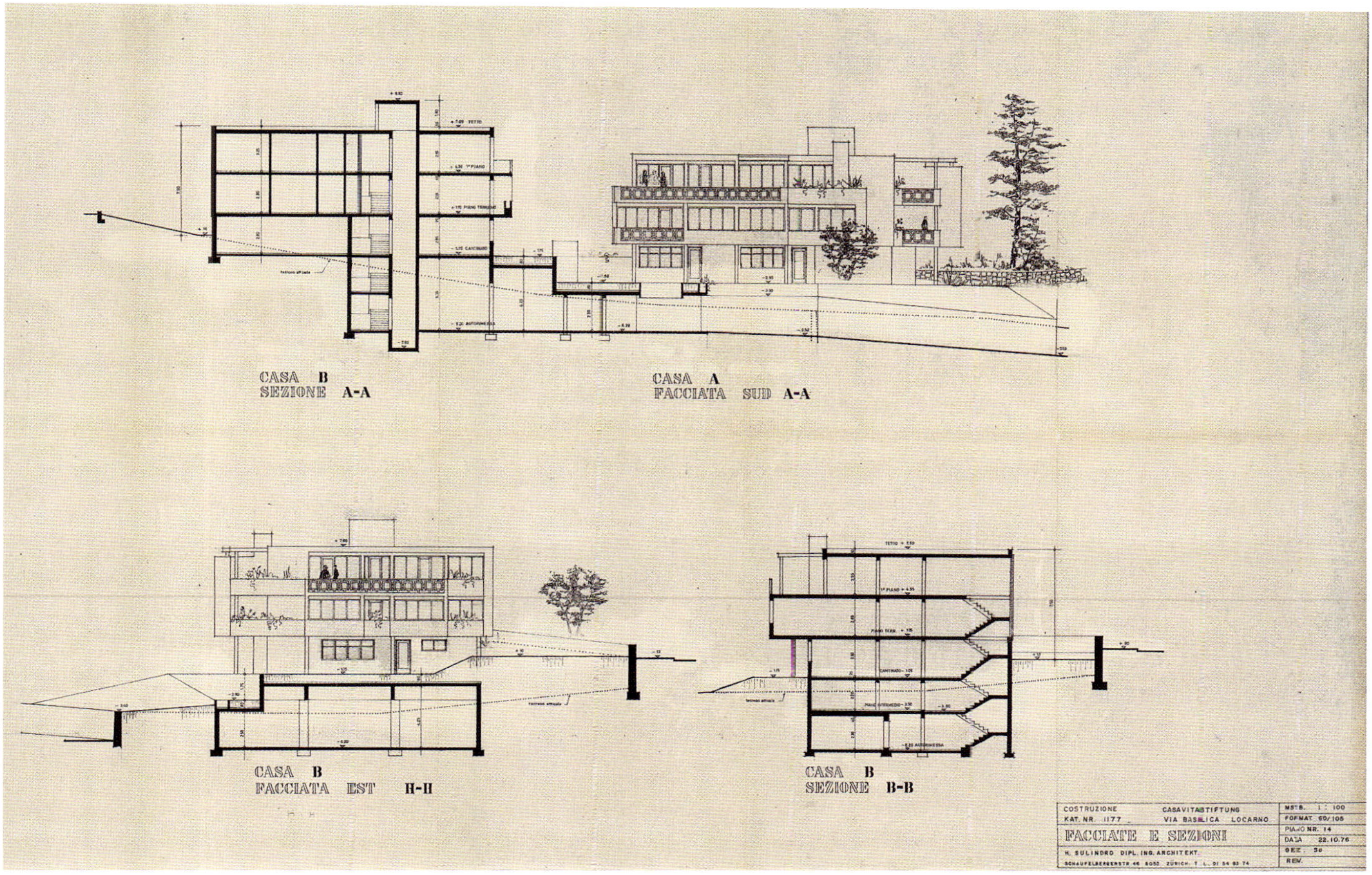

Front view and section of Casa A and Casa B, Locarno, 1979. Architect: Herianto Sulindro.

Source: Private archive Linda Lochmann

Jan Beng Oei, 2022.

Photo: Steffen Oei

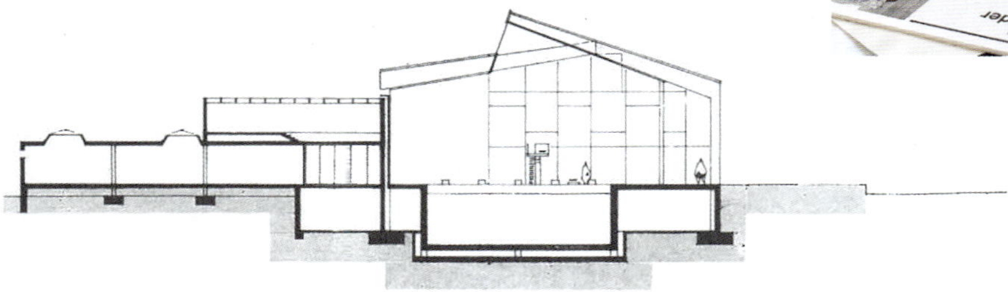

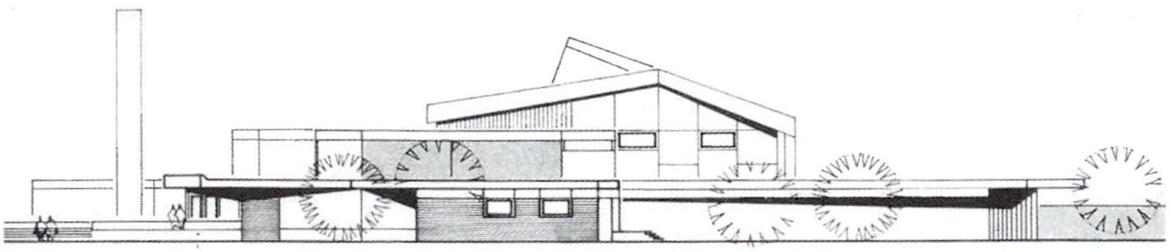

DIPL. ING. JAN BENG OEI
FREIER ARCHITEKT

7012 FELLBACH · AUBERLENSTRASSE 14
WOHNUNG: IRIONWEG 4 TELEFON: 586384

First prize in a competition for a public swimming pool in Fellbach, 1963, unbuilt. Architect: Jan Beng Oei.

Source: Bauwelt 1963 issue 37, p. 1057

Jan Beng Oei
b. 1933
Eduard Kögel

Jan Beng Oei was born in Jakarta into a merchant family. He began studying architecture at the Faculty of Engineering at Universitas Indonesia, Bandung (formerly the Technische Hogeschool Bandung), in 1952. During this time, Oei won a student competition with his design for prefabricated housing; the first prize was a one-year fellowship in the United States through the American Asia Foundation. With fellow student Oen Poo Hauw, Oei first went to California, where he broadened his experience through internships, including two months at Victor Gruen Associates in Los Angeles, California. The practice had just completed the first indoor shopping mall near Minneapolis, Minnesota. Oei also worked for Frank Lloyd Wright (1867–1959) for several weeks at Taliesin West, Wright's winter home and desert laboratory in Arizona.[1]

As a fan of the architects van den Broek & Bakema, Oei left the US in 1957 for the Technische Hogeschool in Delft, where van den Broek was teaching and many of Oei's Indonesian colleagues were already studying. Because of the political tensions between the Netherlands and Indonesia, Oei and some of his fellow students soon transferred to the Technische Universität (TU) in Berlin, where they found another architectural role model in Hans Scharoun. In addition, it was easy to earn money on the side in Berlin to finance their studies. Oei worked in a lottery store, as an extra at the East German film studios in Babelsberg, and also in the offices of the landscape architect Herta Hammerbacher (1900–1985) and the architects Hans Christian Müller (1921–2010) and Hans Scharoun. For the latter, he built 1:20 scale models for the Berlin Philharmonic. Jan Beng Oei received his diploma in April 1960, completing his final project under Professor Kurt Dübbers at the TU Berlin. During his studies, he lived in the Eichkamp International Student Residence designed by Hans Christian Müller.

After graduation, Scharoun got the young architect a job in Stuttgart with the firm of Chen Kuen Lee (1915–2003), a German architect of Chinese descent who was building an apartment house there. Soon after, Oei won first prize in a competition for an indoor swimming pool in Fellbach near Stuttgart in 1963. The city council declared: 'The design by Jan Beng Oei is undoubtedly of high architectural quality.' Nevertheless, the commission went to the duller, second prize-winner – a hotly contested decision in the magazine *Bauwelt*.[2] By winning another competition for the Jakob-Andreä-Haus (completed in 1968) in Waiblingen, a community centre for the Protestant church, Oei could finally realise his first building and open his own practice by the mid-1960s. Today, the three-building ensemble is incomprehensibly on the verge of demolition, despite various conversion concepts developed through a competition.

In Fellbach, where Oei lives, he won a further competition in collaboration with Hans-Dieter Lutz and others for an inner-city redevelopment project that dragged on for several years because of controversial public debates. Located in an area characterised by two- and three-storey gable-roofed buildings, the new mixed-use complex had up to 12 floors and an integrated shopping mall – a testimony to the discourse of 'urbanity through density' circulating in the architectural scene at the time. With his radical concept of a mixed-use urban building block, Oei tested new urbanist ideas that were already criticised during the construction phase up until the end of 1970s and would no longer be possible today.

Two outstanding buildings of his œuvre are the Lindenhalle culture and conference centre in Ehingen (1978–1984) near Ulm and the community centre in Waiblingen (1979–1985) near Stuttgart, both of which Oei's firm was able to design and build by winning competitions. Both follow a similar concept, in which the architect designed everything from the integration into the landscape to the differentiated interior design.

1 'Asian Architects Visit LA Architect', Architect and Engineer, vol. 210, no. 2, 1957, p. 34.

2 tt, 'Projekt für ein Hallenbad', Bauwelt, vol. 37, 1963, p. 1057.

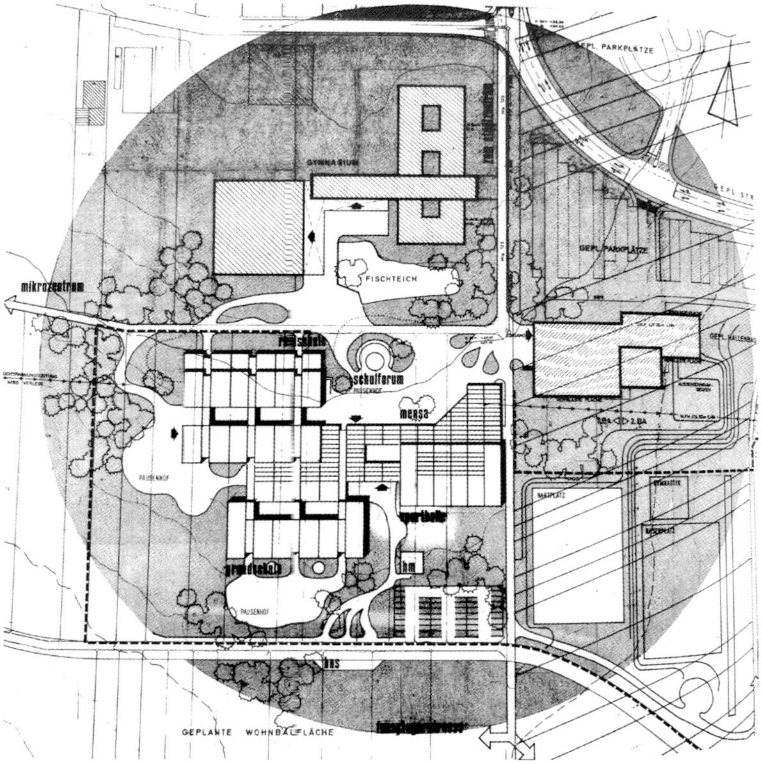

Third prize in a competition for the educational centre Längenholz in Herrenberg, 1973. Architects: Jan Beng Oei, Janos Kenéz.

Source: wettbewerbe aktuell 7/1973, p. 633

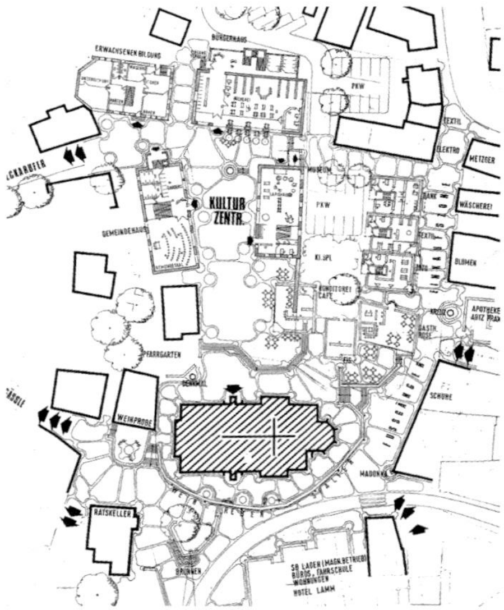

Second prize in the competition for an urban redevelopment in Heilbronn-Sontheim, 1975. Architects: Jan Beng Oei, Janos Kenéz; landscape design: Wolfgang Miller.

Source: wettbewerbe aktuell 9/1975, p. 769

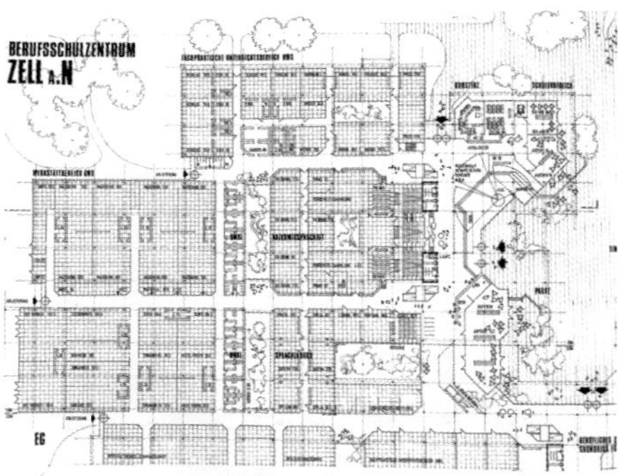

Fourth prize in a competition for a vocational school centre in Zell a. N., 1974. Architects: Jan Beng Oei, Janos Kenéz.

Source: wettbewerbe aktuell 11/1974, p. 109

Fifth prize in the competition for an indoor garden pool in Rebstockpark in Frankfurt/M., 1976. Planning group: Paulus, Oei, Kenéz, Heyd; pool technology: Siegfried Köhler; landscape planning: Prinz, Geiger.

Source: wettbewerbe aktuell 9/1976, p. 557

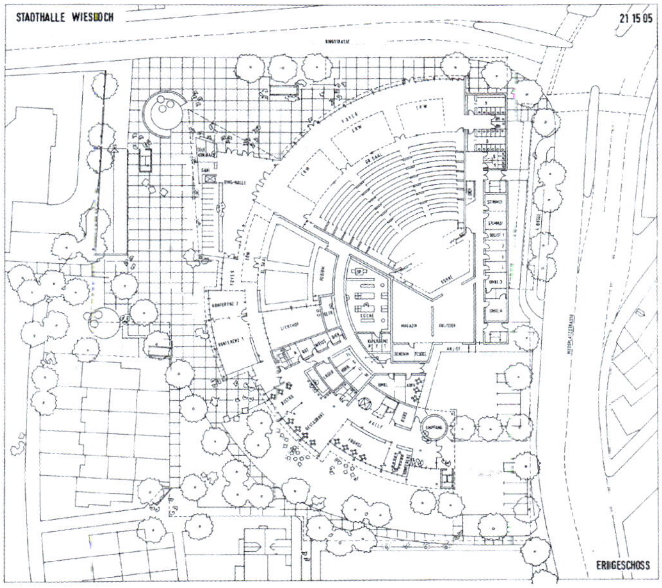

Second prize in the competition for the Palatin Congress Hotel and Cultural Centre in Wiesloch (1988, realised until 1992). Architects: Jan Beng Oei + Partner.

Source: Jan Beng Oei

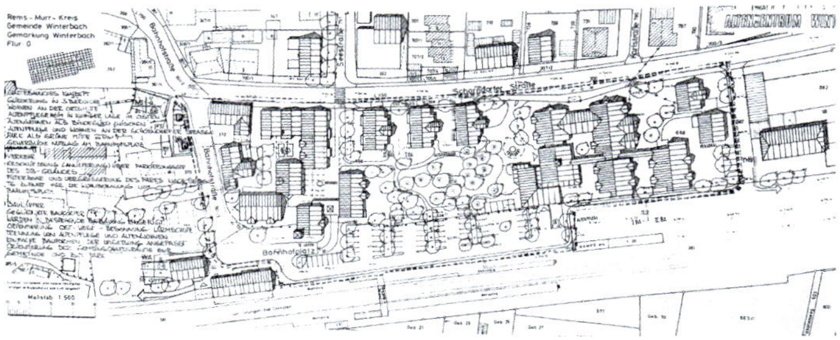

Second prize in the ideas and realisation competition for a centre for the elderly in Winterbach, 1984. Architects: Jan Beng Oei + Partner H. Bromberger.

Source: wettbewerbe aktuell 1/1984, p. 37

First prize in a competition for a public swimming pool in Berlin, 1991, unbuilt. Architects: Jan Beng Oei + Partner Hartmut Bromberger.

Source: Jan Beng Oei

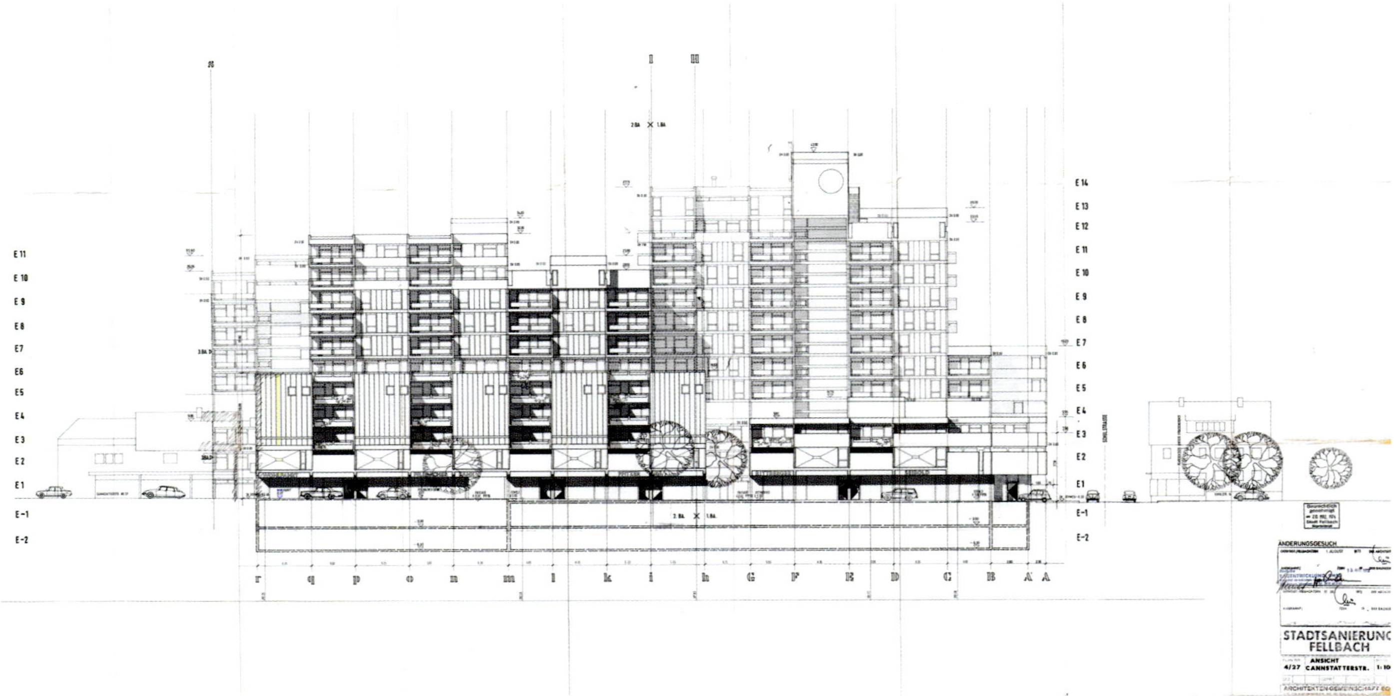

Urban redevelopment 'Wohncity' in the city centre of Fellbach, 1966–1976. Architekten-Gemeinschaft: EOS Kurt Ebinger, Jan Beng Oei, Siegfried Schnell. (See p. 192–195).

Source: Archiv der Stadt Fellbach

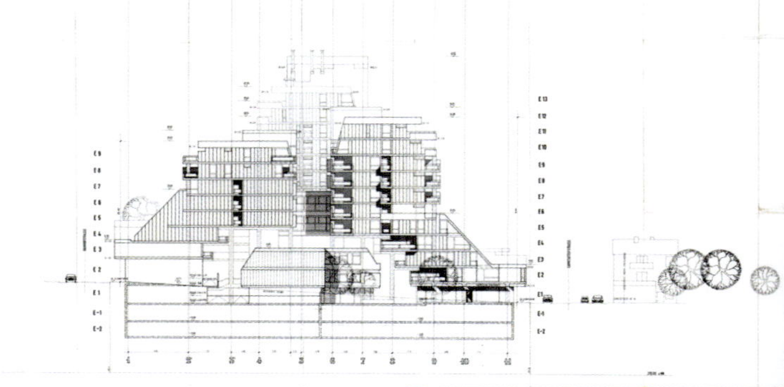

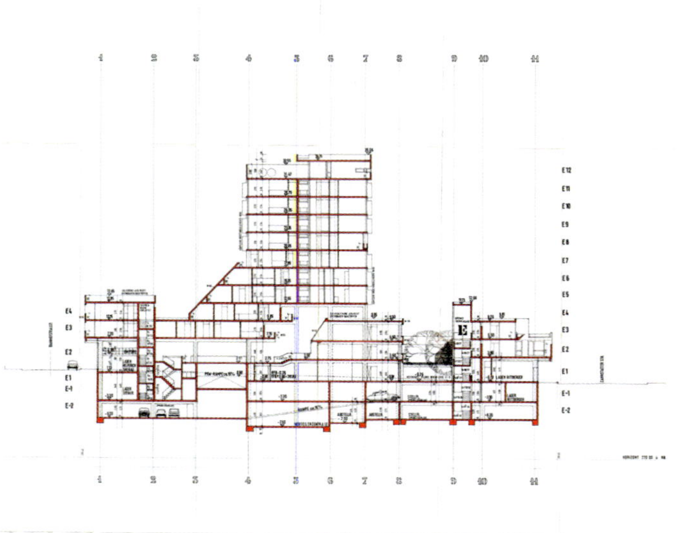

A Entrance Level
1 Vestibule
2 Cash Desk
3 Conference Office
4 Entrance Hall Large Hall
5 Entrance Hall Small Hall
6 Cloakroom
7 First Aid Room
8 Cafeteria
9 Studio
10 Meeting
11 Beer Cellar
12 Bowling Alleys
13 Multipurpose Room
14 Office
15 Staff Stay
16 Kitchen Adjoining Room
17 Orchestra Pit
18 Technic
19 Workshop

B Hall Level
20 Foyer
21 Large Hall
22 Small Hall
23 Stage
24 Restaurant
25 Side Room
26 Conference
27 Kitchen
28 Artist Dressing Room
29 Rehearsal Room
30 Chair Storage

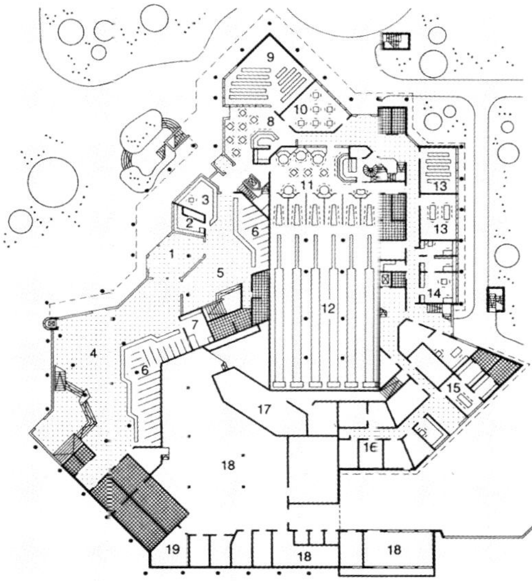

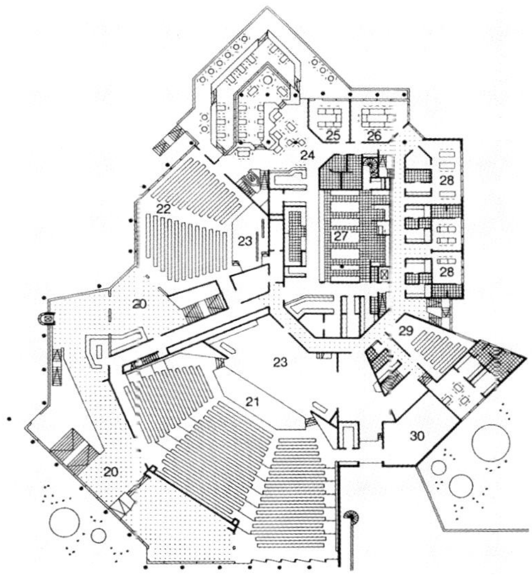

First prize in a competition for Bürgerzentrum Waiblingen, realised 1979–1985. Architects: Jan Beng Oei + Partner Hartmut Bromberger. (See p. 200–203).

Source: Jan Beng Oei

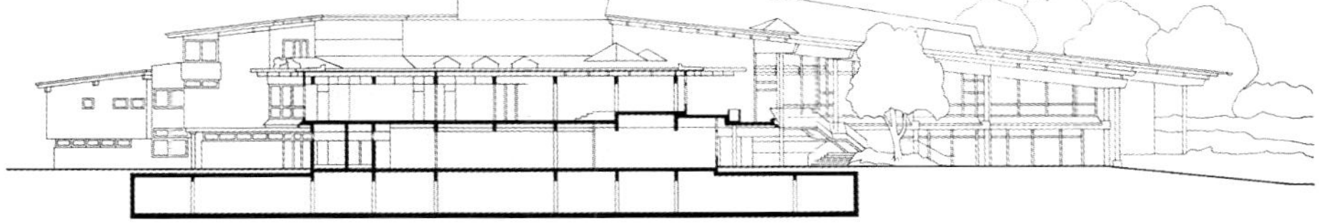

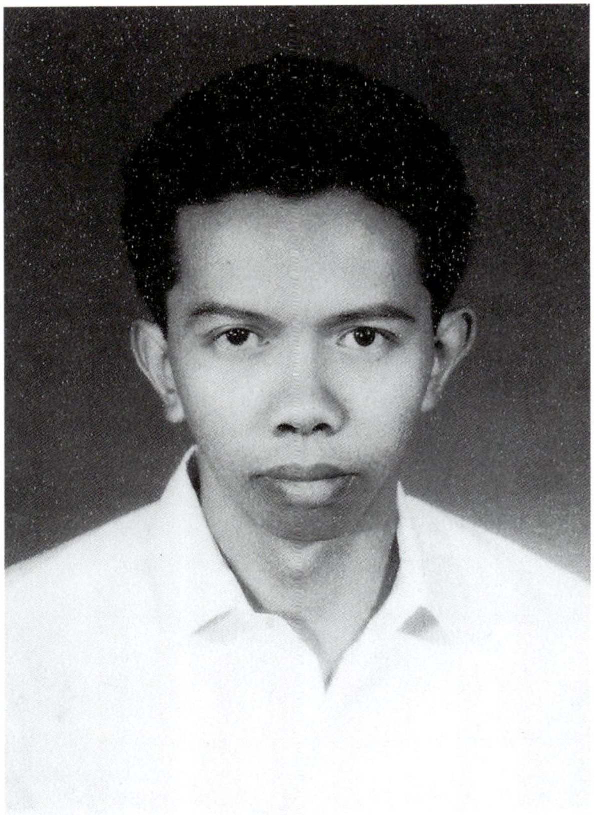

Mustafa Pamuntjak, 1964.

Photo: Private Archive Pamuntjak Family

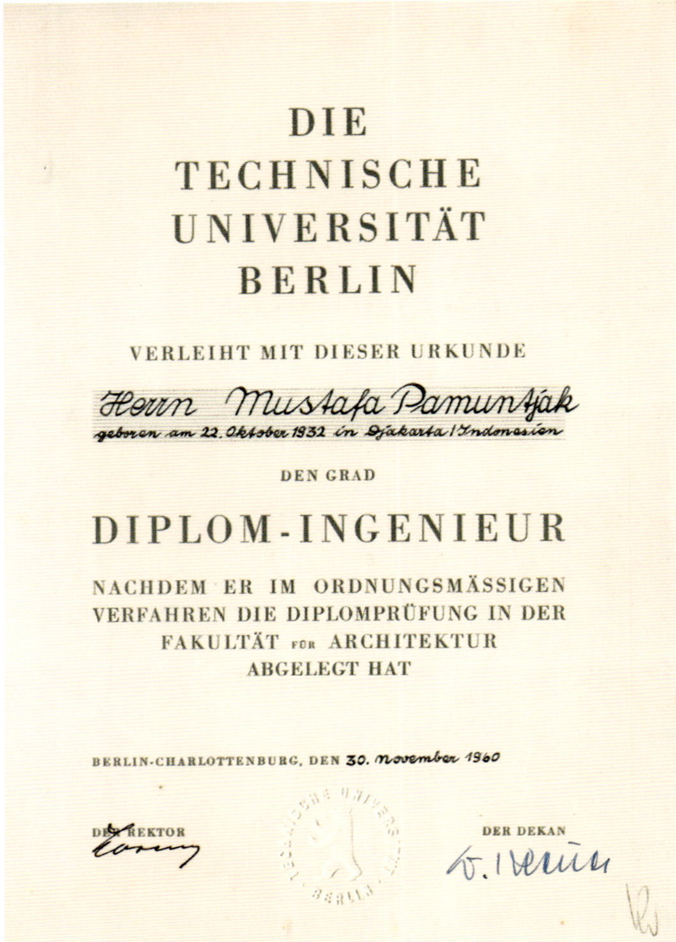

DIE
TECHNISCHE
UNIVERSITÄT
BERLIN

VERLEIHT MIT DIESER URKUNDE

Herrn Mustafa Pamuntjak
geboren am 22. Oktober 1932 in Djakarta / Indonesien

DEN GRAD

DIPLOM-INGENIEUR

NACHDEM ER IM ORDNUNGSMÄSSIGEN VERFAHREN DIE DIPLOMPRÜFUNG IN DER FAKULTÄT FÜR ARCHITEKTUR ABGELEGT HAT

BERLIN-CHARLOTTENBURG, DEN 30. November 1960

DER REKTOR

DER DEKAN

Source: Private Archive Pamuntjak Family

Wedding of Mustafa and Endang Pamuntjak, 1967.

Source: Private Archive Pamuntjak Family

'Ora et Labora' private school (Junior and Senior High School) in Jakarta, 1982. Architect: Mustafa Pamuntjak.

Photo: Private Archive Pamuntjak Family

Mustafa Pamuntjak 1932–2020 Gregorius Jasson, Nadira Adiswari, Siti Arfah Annisa

Mustafa Pamuntjak was born in Jakarta on 22 October 1932 and received his early education there. In 1949, he went to the Netherlands to continue his secondary education at Christelijk Lyceum Leiden. Pamuntjak was inspired to be an architect by the buildings and cities he saw when travelling with his Dutch friends. Following his graduation in 1952, he pursued an architectural education at the Technische Hogeschool Delft.

Due to the diplomatic tensions between the Netherlands and Indonesia in 1957, Pamuntjak moved to West Berlin to study at the Technische Universität, where he was accepted as a seventh-semester student. He was impressed by the learning system, where the professor visited the studio almost daily to confer with the students.[1] Pamuntjak worked on his final project, the design of a broadcasting building, under the guidance of Professor Wilhelm Kreuer and graduated in 1960. He then worked as a junior architect at Kreuer's architectural firm until 1961.

While still a student in Berlin, Pamuntjak and fellow student King-Han Oei submitted a joint contribution to the Paderborn Cathedral Plaza Competition in 1959. The competition sought ideas to redesign the cathedral grounds, and they gained an honourable mention (see p. 52–53).

Upon his return to Indonesia in 1962, Pamuntjak worked as a government employee in several national ministries, tasked with managing macro-scale development on urban and regional planning projects. Starting from the Directorate of Urban and Regional Planning, Ministry of Public Works in Jakarta, he assisted in supervising master plan projects in several cities in Indonesia. From 1968, his work expanded to social housing and neighbourhood improvement programmes when he was assigned as an assistant to the general director for Housing and Urban Planning at the same ministry. He was involved in developing housing policies and monitoring low-cost housing projects, such as the National Urban Development Corporation (Perumnas)[2] and Kampung Improvement Programme (KIP).[3] In 1975, Pamuntjak was assigned by the Ministry of Research as the project director of the Science and Technology Research Centre (Pusat Penelitian Ilmu Pengetahuan dan Teknologi, PUSPIPTEK) in Jakarta. The project was meant to be the largest research body supporting the industrialisation process in Indonesia. Pamuntjak was responsible for managing the entire project until 1979.

Apart from being a government employee, Pamuntjak worked as a professional architect and designed projects for his personal clients from the 1960s onwards. In 1968, Pamuntjak was asked by Han Awal, a former fellow student in Delft and Berlin, to become his partner. Together they founded PT Han Awal & Partners (HAP), where Pamuntjak handled architectural projects ranging from residential houses to public buildings. One of the most notable projects he worked on was the complex of the Faculty of Literature at Universitas Indonesia in Depok (1985–1987), which was built with a tropical architecture approach (see p. 130, p. 204–207).

With experiences in both the ministry and HAP, Pamuntjak established his own practice, Mustafa Pamuntjak & Associates (MPA), in 1995. Besides several public buildings, MPA designed numerous residential buildings. Most of his clients were upper-middle-class families with whom he had networked since the beginning of his career.

1 Pamuntjak, 2017, p. 66.

2 Perusahaan Umum Pembangunan Perumahan Nasional (National Urban Development Corporation, NUDC), commonly abbreviated as Perum Perumnas, is an Indonesian state-owned enterprise engaged in housing development founded in 1974. The establishment of Perumnas is a continuation of the Indonesian government's efforts since 1952 to build decent housing at affordable prices.

3 The Kampung Improvement Programme (KIP), launched in 1969, is the world's first urban slum upgrading project in Jakarta, Indonesia. KIP quickly became a model for transforming slums from illegal settlements into an integral part of the urban fabric.

One of the most noticeable features of Pamuntjak's dwellings is the significant number of openings, with wide sliding glass doors and floor-to-ceiling windows. While large openings provide cross ventilation and plenty of sunlight, they also tend to draw in excess warmth, given Indonesia's tropical climate. However, Pamuntjak's spacious porches act as buffers between the interior spaces and the scorching outdoors, covered by his signature *teritisan* ('canopies') as impactful shading devices. Various ceiling heights and roof angles also create different paths for air circulation.
Pamuntjak's work at MPA continued even after he moved to his home in South Jakarta in 2006. This house was personally designed with the concept of SOHO (Small Office Home Office), which caters to both residential and office functions separated by vertical and horizontal boundaries. Mustafa Pamuntjak passed away in Jakarta on 10 December 2020. He left a legacy of 126 houses and bungalows, at least 40 major construction and renovation designs, as well as other urban-scale projects.

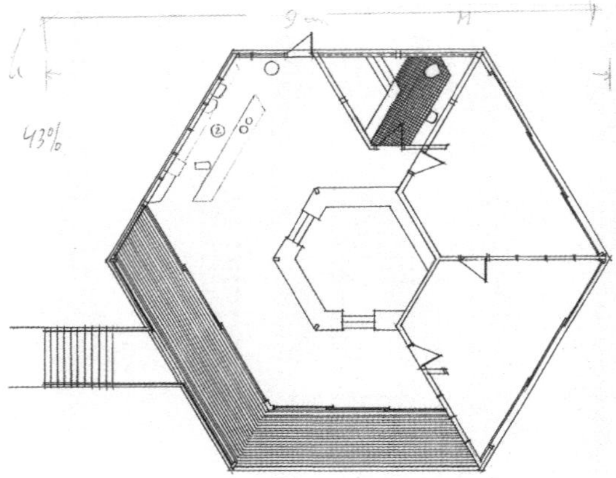

House in Megamendung, West Java, 1971. Architect: Mustafa Pamuntjak. (See p. 212–213).

Source: Private Archive Pamuntjak Family

Residential Extension in Jalan Bangau, Jakarta, 1992. Architect: Mustafa Pamuntjak. (See p. 222–223).

Source: Private Archive Mustafa Pamuntjak Family

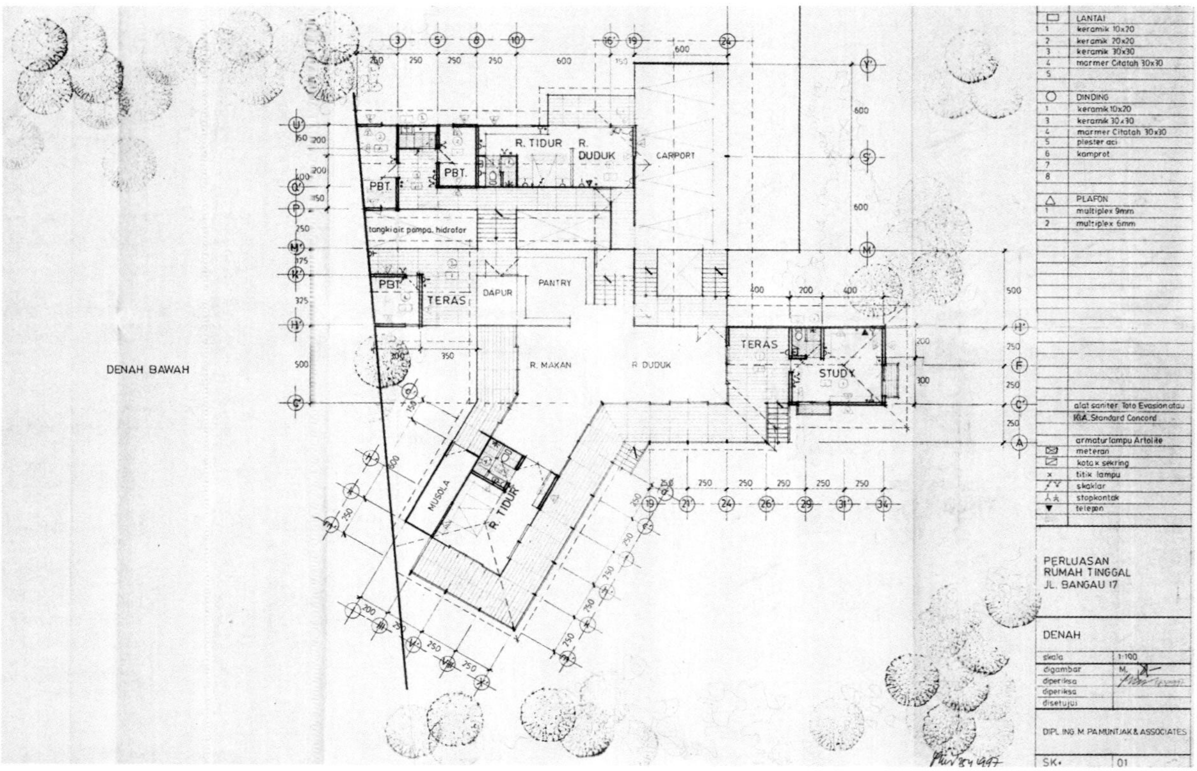

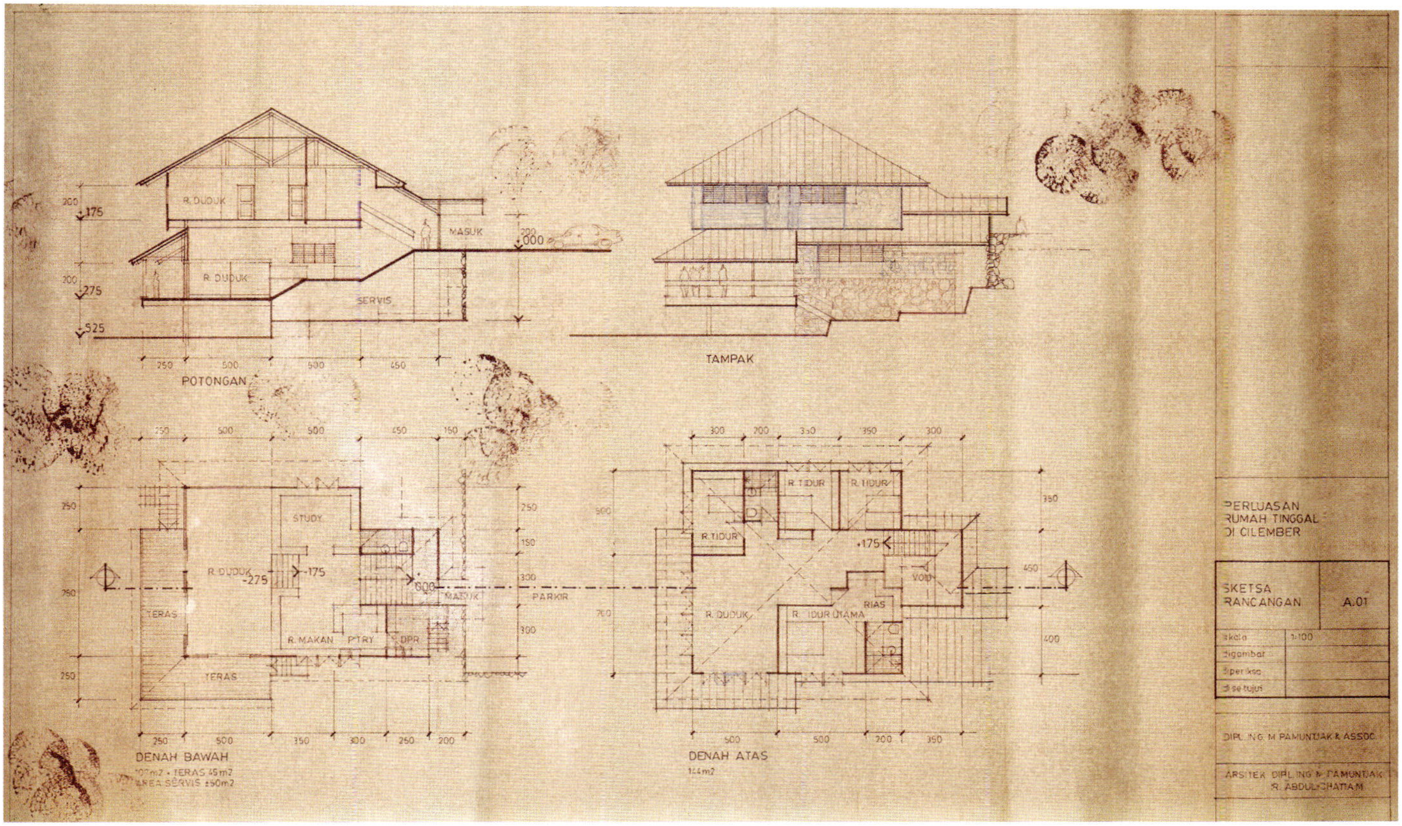

Residential Extension in Cilember, West Java, 1997. Architects: Mustafa Pamuntjak & Assoc. (See p. 214–217).

Source: Private Archive Pamuntjak Family

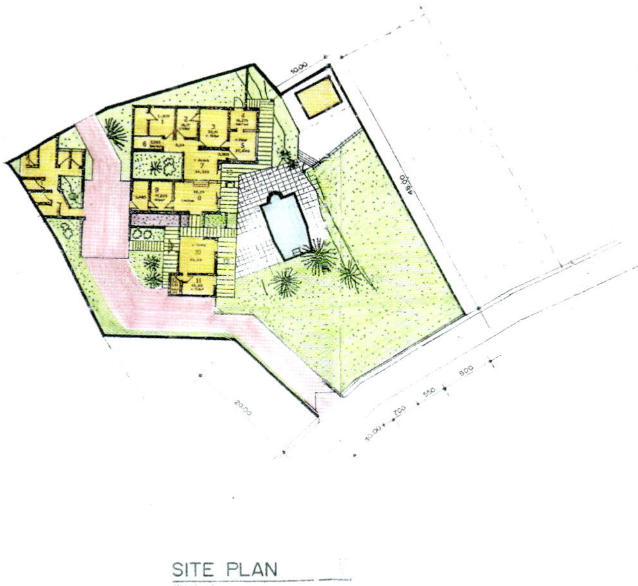

House in Jaya Mandala, Jakarta, 1973. Architect: Mustafa Pamuntjak. (See p. 218–223).

Source: Private Archive Hutabarat Family

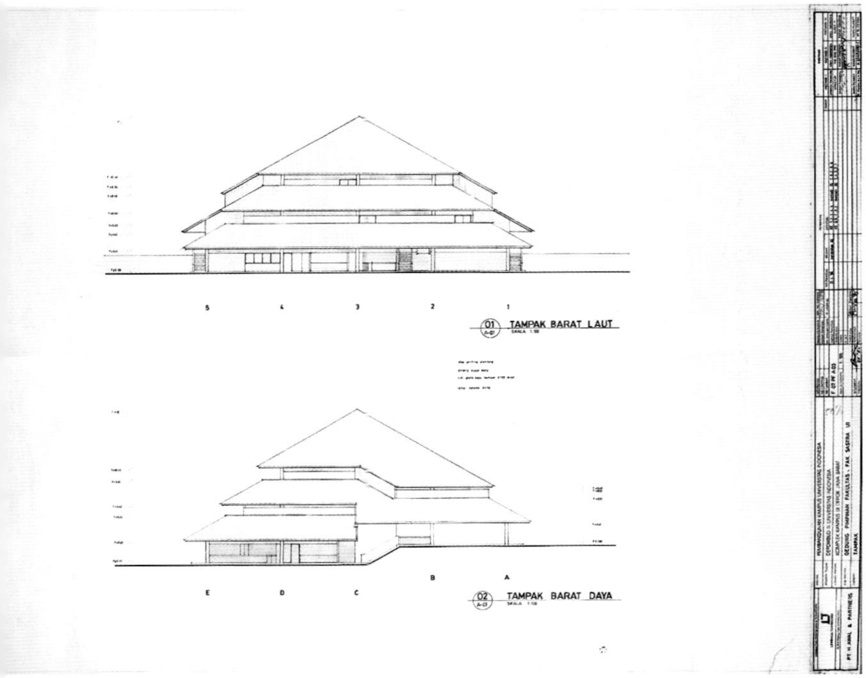

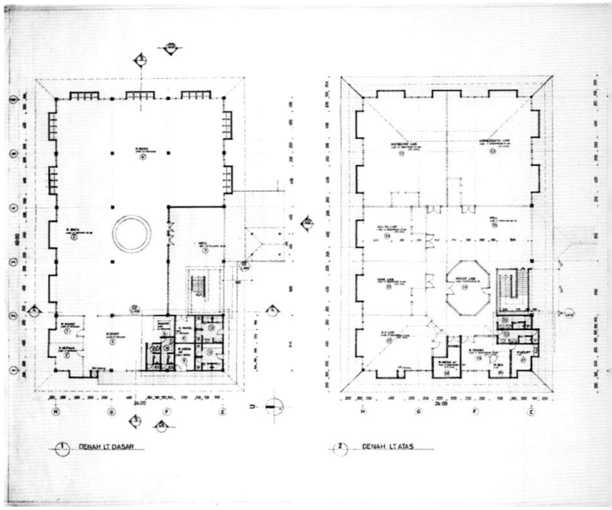

Faculty of Literature, University of Indonesia, Depok, 1985–1987. Architects: Mustafa Pamuntjak, Abdul Chattam / PT. Han Awal & Partners. (See p. 204–207).

Source: Han Awal & Partners

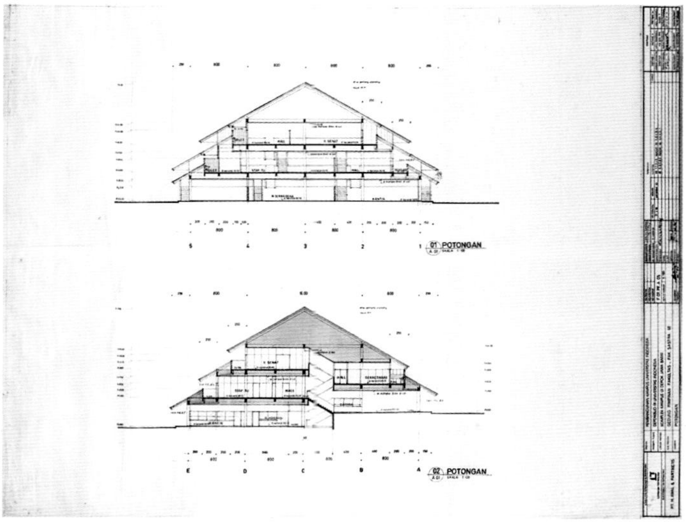

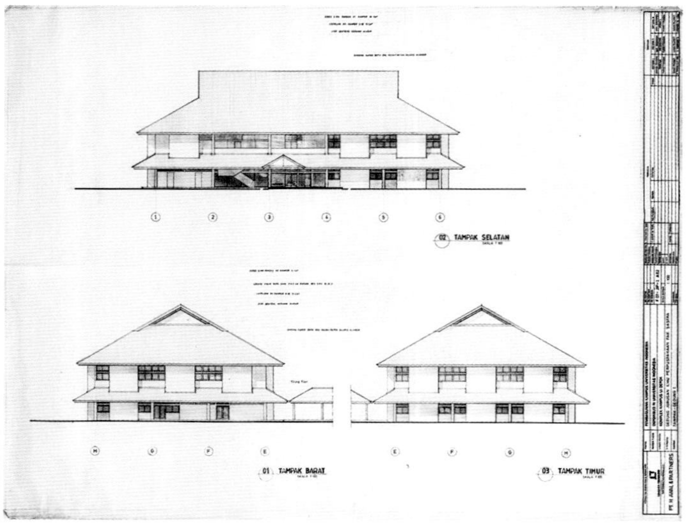

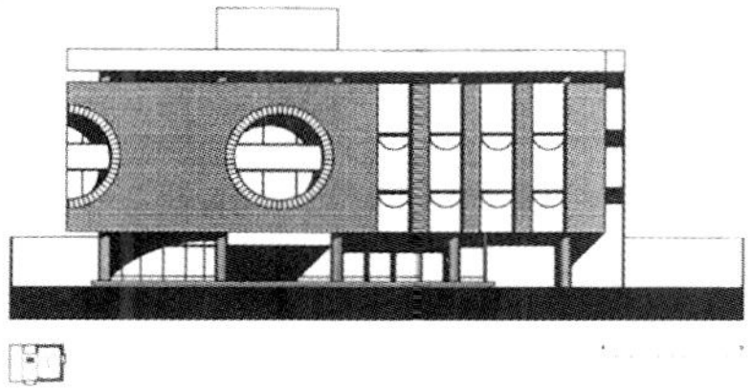

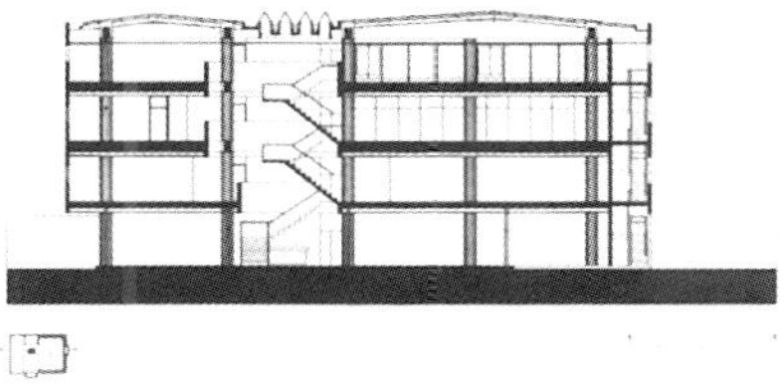

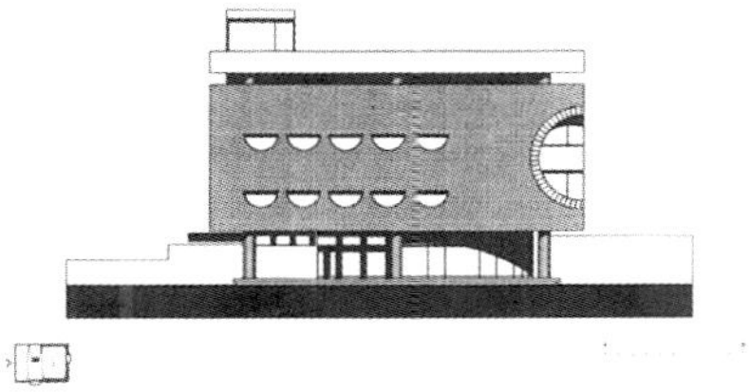

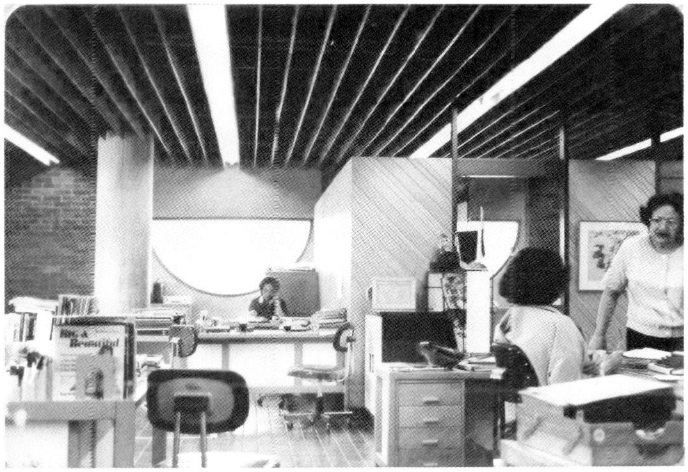

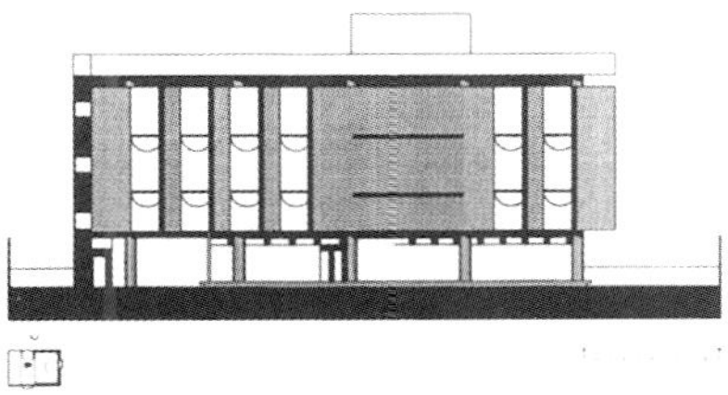

Femina Building, Jakarta, 1982. Architects: Mustafa Pamuntjak & Assoc.

Source: Private Archive Mustafa Pamuntjak Family

Soejoedi as a student
at Universitas Indonesia,
Bandung.

Photo: Soejoedi Family Archive

Farewell memento to
Soejoedi from ITB students.

Source: Soejoedi Family Archive

Soejoedi with the French
Ambassador Pierre Gorce,
1974.

Photo: Soejoedi Family Archive

Soejoedi Wirjoatmodjo 1928–1981 Angeline Basuki

Soejoedi Wirjoatmodjo was born on 27 December 1928 in Rembang on the island of Java. During the Revolusi, the Indonesian struggle for independence, Soejoedi joined the military (1945–1950), where he was appointed chief of staff of Student Army Brigade 17, Detachment II, Region V, in Solo. However, the uncertain life in the militia deteriorated his health, and he was later diagnosed with cirrhosis of the liver.

After graduating from middle school, Soejoedi applied to the Faculty of Engineering at Universitas Indonesia in Bandung (formerly Technische Hogeschool Bandoeng; now Institut Teknologi Bandung ITB). He initially studied mechanical engineering, but in 1951 he transferred to the Faculty of Engineering's Department of Architecture, which had just been established by the Dutch professor Vincent Rogers van Romondt (1903–1974). In 1954, Soejoedi received a scholarship from the French government to study at L'Ecole des Beaux-Arts in Paris, but he was soon dissatisfied. In 1956, he moved from France to the Netherlands and continued his studies at the Technische Hogeschool Delft. The following year, Soejoedi worked as an intern at Kraaijvanger Architects in Rotterdam. During his studies in Delft, he was involved in the ATAP study group along with Bianpoen, Han Awal, Mustafa Pamuntjak, and other Indonesian architecture and art students.

The following year, Indonesian students on national scholarships were advised to leave the Netherlands due to the escalating conflict between the two nations over West Guinea. Soejoedi, along with Han Awal, Mustafa Pamuntjak, and others, went to Germany to study at the Technische Universität in West Berlin. He completed internships at the architectural firms Kasper in Freiburg (1958) and Hentrich und Petschnigg in Dusseldorf (1960–1961), the latter of which influenced his later work in Indonesia.[1] Under the supervision of professor Wilhelm Kreuer, Soejoedi completed his final design project for an Islamisches Refugium (*pesantren* or Islamic boarding school) with cum laude.

Upon returning to Indonesia, Soejoedi received a teaching post at ITB together with Suwondo Bismo Sutedjo, who had just returned with an architecture degree from Hanover. Soejoedi replaced the recently retired Dutch professor van Romondt as head of the School of Architecture at the ITB. His homecoming was eagerly anticipated, and his thesis from Berlin was exhibited at the school.

Besides his academic career, Soejoedi designed several government buildings and private houses. He joined the architectural firm Estetika in Jakarta, where Han Awal also worked back then, and became the head of the Bandung branch, which he managed from his garage. His early works for Estetika include the redesign of Braga Permai in Bandung, a historical colonial café built in 1918, and the official residences of ITB lecturers. Later, he established his own architectural practice, Prakarsa, which focused mainly on residential buildings. In 1963, Jajasan Kerdjasma Arsitek (Architecture Collaborative Foundation) ITB appointed him as the Head of Special Project Airport Tuban Bali (1963–1969; now Bandar Udara Internasional Ngurah Rai), and Soejoedi stayed in Bali for that time.

After Soejoedi was appointed architect to the Ministry of Public Works and Electricity in 1964, he won the competition for a new building complex for the Conference of New Emerging Forces (CONEFO)[2] and moved to Jakarta. Construction began in April 1965 and was to be completed before the Independence Day celebrations on 17 August 1966. However, the project was overshadowed by the political situation after 30 September 1965, when six Indonesian army generals were assassinated in a failed coup d'état. Construction was interrupted

1 See F. Christian J. Sinar Tanudjaja (ed.), ARSITEK DAN KARYANYA Dibalik Sosok Karya SOEJOEDI (Yogyakarta: Penerbitan Universitas Atma Jaya Yogyakarta, 1991).

2 The Conference of New Emerging Forces (CONEFO) was formed in 1965, shortly after Indonesia withdrew from the United Nations due to the confrontation between Indonesia and Malaysia.

and resumed only in 1967 under the New Order regime. The complex was renamed the MPR/DPR Building (the People's Representatives Council) and was finally completed in 1984.

In 1969, Soejoedi founded the architectural firm PT. Gubahlaras to continue work on the MPR/DPR project. Other significant projects followed, such as the Kedutaan Besar Perancis (French Embassy, 1969–1973, demolished), the Duta Merlin Hotel (1970, unbuilt), and the Pusat Grafika Indonesia (1971), all in Jakarta, the Kedutaan Besar Republik Indonesia (Indonesian Embassy) in Kuala Lumpur (1974–1976), the Bank Ekspor Impor Indonesia in Pematang Siantar (1976–1978), the Sekretariat ASEAN in Jakarta (1978–1981), the Kedutaan Besar Republik Indonesia (Indonesian Embassy) in Belgrade (1979–1981), the Departemen Perhubungan (Transportation Agency) in Jakarta (1980–1982, now Kementerian Perhubungan), the Pusat Kehutanan (Forestry Centre) in Jakarta (1976–1983), the Departemen Pertanian (Agriculture Department) in Jakarta (1980–1984, now Kementerian Pertanian), and the Bank Ekspor Impor Indonesia in Balikpapan (1981–1983, now Bank Mandiri). Soejoedi was also responsible for the design of the Indonesian National Pavilion at Expo '70 in Osaka, Japan.

Soejoedi was a dedicated worker, juggling between projects day and night, but his weak physical condition was a lifelong challenge. A friend invited him to stay in his residence in Magelang, where the environment was better than in bustling Jakarta. Soejoedi died there on 17 June 1981.

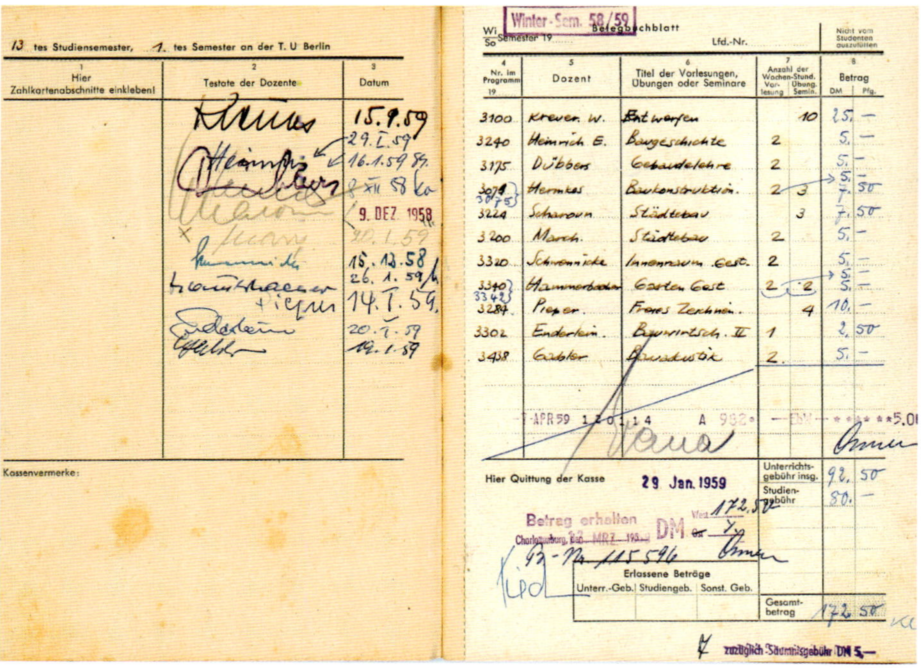

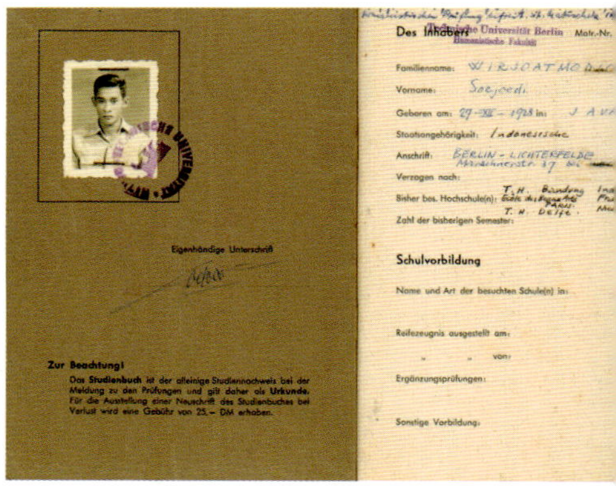

Studienbuch TU Berlin (1958–1960).

Source: Soejoedi Family Archive

CONEFO project (now DPR/MPR, The People's Representatives Council), Jakarta, 1964. Architects: Soejoedi Wirjoatmodjo & Team.

Source: Gedung MPR/DPR RI: Sejarah dan Perkembangannya, Museum DPR

The MPR/DPR building (former CONEFO project) in Jakarta. Architects: Soejoedi Wirjoatmodjo & Team. (See p. 178 – 181).

Photo 1977: TEMPO/ Lukman Setiawan; 32/69/77; 20030911

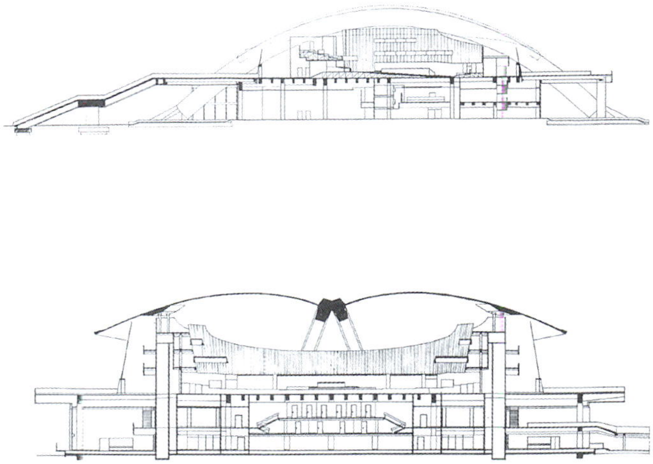

Two sections, CONEFO project (now DPR/MPR, The People's Representatives Council), Jakarta, 1964. Architects: Soejoedi Wirjoatmodjo & Team.

Source: Gedung MPR/DPR RI: Sejarah dan Perkembangannya, Museum DPR

Perspective drawings and floor plan, Duta Merlin Hotel (1971, unbuilt).

Source: Soejoedi Family Archive

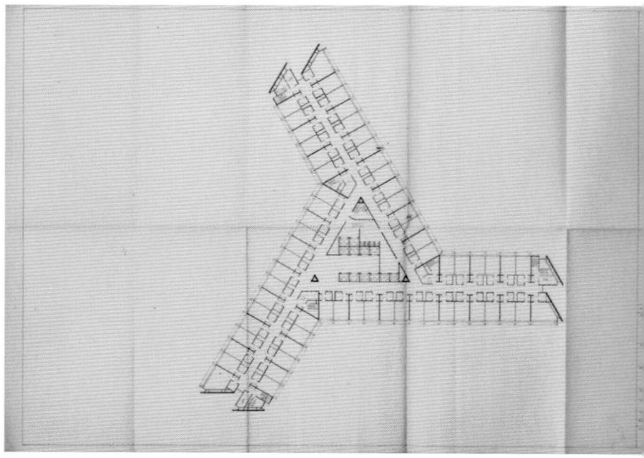

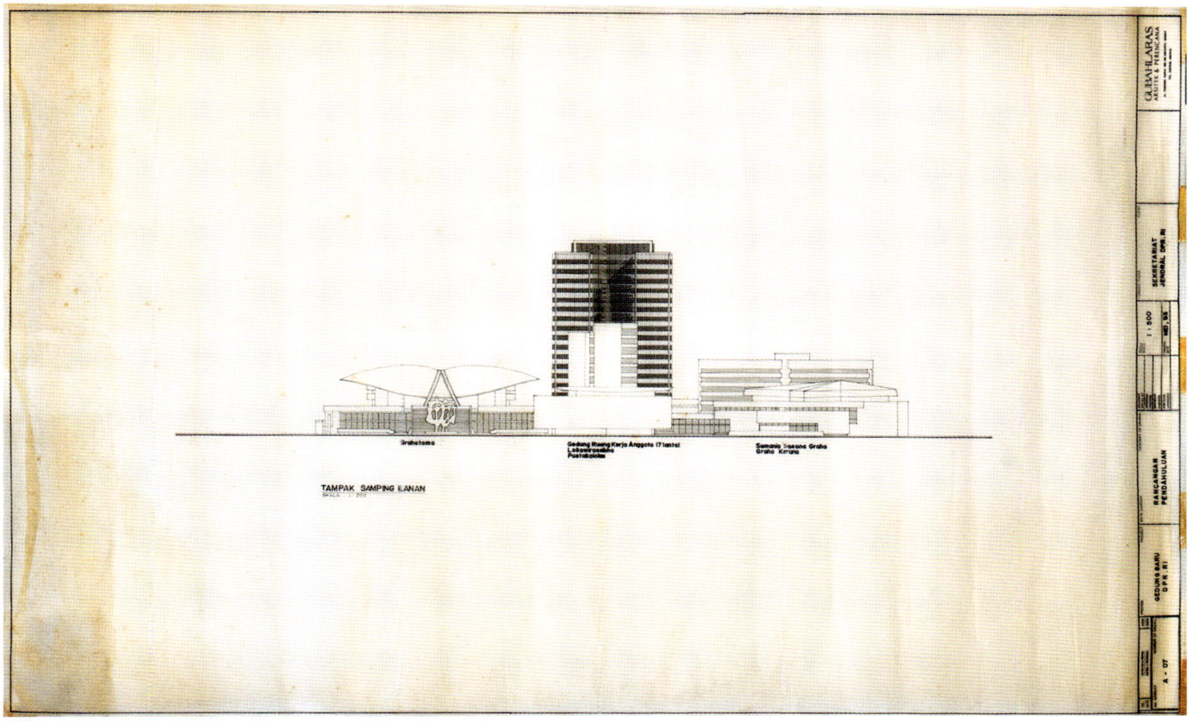

In 1993, PT. Gubahlaras, which continued after Soejoedi's withdrawal, was asked to add a 17-storey tower to the DPR/MPR building (realised).

Source: Soejoedi Family Archive

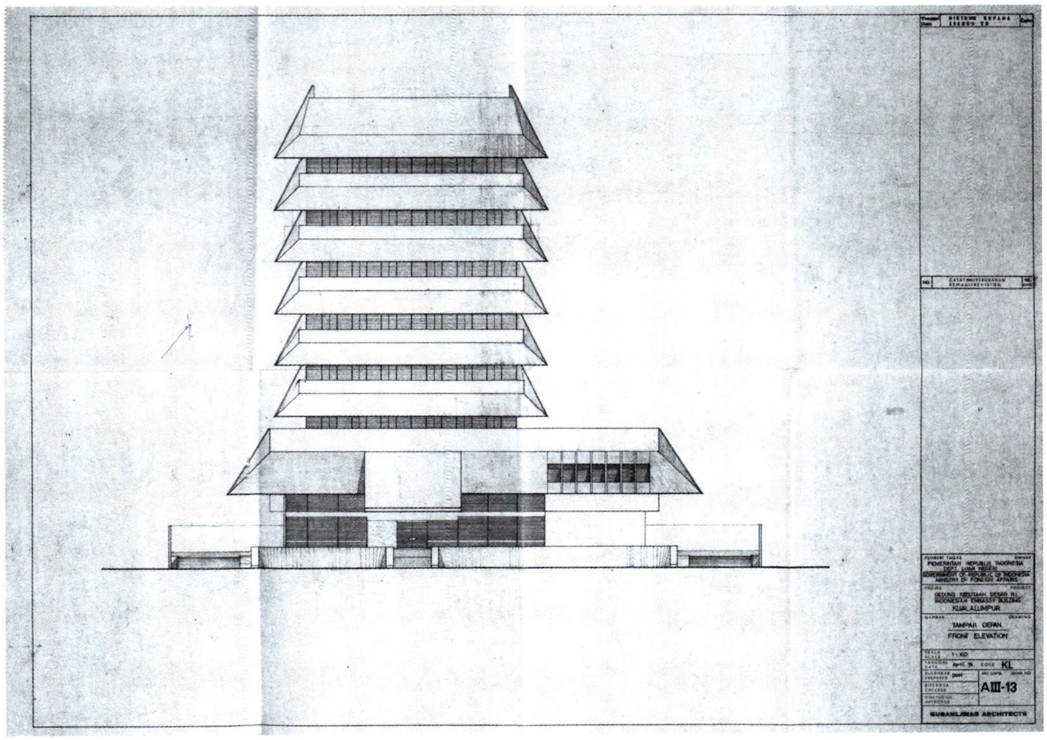

Kedutaan Besar Republik Indonesia (Indonesian Embassy), Kuala Lumpur, Malaysia, 1974. Architects: PT. Gubahlaras/ Soejoedi Wirjoatmodjo.

Source: Soejoedi Family Archive

Kedutaan Besar Republik Indonesia (Indonesian Embassy), Kuala Lumpur, Malaysia, 1974–1976. Architects: PT. Gubahlaras/Soejoedi Wirjoatmodjo.

Photo 1981: TEMPO/Ed Zoelverdi; 24A/133/1981; 24A13303

Secretariat of the Association of Southeast Asian Nations (ASEAN) in Jakarta, 1978–1981. Architects: PT. Gubahlaras/ Soejoedi Wirjoatmodjo. (See p. 182–183).

Photo 1982: TEMPO/Ed Zoelverdi; 42A/069/1982; 42A06910; and Photo 1981: TEMPO/Ed Zoelverdi; 24A/017/1981; 24A01702

The Department of Transportation building seen from above in Jakarta, 1980 – 1982. Architects: PT. Gubahlaras/ Soejoedi Wirjoatmodjo.

Photo 1983: TEMPO/Maman Samanhudi; 17B/147/1983; 17B14710

Pusat Kehutanan (Forestry Centre; now Manggala Wanabakti – The Ministry of Environment and Forestry), Jakarta, 1976–1983. Architects: PT. Gubahlaras/ Soejoedi Wirjoatmodjo and Noerpontjo. (See p. 184–189).

Photo 1983: TEMPO/Maman Samanhudi; 16B/052/1983; 16B05203

Bianpoen in Hanover, 1958.

Photo: Private Archive Bianpoen Family

Bianpoen at his PhD ceremony, Rotterdam, 1983.

Photo: Private Archive Bianpoen Family

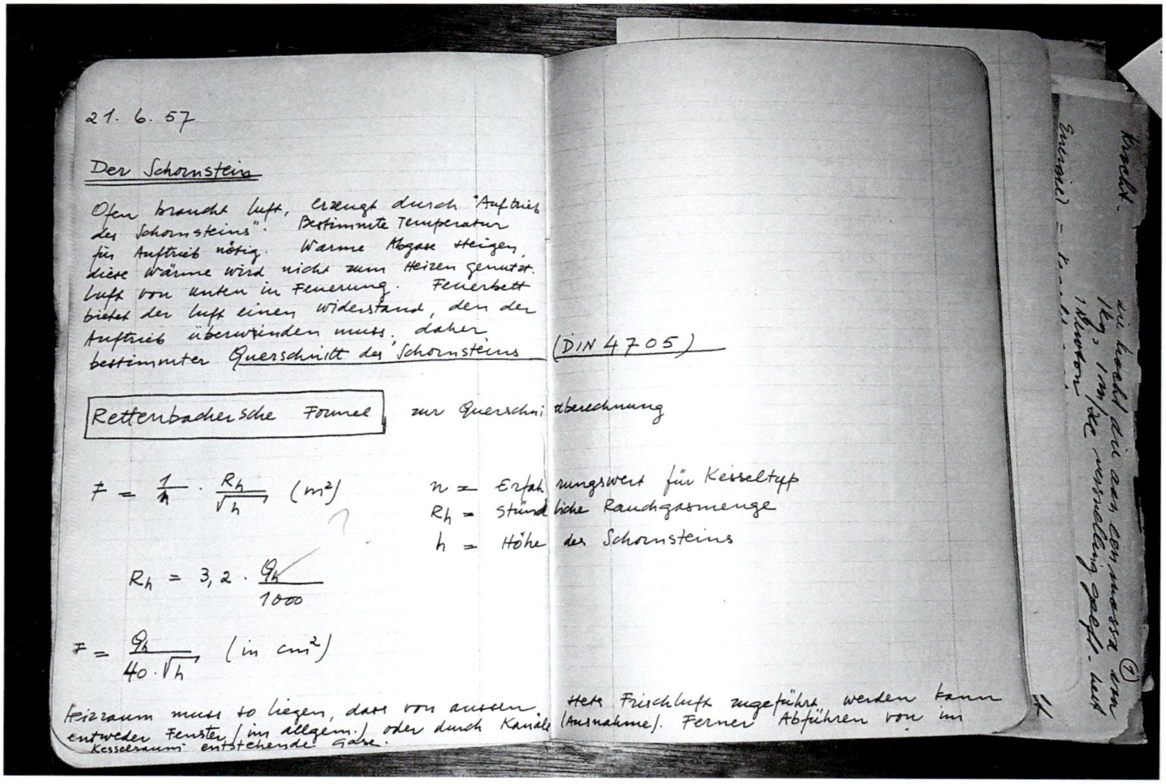

Notes about chimneys from his studies in Hanover, 1957.

Source: Private Archive Bianpoen Family

Bianpoen
1930–2020
Fernisia Winnerdy, Adetania Pramanik, Jesslyn Amanda

Bianpoen (born LIEM Bian Poen) was born in Mojokerto, Java, on 21 February 1930. His father was a timber merchant whose name is mentioned in connection with the renovation of a historic Chinese temple in the 1930s. For his early education, Bianpoen went to Europeesche Lagere School (ELS) in Mojokerto and then Hogere Burgerschool (HBS) in Surabaya, where he met Han Awal. In 1951, Bianpoen left Indonesia to study architecture at the Technische Hogeschool Delft in the Netherlands on a scholarship from the Indonesian government. With several other students, including Han Awal, Soejoedi Wirjoatmodjo, Suwondo Bismo Sutedjo, and Mustafa Pamuntjak, he was active in various organisations. As a member of the ATAP group, a loosely organised network of Indonesian architecture and art students at the universities in Delft and Amsterdam, he travelled to various cities abroad and organised group activities. Around 1957, Indonesian students were advised to leave the Netherlands due to the growing political tensions between the Netherlands and their home country. Bianpoen, together with Suwondwo, continued his studies at Technische Hochschule Hanover in West Germany, where he received his diploma as Diplom-Ingenieur in March 1961.

Bianpoen's career started at the Hanover City Planning Office, where he worked as a junior planner for a year. In 1962, he and his family – he got married in Münster, West Germany, in 1959 – moved back to Indonesia, where he taught architecture at the Bandung Institute of Technology (Institut Teknologi Bandung, ITB) and reunited briefly with Suwondo and Soejoedi as fellow lecturers. In 1963, Bianpoen relocated to Jakarta, where he was granted a small house by the Indonesian government; he and his wife lived there until their eighties. Back in Jakarta, Han Awal introduced him to Ir. Wastu Pragantha (1935–2011), who helped him obtain work in the Jakarta City Planning Office. There he started as a senior planner, commencing his two-decade career as an urban planner and researcher in the civil service.

As head of the Advisory Council for Architecture in Jakarta from 1965 to 1974, Bianpoen was responsible for approving the architectural designs of major buildings in the Indonesian capital. During these years, he was also active in the design of church projects in Jakarta: the Gereja Kristus Raja in Pejompongan (1964–1967), the Gereja St. Kristoforus in Grogol (1967–1970), and the Gereja Maria Bunda Perantara in Cideng (1972–1974). Bianpoen also worked with Han Awal on a dormitory for nurses at St. Carolus hospital in Jakarta (1972).

From 1974 to 1986, Bianpoen served as the head of the Centre for Urban and Environmental Research and Development (Pusat Penelitian dan Pengembangan Perkotaan dan Lingkungan-PPPPL-DK, P4L-DKI). During his leadership, the governmental institute conducted over 100 research projects, some of which were featured in its bi-monthly journal *Widyapura* (see p. 172–175). The centre was also responsible for the city's regulations and standards concerning the environment, urban planning, fire prevention, water quality, air and noise pollution, and parking. In the early 1980s, Bianpoen collaborated with the School of Economics at Erasmus Universiteit Rotterdam for some of P4L-DKI's research and published in this context his dissertation: Research and Development for Urban Management: Case Jakarta, which earned him a doctoral degree in 1983.

In 1986, after witnessing the country's poor progress in solving population, social, and environmental problems, specifically the inaction of the officials in his Jakarta City Planning Office, Bianpoen decided to resign from his post and focus more on education and research. Between 1985 and 2005, he applied his two decades of experience as a consultant for numerous environmental impact assessments in the urban and environmental consultancy firm PT. Purwokanthi Kusumo. He was also a member of the Indonesian Institute of Architects (IAI) throughout his career, particularly in the human settlement working group, and a member of the Environmental Evaluation Committee for the City of Jakarta (Komite Evaluasi Lingkungan Kota Jakarta) from 2005 to 2009.

Bianpoen continuously passed on his knowledge to younger generations over five decades. While a civil servant, he was also a lecturer and head of the Research Centre for Technology and Human Settlement at the School of Architecture of Tarumanagara University in Jakarta from 1963 to 1994. His longest academic and research position was at the Universitas Indonesia (UI) Jakarta from 1967 to 2017, where he reunited with Han Awal and Suwondo, the Chair of the Architecture School, Dean of the Faculty of Engineering, and a professor at UI from 1970. At UI, Bianpoen taught courses and advised students in the undergraduate architecture programme, the postgraduate environmental science programme, and the postgraduate anthropology programme. He was also a lecturer at the School of Architecture of Merdeka University, Melang (Jurusan arsitektur, Universitas Merdeka, 1994–2004) and the School of Design of Pelita Harapan (Universitas Pelita Harapan) Karawaci in Tangerang (1996–2017). His teaching and mentoring activities ranged from urban planning to social and environment-related subjects.

When preparing material for discussions, classes, seminars, workshops, or publications, he always cited real issues, data, and anecdotes, often in the form of collages made with newspaper articles and books. Until he passed away on 1 September 2020, Bianpoen continued his habit of cutting out newspaper articles and marking their corners with colour codes, whose meaning only he knew.

Gereja St. Kristoforus (St. Kristoforus Catholic Church) under construction, Jakarta, 1967–1970. Architect: Bianpoen.

Photo: Private Archive Bianpoen Family

Side.elevation.
View from the Convent.

Approach to church yard.
View from the parking area.

Detail of tabernacle.
Made of anodized aluminum.

Interior view.

Gereja St. Kristoforus (St. Kristoforus Catholic Church) after completion, Jakarta.
Top image, left: Suwondo family; right: Bianpoen
Architect: Bianpoen.

Source: Private Archive Bianpoen Family

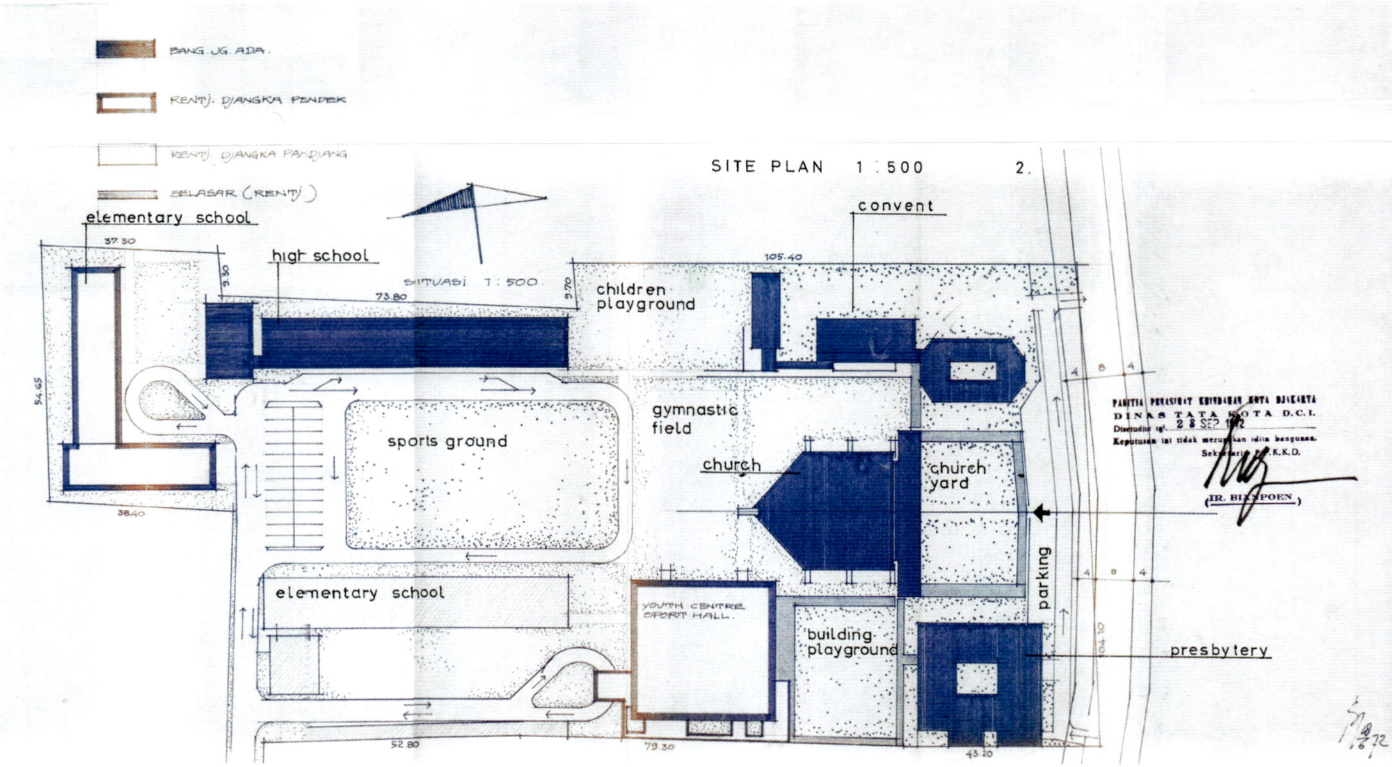

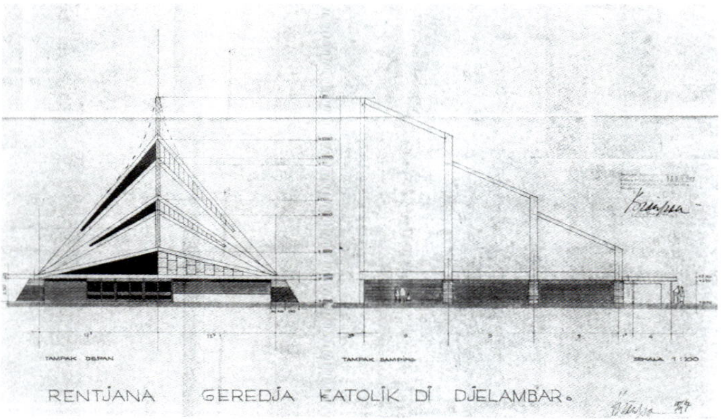

Site plan, side view, and front of Gereja St. Kristoforus, Jakarta, 1967–1972. Architect: Bianpoen.

Source: Private Archive Bianpoen Family

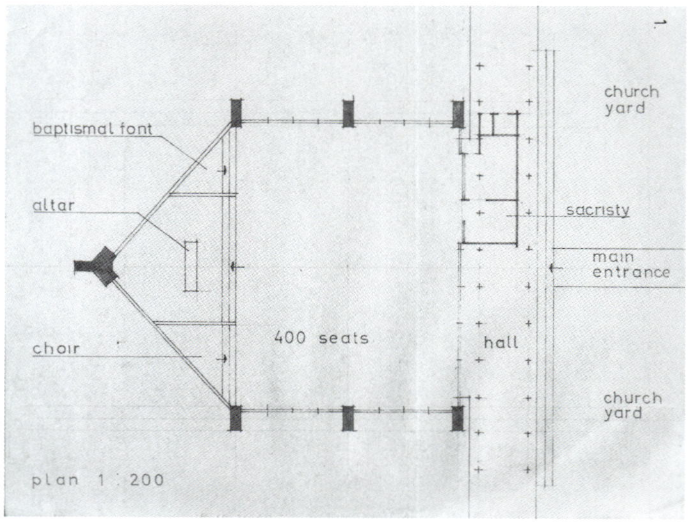

Plans of Gereja Maria Bunda Perantara Cideng, (Our Lady of Intercession Catholic Church, Cideng), Jakarta, 1974 (see p. 208–209).
Architect: Bianpoen.

Source: Private Archive Bianpoen Family

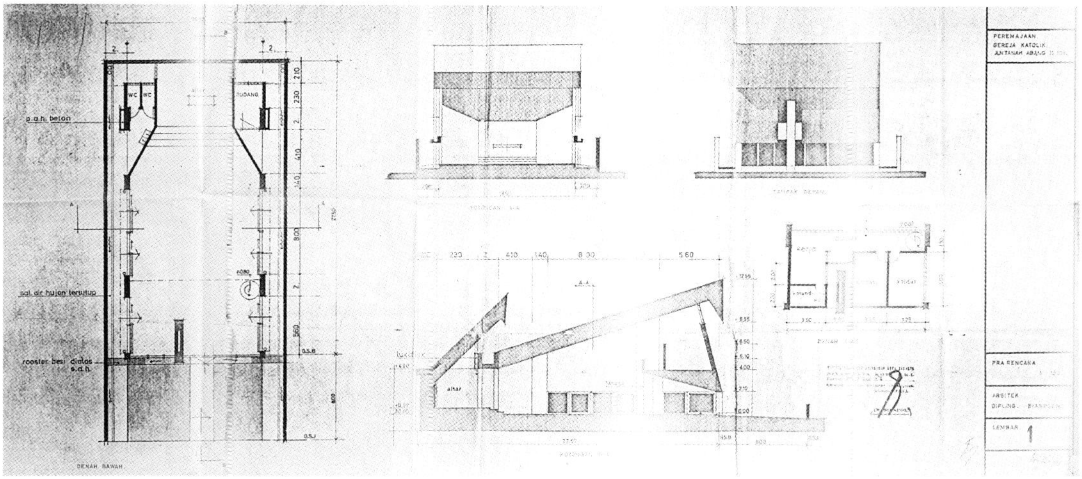

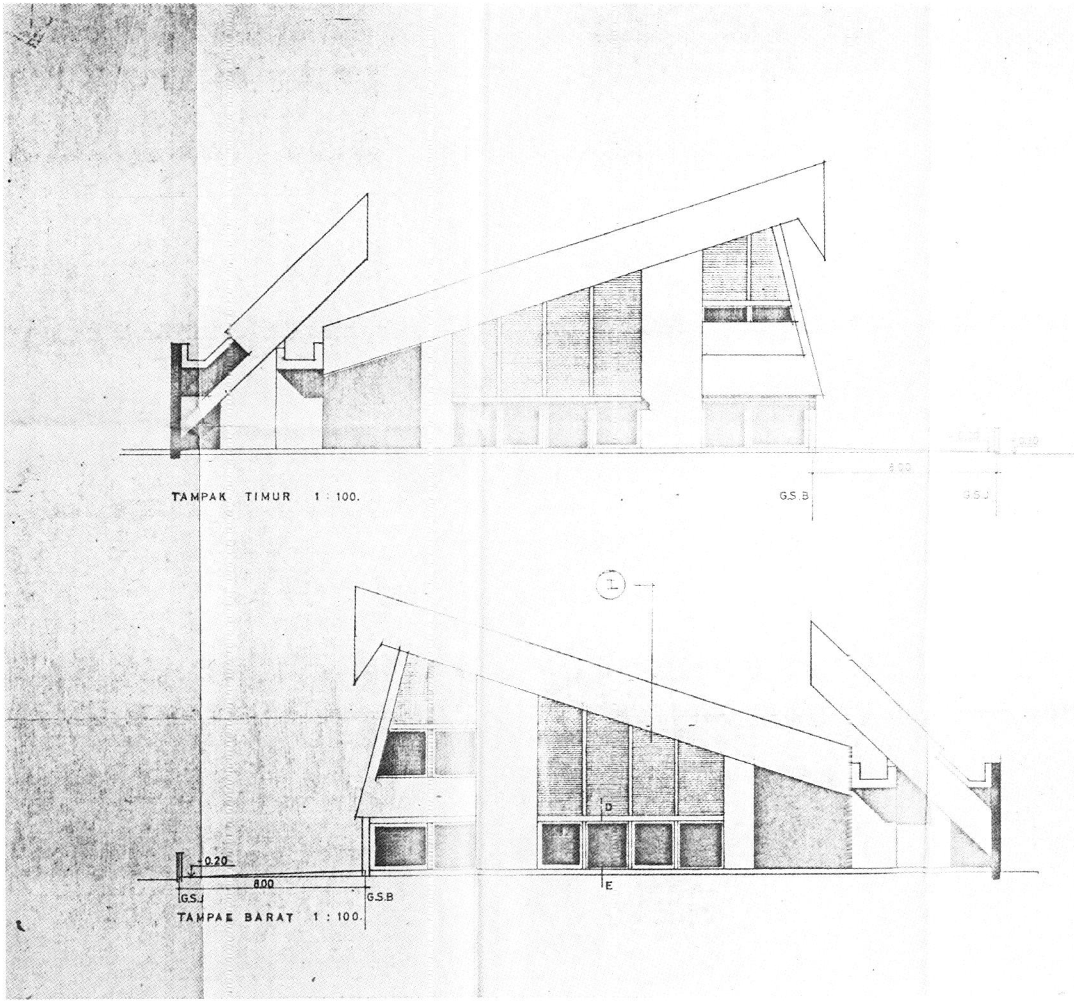

Suwondo Bismo Sutedjo, early 1990s.

Photo: Suwondo Family Archive

House in Seefeld at Ammersee, near Munich, 1975. Architect: Suwondo.

Photo: Suwondo Family Archive

Charles Jencks with Suwondo and Wan Jin (Kan Wancin), early 1990s.

Photo: Suwondo Family Archive

Suswondo Bismo Sutedjo 1928–2019 Hedista Rani Pranata

Suwondo Bismo Sutedjo was born as Raden Bisom Sutedjo on 2 June 1928 in Pekalongan, Java. His great-grandfather was M. Aboekasan Atmodirono (1860–1920), the first Indonesian architect.

Bismo started his early education at the Europeesche Lagere School I (ELS) in Bogor. While there he stayed with his uncle Boesono Daroesman, a veterinarian who happened to be best friends with the famous Indonesian architect Friedrich Silaban (1912–1984). His uncle's frequent conversations with Silaban inspired Bismo to become a *bouwkundig ingenieur* ('civil engineer'). Bismo joined the military from 1945 to 1947 and managed to finish his senior high school at Sekolah Menengah Atas (SMA 1) in Yogyakarta in 1948.

In 1949, Bismo attended a civil engineering course at the Technische Wetenschappen at Universitas Indonesia (UI)[1] in Bandung, as there were still no dedicated architecture schools in Indonesia at that time. After only a few months, he was given the opportunity to study architecture at Technische Hogeschool (TH) Delft.

Unfortunately, Bismo fell ill with severe tuberculosis in June 1951 and had to put his studies on hold. After fighting the disease for roughly three years, his health finally improved. In February 1954, out of gratitude for his recovery, he changed his first name to Suwondo, converted to Christianity, and continued his studies.

In Delft, Suwondo actively participated in Dutch and Indonesian student organisations. He also belonged to the informal Indonesian student organisation ATAP along with Han Awal, Bianpoen, Mustafa Pamuntjak, Soejoedi Wirjoatmodjo, Kan Wancin, and many others. In 1957, Suwondo obtained a C-II diploma as a *bouwkundig ingenieur* (b.i) from the TH Delft.

Shortly afterwards, the conflict over Papua broke out between the Netherlands and Indonesia, forcing all government-sponsored Indonesian students to leave the Netherlands. Suwondo decided to move to West Germany and continued his studies at Technische Hochschule Hanover, where he graduated as Diplom-Ingenieur in the discipline of architecture in 1961.

In the same year, Suwondo returned to Indonesia and embarked on an academic career as a lecturer at ITB. During this time, he married Kan Wancin. Suwondo was a lecturer in architecture at ITB from 1961 to 1970 and head of the architecture department from 1966 to 1969. In 1970, he joined Universitas Indonesia (UI), where he was head of the architecture department from 1972 to 1976. From 1974 to 1978, he was dean of the Faculty of Engineering at UI and taught there from 1988 to 1993. As a scholar, Suwondo wrote numerous articles and lectured at symposia and seminars. His topics ranged from architectural design to urban planning, urban housing, and architectural education.

His architectural works were quite diverse. He designed residential buildings in Bandung, Bogor, Jakarta, Munich (West Germany), and Pennsylvania (USA); commercial buildings such as Hotel Metro in Semarang (1970) and Kantor Decocitas in Jakarta (1992); hospitals such as Rumah Sakit Pertamina in Cirebon (1973) and Rumah Sakit Pertamina in Cilacap (1975); schools such as Sekolah Islam Tugasku (1998); and the Ministry of Cooperatives and Kantor Departemen Koperasi (SMEs, 1998).[2] He carried out most of these projects with the firm PT Tetrahedra.[3] Suwondo also served as a design consultant for several institutions and organisations, such as Pertamina[4] (1970–1975), Bank Indonesia (1986), and Bank Pembangunan Indonesia (BAPINDO, 1988–1994), and was director for Museum Affairs at

1 Later known as Technische Hogeschool Bandoeng (now Institut Teknologi Bandung, or Bandung Institute of Technology).

2 Kantor Departemen Koperasi is now known as Kementerian Koperasi, Usaha Kecil dan Menengah.

3 Tetrahedra was an architectural firm founded in Jakarta in 1980. Hartomo was its chief director with Suwondo and Ir. Bambang Barata as directors.

4 Pertamina is a state-owned oil and natural gas company in Indonesia.

the Cultural Directorate of the Ministry of Education and Culture (1975–1980), among others.
He was also involved in national and international architectural organisations. From 1980 to 1990, he was a member of the Assembly of the Ikatan Arsitek Indonesia (IAI; Indonesian Architects Association) and served as its chairman from 1982 to 1988. Moreover, he represented Indonesia in the Habitat working group of the Union Internationale des Architectes (UIA).
Despite his frequent travels, Suwondo was a family man and never forgot to send postcards home. Not only his only son but also many of his students looked up to him as a beloved and respected role model. Suwondo Bismo Sutedjo passed away in October 2019.

Studio House of Suwondo family, Jakarta.

Photos: William Sutanto

Pertamina Cilacap Hospital in Cilacap at the southern coast in Central Java, 1975. Architect: Suwondo.

Source: Suwondo Family Archive

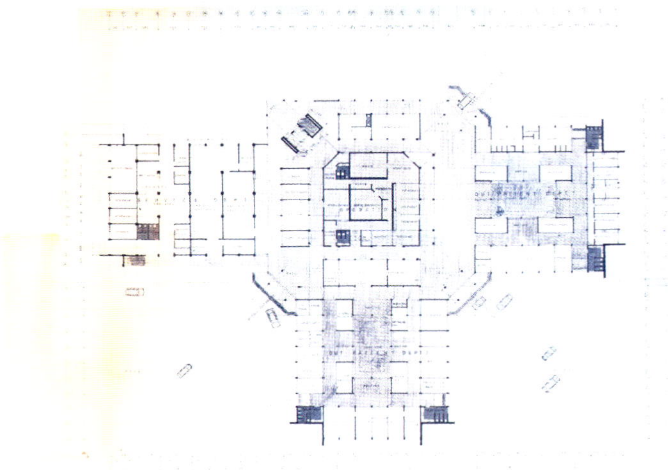

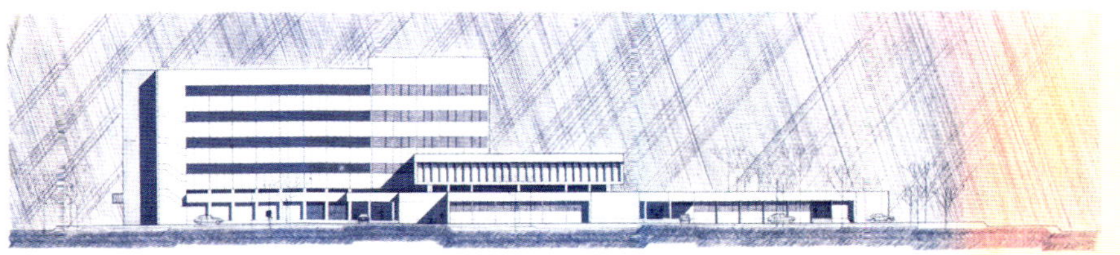

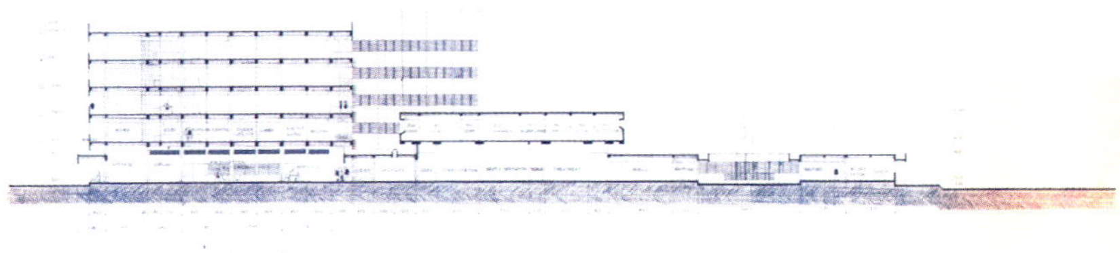

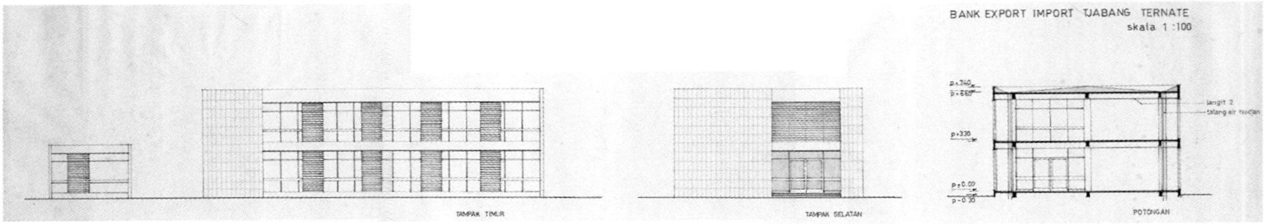

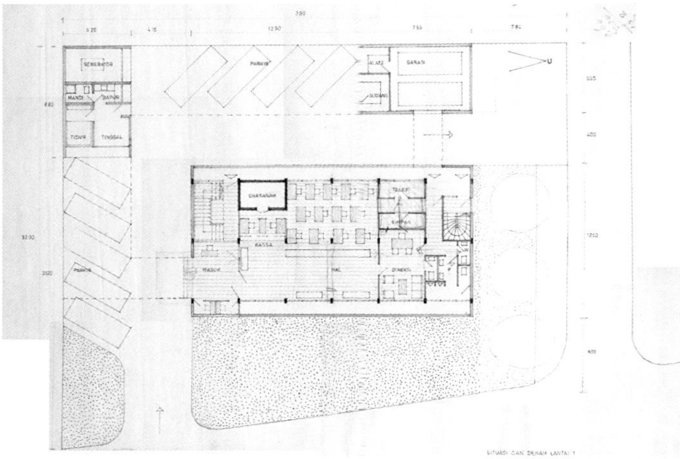

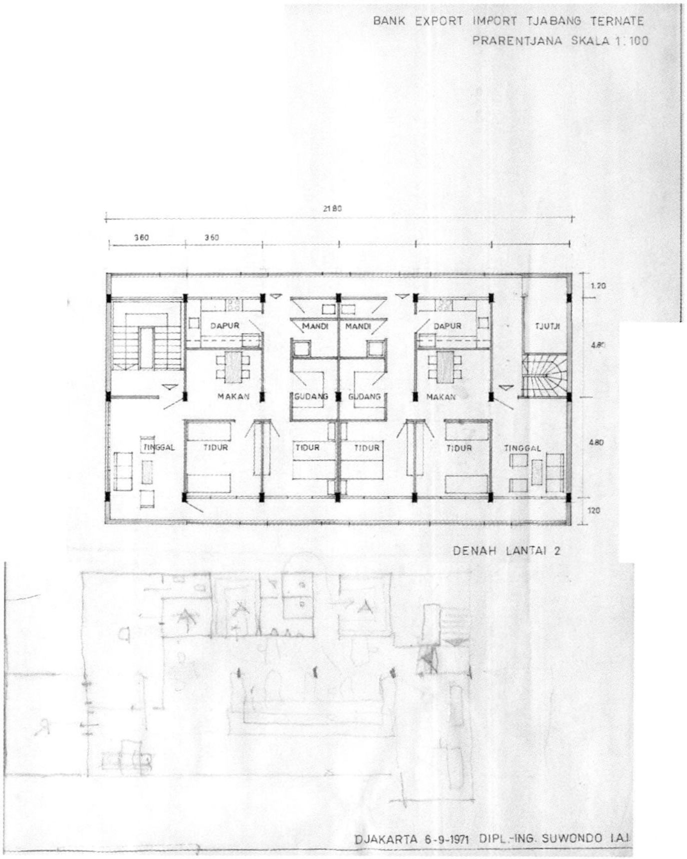

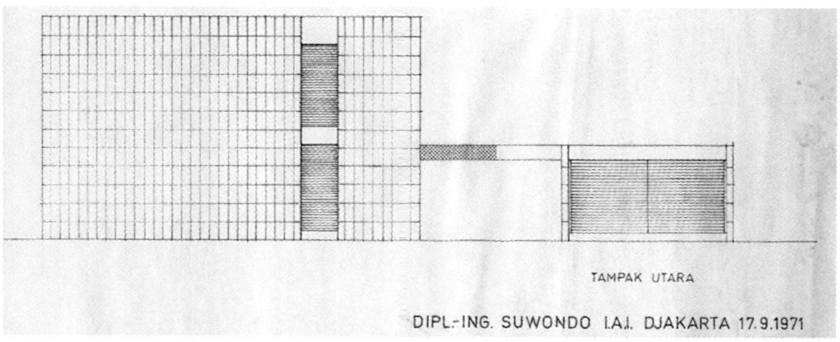

Bank Export Import, 1971.
Architect: Suwondo.

Source: Suwondo Family Archive

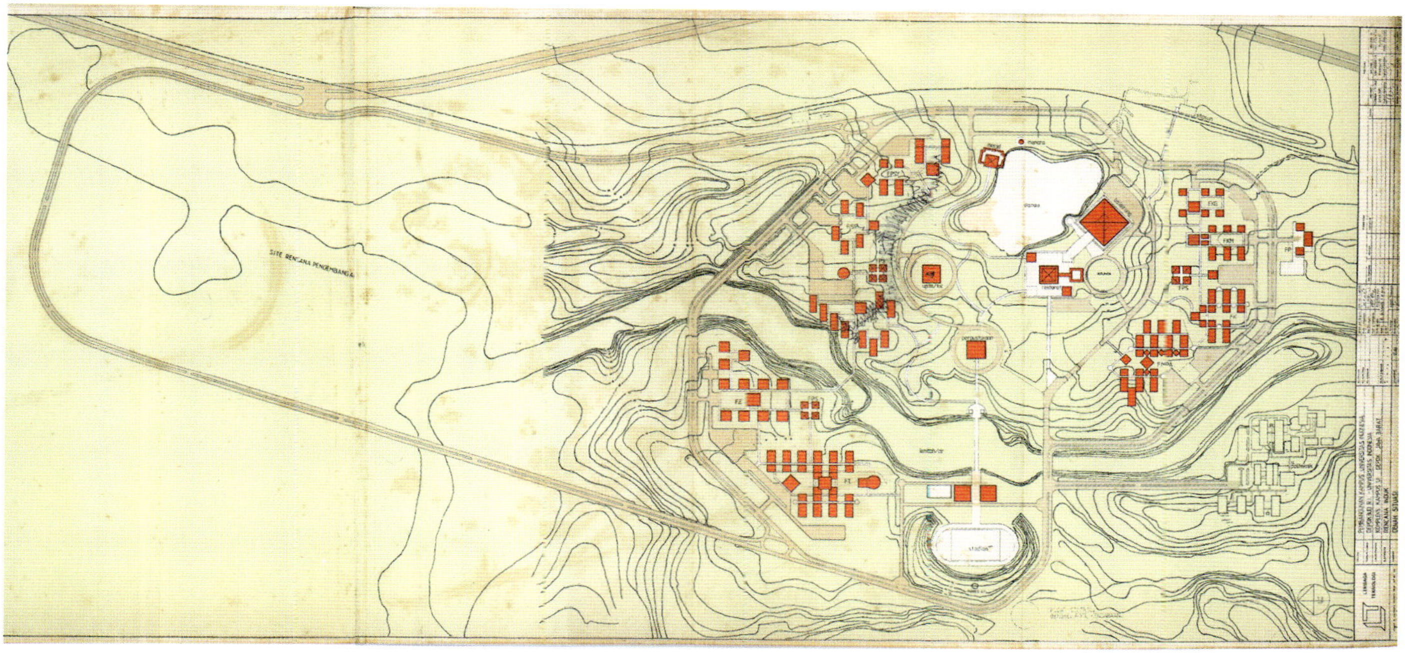

Pembangunan Kampus Universitas Indonesia Depdikbud. Kompleks Kampus Depok. Rencana Induk. Denah Situasi. (Development of the Indonesian University Campus of the Ministry of Education and Culture. Depok Campus Complex, Master Plan, 1984). Architects/Planers: Gunawan Tjahjono, Budi Adelar Sukada, Triatno Yudo Harjoko, & Hinurimawan under Lembaga Teknologi (LEMTEK) Universitas Indonesia. Supervisor/Coordinator: Suwondo.

Source: Mustafa Pamuntjak Family Archive

The main hall (Balairung) and rectorate building of the University of Indonesia as shown in the master plan.
Architects: Gunawan Tjahjono, Budi Adelar Sukada, Triatno Yudo Harjoko, & Hinurimawan under Lembaga Teknologi (LEMTEK) Universitas Indonesia.

Photo: Badan Pengembangan Universitas dan Pengelolaan Logistik, Universitas Indonesia

Y. B. Mangunwijaja, 1991.

Photo: Gerry van Klinken

Y. B. Mangunwijaya joins farmers' protest at Boulevard UGM in Yogyakarta, 1999.

Photo: Ln Idayanie

Y. B. Mangunwijaya at his home in Yogyakarta, 1985.

Photo: TEMPO/Yuyuk Sugarman

Ceramics inaugural exhibition at Bentara Budaya Museum, Jakarta, 1986. Architect: Y. B. Mangunwijaya.

Photo: TEMPO/Maman Samanhudi

Yusuf Bilyarta Mangunwijaya 1929–1999

Eduard Kögel

Priest, architect, and poet Yusuf Bilyarta Mangunwijaya, often referred to as Romo (Father) Mangun, was born in Java into a Catholic family. In 1950, he decided to become a priest and commenced studies at the Sancti Pauli Institute of Philosophy and Theology in Yogyakarta. Although the bishop ordained him as a priest in September 1959, he sent him to Bandung the very next day to study architecture. As Mangunwijaya later explained: 'He [the Bishop] wanted church buildings, and in general, the Catholic liturgy in Indonesia wanted to reflect the universal substance of the Christian faith in authentic indigenous expressions.'[1] The following year he moved to Aachen, West Germany, where he studied architecture at the Rheinisch-Westfälische Technische Hochschule (RWTH) until 1966. We can assume that in Aachen, he saw the radically modern buildings of Rudolf Schwarz (1897–1961), such as the School for Women Social Workers ('soziale Frauenschule') built in 1929–1930 as well as the churches of St. Corpus Christi (1930) and St. Boniface (1961).

For a student with a particular interest in modern church buildings, the architecture department in Aachen was filled with inspiring role models. Willy Weyres (1903–1989), the master cathedral builder in Cologne, taught architectural history and monument preservation and was a proponent of a modern approach to church building. Hans Schwippert (1899–1973), who was responsible for the reconstruction and conversion of St. Hedwig's Cathedral in East Berlin from 1956 to 1963, taught material studies and housing construction. He was succeeded in 1963 by the church architect Gottfried Böhm (1920–2021), whose expressive church of St. Hubertus in Aachen was completed in 1964. A few years earlier, Böhm had designed a small church complex for the Taiwanese village of Jīngliáo, built from 1955 to 1961. His design reflects his attempts to respond to the local context in an abstract manner. Eleanor von Erdberg (1907–2002) joined the architecture department as a lecturer in 1951 and, in 1961, became an adjunct professor of Asian art and architectural history. Erich Kühn (1902–1981) was chair of urban and regional planning. Starting in 1963, his colleague Liborius Schelhasse (1930–2012) was instrumental in setting up the seminar 'Planning Fundamentals for Developing Countries', about which Mangunwijaya later said: 'Liborius Schelhasse managed to open my eyes to see the real problems of architecture in developing countries. He widened my horizon to discover and explore the other side of the moon. Aesthetic dimensions remained important, of course, but that was not the core of the problem in developing countries, and maybe it was not even the problem of architecture of our whole global civilisation.'[2]

After returning to Indonesia, Mangunwijaya designed more than 80 buildings between 1967 and 1998, 29 of them church projects. He also taught at Gadjah Mada University in Yogyakarta until 1982. After the end of his active career as a teacher, he wrote the book *Wastu Citra*, which included images of the churches by Gottfried Böhm and Rudolf Schwarz.[3] Citing examples from different periods and various parts of the world, the book laid out Mangunwijaya's approach to modern architecture, combining local resources with contemporary solutions.

Mangunwijaya designed his first church, St. Mary Assumpta, in Klaten in Central Java (1967–1968). Its column-free interior is enclosed at the front by folded walls whose openwork filter the light. A narrow slit between the roof and the walls also allows natural light to

1 When Yusuf Bilyarta Mangunwijaya received the Ruth & Ralph Erskine Award in 1995, he wrote a speech reflecting on his architectural views and career. Since he could not go to Stockholm for health reasons, Eko Prawoto read the manuscript in his place. See <http://suraoriginal.blogspot.com/2018/02/words-of-gratitude-for-granting-of-ruth.html> accessed 25 June 2022.

2 Ibid.

3 Mangunwijaya, 2009.

enter the space. While his admiration for Le Corbusier's Ronchamp Chapel is palpable in this structure, Mangunwijaya's ideas also drew on elements from the local culture.[4]

After his studies, Mangunwijaya focused his work on life in the slums. The Kali Code River Redevelopment Project in Yogyakarta (1980–1985), which received the Aga Khan Award in 1992, is one of his biggest projects in this respect. The architect also lived in the *kampung* (Indonesian for 'informal settlement') during the project. Working with a relatively small budget, he enlisted the help of volunteer art students to help complete new permanent housing for the riverside settlement using simple materials such as bamboo.[5]

Mangunwijaya was awarded the Ruth & Ralph Erskine Award in Stockholm in 1995. In his speech, delivered by his friend Eko Prawoto, he noted: 'I learned from my lecturers [...] in Aachen and from the best examples of the old and modern architecture of Central Europe, to find the inner link between truth and beauty, which revealed to me how good and genuine architecture should be built. Not as mere fancies, but as manifestations of the European mind and *Lebensanschauung* [German for 'worldview'], as expressions of the meaning and sense, the symbolisation, and the inner meaning of architectural buildings, in other words: the unity of Truth and Beauty, which was formulated by Thomas Aquinas as: Pulchritudo splendor ordinis est.'[6]

4 Napitupulu, 1/2003, p. 91.
5 Abbad Al Radi, <https://www.archnet.org/sites/752> accessed 25 July 2022.
6 Y. B. Mangunwijaya, Ruth & Ralph Erskine Award speech (see note 1).

Maria Asumpta Church in Kladen near Yogyakarta, 1967–1968. Architect: Y. B. Mangunwijaya.

Photos: Eko Prawoto

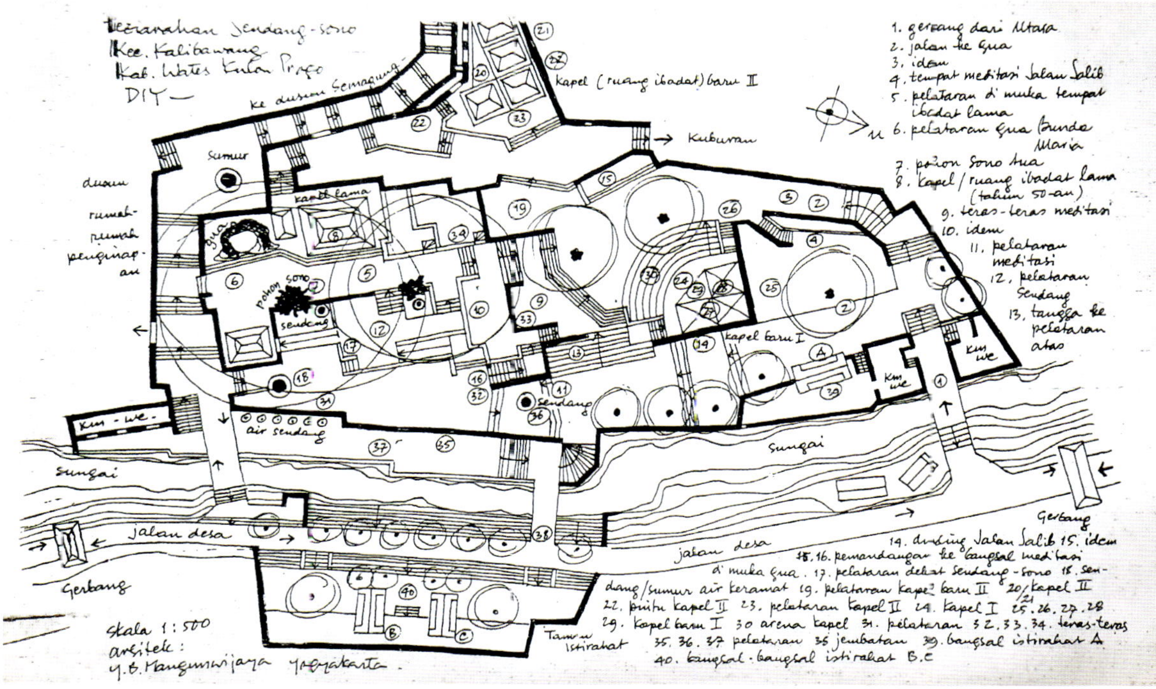

Sketch of the Sendangsono retreat near Yogyakarta, 1972–1991. Architect: Y.B. Mangunwijaya.

Source: Archive Yori Antar Awal

Sendangsono near Yogyakarta, 1972–1991. Architect: Y.B. Mangunwijaya.

Photo: Eko Prawoto

Youth Centre at Wisma Salam Catholic retreat in Salam near Yogyakarta, 1975. Architect: Y.B. Mangunwijaya.

Photo: Eko Prawoto

Kampung Cali Code, Yogyakarta. Architect: Y. B. Mangunwijaya.

Photo: TEMPO/ Rully Kesuma; R1A/209/95; 20010608

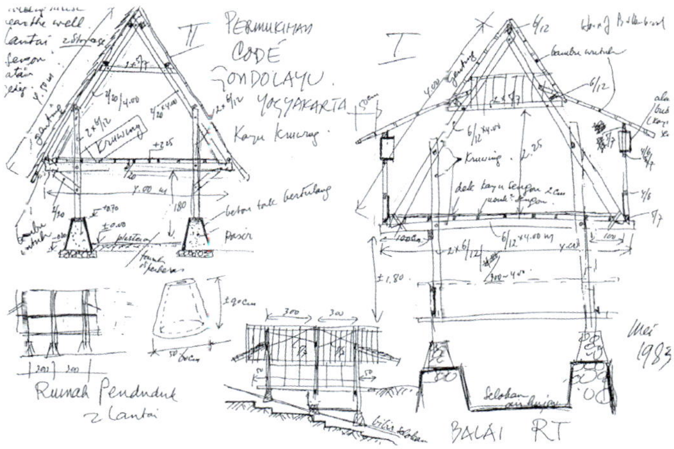

Kampung Cali Code, Yogyakarta, 1983–1987. Architect: Y. B. Mangunwijaya.

Photo: Eko Prawoto

Sketches for buildings in Kampung Cali Code, Yogyakarta. Architect: Y. B. Mangunwijaya.

Source: Aga Khan Development Network

Eddy Heryadie, Hoemar Tjokradiatmo, Po Hin Thung, and King-Han Oei

Eduard Kögel, Moritz Henning

Of the 12 architects whose lives we researched for this book, eight returned to Indonesia permanently. Four of them remained in Europe: Jan Beng Oei and King-Han Oei settled in Germany, Herianto Sulindro in Switzerland, and Po Hin Thung in the Netherlands. The accounts in this book focus on the lives and works of Bianpoen, Han Awal, Herianto Sulindro, Jan Beng Oei, Mustafa Pamuntjak, Soejoedi Wirjoatmodjo, Suwondo Bismo Sutedjo, and Yusuf Bilyarta Mangunwijaya. The other four graduates from the Technische Universität (TU) Berlin – Eddy Heryadie, Hoemar Tjokradiatmo, Po Hin Thung, and King-Han Oei – are briefly introduced here.

Eddy Heryadie, early 1950s.

Photo: ITB Brochure, 1993

Eddy Heryadie was the last of the Indonesian students to receive his diploma from the TU Berlin in 1961. He had graduated from Universitas Indonesia in Bandung in 1955. After studying in Berlin, Heryadie returned to Bandung, where he worked in the city planning department. As the head of the office, he travelled to Braunschweig in December 1964 at the invitation of the German Academic Exchange Service (DAAD). The first twinning between an Indonesian and a German city was established between Bandung and Braunschweig in 1960. To learn about German planning culture, Heryadie first spent time at the Braunschweig planning department, then the Berlin planning department in January 1965, followed by a month at the Dusseldorf planning department before returning to Indonesia. The only available information about his subsequent career is that he retired from service in the Jakarta Provincial Government in the early 1990s.

Hoemar Tjokrodiatmo, early 1950s.

Source: ITB Brochure, 1993

Even those who did not remain in Europe permanently continued to maintain good relations with Germany. After receiving his degree in 1960, Hoemar Tjokradiatmo worked in Berlin in the architectural firm of Franz Mocken, who served as the contact architect for Hugh Stubbins on the Kongresshalle (Congress Hall) and later oversaw the new Benjamin Franklin Hospital building. Tjokradiatmo returned to Indonesia in 1964 but came back to Germany in 1968 and worked in interior design for six years. After returning permanently to Indonesia he launched his own interior design firm in Jakarta in the mid-1970s. His work helped to draw attention in the country to this field of design and reunited him with some of his former fellow students. For example, he was responsible for the interior design of Soejoedi Wirjoatmodjo's ASEAN Secretariat Building in Jakarta (1978–1981).

Po Hin Thung, 1993.

Source: Courser, 10.6.1993, p. 9

Po Hin Thung was born in 1933 in Sukabumi, Java, where he had been a student at the Catholic Lagere School and Middelbare School. In 1952 he went to study in Delft, then studied in Rome from 1957 to 1959, and graduated in Berlin in 1960. Thung went on to work in various capacities in the Netherlands, Germany, Italy, Indonesia, Kenya, Sri Lanka, Suriname, and Zambia, in the field of development aid, among others. From September 1982 to May 1983, he worked at the university in Suriname and from 1986 to late 1987 with Prof. Chris J. L. Bertholet (1929–2019) and Dr. P. J. Lapperre in Zambia. During this time, he developed the topic for his dissertation, which addressed the ineffectiveness of development aid and used Sri Lanka as an example. Thung worked on his dissertation between 1988 and 1993 and defended it at Technische Universiteit Eindhoven.

Sien and King-Han Oei, late 1950s.

Source: Private Archive Suwondo Family

King-Han Oei was born in Jakarta in 1931 and moved to Delft with his wife in 1952 to study architecture. Due to the political circumstances, he left the Netherlands in 1957 and transferred to the TU Berlin, where he graduated in 1960. While still a student, Oei, in collaboration with Mustafa Pamuntjak, won a price in an ideas competition to design the outdoor premises of the cathedral in Paderborn. Oei was expected to return to Indonesia after gaining his diploma. However, due to the challenges faced there by ethnic Chinese at the time, the Oeis settled in Cologne, where they had relatives.

Oei's professional career began in 1960 in the architectural practice of Professor Heinz Haunschild. Two years later, he joined the practice of Heier & Monse, where he soon became a partner. In 1966, Kwee Hin Goan (b. 1932), an Indonesian colleague who had fled the political conditions in Indonesia, worked at the same office for a short time. King-Han Oei retired in 1996. In 2003 he played a small role in the 'Nasi Goreng' episode of the German television series *Mit Herz und Handschellen* ('With Heart and Handcuffs'). He died in Cologne in November 2021.

Heier, Monse & Partner participated in numerous competitions and, from the 1960s to the 1990s, realised several educational and research buildings, including secondary schools in Rodenkirchen (1967) and Lohmar (1978), a training centre for the construction industry in Kerpen (1980), the Fraunhofer Institute for Production Technology in Aachen (1988), and the Institute for Genetics at the Universität zu Köln in Cologne. In 1967, the practice received the Cologne Architecture Prize for the Bayer AG Application Technology Laboratory in Cologne-Flittard.

No. 11 - 12 Th. I/1978
Edisi Khusus

No. 5 - 6 Th. I/1977

Widyapura

Masalah Lingkungan Hidup

Masalah Lingkungan Jakarta
Bianpoen

Lingkungan, Pengembangan Tatakota, Tatawilayah & Perencanaan Nasional
R.E. Soeriaatmadja

Inventarisasi Kwalitas Air Permukaan Teluk Jakarta Timur
Wahyu Santoso, Aboeyoewono, Jaspar Bilal, Irwandi Bachtiar.

JURNAL PUSAT PENELITIAN MASALAH PERKOTAAN DAN LINGKUNGAN

POSITIONS

Independence and Architecture
Han Awal

Independence and Architecture was written for Universitas Merdeka Malang and published on 13 November 1993. In this paper Han Awal expressed his dissatisfaction with architecture education and practice situations in Indonesia.

Footnotes by the translator.

Preface

When we hear or read the word INDEPENDENT, our mind unavoidably also thinks of the definition of DEPENDENCE.

The meaning of independence is related to FREEDOM; clearly, independence is a behavioural attitude derived from freedom. In Dutch, the word independent is *onafhankelijkheid* – 'in-dependence'. Therefore, when we have a free spirit, we are not dependent on anything or anyone. We manage ourselves, as independence without management is ANARCHY.

The word INDEPENDENT bears the meaning of FREE – free of dependency.

In order to reach this point, one has to dig for knowledge and skill so that anything he is working on is done accordingly. If he has enough knowledge and skill, he shall reach a certain LEVEL OF COMPETENCE.

The mission of the university (as told by philosopher José Ortega y Gasset[1] around 50 years ago) is to teach people to think and act independently wherever they are. He asserted that humans are capable of independently freeing themselves from any problems they face under any circumstances. This mission continues to be embraced by modern universities everywhere.[2]

The Connection with Architecture

This is hard to think about. Our architecture education is very dependent on many factors. We depend on rules that support the curriculum, which hopefully provides a level of competence that will generate independent bachelors of architecture – in other words, architects who think and create independently, who are skilled in their profession.

Is there any independence in architecture? Is architecture, as a discipline, highly connected, i.e., dependent on other disciplines? Of course, there are connections, but as a communal expression, architecture clearly reflects the form of living in a community of a given period.

Therefore, architecture cannot be separated from living in our community. If we do not change, then architecture is merely following a trend. Architecture reflects the community's nature and character in certain places.
It is an open secret that investors prefer foreign architects for their developments, buildings, or master plans. Foreign architects are considered more skilled, capable of planning better, and more artistic in their work. Furthermore, they have added marketing appeal (taking advantage of our inferiority?) and offer more financial benefits (the economic boom has passed in their countries). Sometimes they lack creativity, repeating things they have done before, or proposing a rejected design that is received well in our country.

In this context, the architecture we get is not the architecture that derives from our independence; on the contrary. Here the architects are challenged to take the available opportunities or win the competition. Intentionally or not, our cities are being ruined by imported products and unsuitable, brutal imitations. Independence in architecture is when we understand the rules, are creative, and develop a structure that enriches

1 José Ortega y Gasset (1883–1955), Spanish philosopher.

2 José Ortega y Gasset, *Mission of the University*, trans. with an introduction by Howard Lee Nostrand (Princeton: Princeton University Press, 1944).

the environment. In any style, architecture is dependent, but this is not the dependency to plagiarise.

It might sound contradictory: independent but dependent? As explained, architecture is highly dependent on other disciplines; they influence each other. In architectural styles such as constructivism, the changes sent shockwaves throughout the discipline and beyond. Other fields can limit or inspire architectural development. Architecture's dependency on different disciplines and the tendency for architects to adapt creatively contribute to its further development.

Tradition, with its principles, serves as a foundation upon which new and positive influences can be adapted widely and creatively, contributing positively to the development of the field. The reflex to blindly reject what is new is not the same as being independent, but traps us inside tradition instead.

Architecture recognises many styles.

Independence and Dependence in Architecture
It has been said that we cannot be separated from our various influences, whether thoughts or daily activities. The ability to take independent action, informed by influences from multiple disciplines, is a characteristic of the architect.

Independence in thinking or creating something that has never been done before is a valuable contribution to the development of architecture.

Theoretically, every architectural design is dependent on various factors. Each has a different site; therefore, the result should be different unless an area is designed uniformly, as in a building estate.

Plagiarism or copying cannot be categorised as good architectural work since it denies its site and environment. This is the challenge for true independence.
Other than that, the phenomenon of imported architecture brought in by developers often bluntly establishes inauthentic designs. Designs that were already built or rejected by their countries of origin are repurposed with minor changes here for the sake of business efficiency. These proposals are well received by many developers who claim that local architects are too slow or their fees are too high, while foreign consultants are fast – as fast as a week – and their fees are negotiable. If we understand the background, then, of course, we can do the same. After all, it is a profitable business transaction.
We should be able to choose which influences we adapt and be true to our approach and principles. Both as an independent nation, free and liberated, and in our role as architects, we are independent in our actions. It does not matter who commissions us as long we understand the terms and conditions and apply them adaptively to our new works. These new works are the candidates for the Indonesian Institute for Architects (IAI) Award, so we put in maximum effort and translate our dependencies by learning from experience. We should try to avoid repeating the mistakes of others, not here or anywhere in the world. We need to communicate and read a lot about architecture and architectural criticism. We also need a healthy practice of reflection so we can avoid making shallow decisions.

Architects today are challenged by the fast-growing business. Even well-arranged environments are ignored because of their high strategic value; they are exploited at all costs. If needed, there is no hesitation to destroy a site.

Architects need to be independent at all stages. We need to start in college, and as mentioned before, it should be the university's mission to teach and guide students to become fully independent. After receiving their degrees, architects must be able to defend themselves.

Independence in thinking comes before independence in action. It is impossible to be independent in thinking without being critical. Students should not be naive and blindly accept what lecturers and teachers say; they need to understand the words and the definitions.
Aspiring architects, therefore, need to be trained early to be critical and able to ask questions, even if they sound ridiculous at first or do not make sense; thought acrobatics is a healthy exercise of the mind. Participating in architecture

discussion groups is a good way to examine our concerns in architecture and society. They will lead to understanding and respect for each other and train students to think critically. It will decrease their dependencies without losing respect for others and their opinions.

Dialogue between lecturers and students is important so that when the aspiring architects begin their own practices, they are prepared to face different tasks.

It was mentioned that we gain knowledge at university. We try to understand deeply so that in our practice, we are proficient and skilled in applying our knowledge to create a beautiful and valuable synthesis for the public.
During architectural studies, good training can be found in our case in the colloquium, where students have a chance to explain and defend their designs, while others can oppose and disagree on what they consider to be design weaknesses. At first, it may seem unusual, even unethical, to criticise others' work. Supposedly, our 'eastern' nature does not allow us to do such a thing; it is better to keep criticism to ourselves.
If lecturers understand the reason for the colloquium, there will not be any consequences that affect the score. However, we must realise that this can show the design's weaknesses at an early stage. Here, an atmosphere of criticism without sentiment can lead to mutual respect. Students and lecturers will feel committed to a higher common goal: objectivity, which is one of the absolute conditions for independence.
Maturity of thinking is a process that cannot be forced; it is obtainable through different ways. Besides gaining knowledge through training, lectures, and reading, discussions are another highly effective method.
If possible, the lecture room should be an arena of amiable discussion. If needed, we can be passionate when talking about our discipline, that of architecture, which will later be part of our flesh and blood. Sometimes we also need to be proficient in evaluating our own works and those of our colleagues within the timeline that we call history in the making.
Let us look at several works that recently won the IAI Award and see how far a sense of independence can be found in these works.

Winner of the IAI Award 1993
Tropical Retreat in Central Java by Mangunwijaya

In his design, Mangun placed the structures strategically and translated the programmes simply, creating a fascinating sense of unity in the complex (p. 155).
He would not be Mangunwijaya if he did not include rich features in his buildings.
Working with a minimal budget, he used standardised, modular elements for the windows and doors. After deciding on their forms, he worked with the local artisans and nuns at the retreat to place the windows and other openings in random patterns. This resulted in a lively composition on the wall surfaces, a *Spielerei* – a clever game, which actively involved everyone during the construction. Imagine the enthusiasm of everyone, especially the artisans who worked on it.
The priest architect worked independently. He is clearly highly creative, knowledgeable, and skilled in his use of materials, with his immense spirit pervading the modest arrangement of the buildings.
Mangunwijaya succeeded in making a statement through these modest buildings. He was not tempted by modern materials or acrobatic structures but started with fundamental architectural principles. The famous architect Le Corbusier, who also made a window composition at his chapel in Ronchamp, France, might have inspired his innovation, even though its execution was different.

No less important is his work in Kali Code, Yogyakarta, where he exercised maximum innovation with traditional-looking architecture (p. 157). The community hall and its auxiliary buildings magically transformed a slum into an attractive place where people are humanised. This was indeed the aim of the planning concept, which received the Aga Khan Award last year. Such innovation could not have been achieved without the priest's independence and maturity of spirit in maintaining a connection with the context and tradition. With a modest budget and unconventional approach, this approach produced the best possible result.

It seems that creative independence is not separate from a strong character daring to make an architectural statement despite the risks.

Another good example is in Malang itself: Hotel Tugu Park, which we all know. It also won the IAI Award two years ago, thanks to the owner's appreciation for a harmonious environment, especially the heritage environment. As many know, the hotel was permitted to be built higher for commercial purposes. Instead, an independent approach was taken with respect for the environment and it was received with widespread appreciation. The architecture is not innovative, but rather follows the rhythm and style of the surrounding pre-existing architecture and increases the environmental value of the *alun-alun* plaza.

Several other notable works by young architects, such as the experimental innovation by Sarjono (b. 1963[3] who graduated from Universitas Parahyangan), draw on current architectural styles, analyse their construction, and seek a new direction. For this work, Sarjono achieved an honourable mention. If the architect is willing to continue his experiment to find an independent style, there is no doubt that his works will achieve more awards in the future.

There are many more works that cannot be mentioned here. Still, one last example is by Martono Yuwono (†2019),[4] which also received an honourable mention from IAI a few years ago: Kampung Nelayan (a fishing village) in North Jakarta. Its architecture cannot be separated from traditional principles of rhythm, which helps to shape an appealing environment. This is something that Martono Yuwono, a preservation expert, was well aware of.

Today we are faced with even more challenges as the commercial world aggressively tries to dictate the rules.

Architects must be tough and independent in order to face these challenges. They must work without hesitation to find the best solution and develop their own creations to assert their independence. As Rabindranath Tagore has said, a nation's independence is only meaningful when its people are free and independent.

That is all.

Translation: Angeline Basuki

Sources:

Ortega y Gasset, Jose, *The Mission of the University.* Trans. with an introduction by Nostrand, Howard Lee (Princeton, NJ: Princeton University Press, 1944).
Tagore, Rabindranath, 'Filsafat Kemerdekaan'
Armytage, W.H.G., *A Social History of Engineering* (London: Farber & Farber, 1961).
Finch, James Kip, *The Story of Engineering* (New York: Anchor Books, 1960).
Andreas Johannes Wiesand, et al., *Beruf Architekt* (Stuttgart: Gerd Hatje, 1984).

3 Sardjono Sani graduated from Parahyangan Catholic University Bandung in 1987 and received a master's degree in Architecture from the University of Colorado, Denver, USA, in 1990. He began his career in Modula Consultant Office (1985–1986). Later, he worked at Harmonica Office, Craig Hodgetts & Hsin Ming Fung Design Associate (1990–1991). In 1992, he established Bias Teknoart Kreasindo, an architecture firm located in Jakarta.

4 Martono Yuwono graduated from ITB in 1969. He is an architect, writer, and heritage expert. He was chief of Sunda Kelapa Maritime Tourism Management Body between 1995–2006 and founder of Yayasan Pelestari Budaya Bangsa (Nation Culture Preserver Foundation) in the early 1990s. He also wrote a number of papers and books focused on maritime heritage in Jakarta.

A Conception of Indonesian Architecture
Yusuf Bilyarta Mangunwijaya

This paper was presented at the Second National Congress of the Indonesian Institute of Architects (Ikatan Arsitek Indonesia) in Yogyakarta on 2 December 1982.

Footnotes by the translator

I. Architecture, a Form of Human Language

Architecture (from Ancient Greek: *arkhi* meaning head, chief, master; *téktōn* meaning stone mason, builder, creator; *arkhitéktōn* meaning master builder) in a limited sense, and *wastu* (from Sanskrit: *vāstu* meaning norm, building order, spatial order, formal order)[1] in a comprehensive sense, always come from within, from the core, inner self, worldview, life attitude, and national culture; from universal beliefs of the community, real and historical. It is not abstract, not uniform for all nations and age groups, but dynamic and always the scene of controversies and bittersweet struggles. It is like language, because architecture or *wastu* is a form of human language.

Language is not a complement, external addition, or a mere incidental or accidental attachment to human beings. It is often said that humans speak (have language), but it is much more so that language is an inherent part of being human. Language, as well as architecture or *wastu,* is part of the constitutive nature of humans. It is like the light in fire and wetness in water. This is why the modern phenomenological philosopher Merleau-Ponty[2] writes about 'the soul that inhabits the body ... the meaning of inhabiting the word ... the eyes inhabit exists like humans inhabit their house', even '... human inhabits objects ... *le corps habite l'espace et le temps* (the body inhabits space and time)'. Because architecture or *wastu* is a form of human language, it also embodies values and meanings embraced by people in a certain space of time. And it is always real in its historical realisation, not abstract. Abstraction can only help for theoretical reflection, and it also presupposes the absence of some variables, which for the sake of clarity, requires simplification.

From all of that, we see how architecture or *wastu* not only reflects, but, more deeply, is the embodiment of the state of the soul in the subject who created the architecture. If the expression of architecture or *wastu* turns out to be classic and majestic, elegant, and well-balanced, then the ideals, values, and cultural will of the creators must be majestic, elegant, and well-balanced as well. If the architecture, in reality, is full of vital motion and dynamic emotions, it can be ascertained that the desires, attitudes, and values of the creators are dynamic, moving, vibrant, and against the static condition.

A well-known example is the architecture or *wastu* in the southern part of Central Java and Bali. In its essence, the architecture of the southern part of Central Java is no different from the style and atmosphere of the local dances. Likewise, Balinese architecture or *wastu* cannot be imagined without all the dynamic movements of the dances, the gong music, as well as the language style and intonation of Balinese oral literature. The essence of Shinto values also manifests in Japanese architecture and other architectural expressions in a modern way.

This is how the mathematical man from the industrial world expresses himself in Mies van der Rohe's style of architecture. And the cultured people of the Second Industrial Revolution, who are highly electronic and cybernetic, created the Centre Pompidou near the Eiffel Tower in Paris, which is more like a complicated tool rather than a building in the classical sense. But from the other side, we can also see that in a chaotic state of culture, with the somersault of values, we also get a chaotic, not to say anarchistic, form of architecture and spatial structures.

II. Three Tendencies

Our nation's culture is subtly in transition. We are in the *Kawah Candradimuka,*[3] a hotbed of clashing values, con-

1 *Wastu*, a word appropriated by Mangunwijaya.

2 Maurice Merleau-Ponty (1908–1961) was a French phenomenological philosopher.

3 Kawah Candradimuka is a volcanic crater in central Java and an idiom in Indonesian that means a place where one can train to acquire a strong character.

flicting psychological conditions, and trial and error. Each trial and error demands a high price, feels bitter in its implementation, and often leads to frustration – not only in the field of architecture or *wastu* but also in literature, physics, technology, industrialisation, and the economic and political order. Our nation is experiencing a severe crisis of values, a crisis of spatial structures, even in its personality and identity.

Is there any educated architect among the Javanese at this time who still can create an authentic Javanese joglo[4] pavilion? Whose material or size truly grows from within and is not a mere patch, as reflected by Merleau Ponty's phenomenological analysis? What we get are only Indo-European mixed-style joglos. That is understandable and perhaps not wrong. Because our generation is more or less like the character of Setadewa in the novel *Burung-Burung Manyar*[5] (1981): the Indo-European born in the Archipelago, but whose education and desires are similar to those of the *wong Londo* ('the Dutch').

Which of us still has the perseverance and intention to dive into the *jagad gede* (macrocosm) and *jagad cilik* (microcosm) of Javanese, Minangnese, Sundanese, Balinese, Malukunese, and so on?[6]

On the one hand, this is precisely what the current generation did not expect after the 1928 Youth Pledge[7] (*Sumpah Pemuda*), whose aim was to unite the nation and culture of Indonesia. On the other hand, the process of Indonesianisation is not a finished product but a hard struggle in a long historical process. And the historical process is not determined solely by indigenous factors. The external influence of the 'Earth, One Spaceship' generation,[8] is not a mere fad but a real tendency in an unstoppable process. Even Takdir Alisjahbana[9] fearlessly said that he would not mourn losing his Indonesian identity as long as he managed to find his identity in the wider global culture. This is similar to the 1928 generation, who did not cry and were even proud of losing their ethnicity for the sake of finding a broader Indonesian identity. We may or may not agree with the ideas of Takdir Alisjahbana, as long as we know and honestly recount the reality that has shaped each of us, and test objectively to what extent his words are true or false. This also pertains to the field of architecture or *wastu* that we are currently working on. Because it is a mere fantasy in broad daylight to demand an architecture or *wastu* with Indonesian characteristics that express the (real) values embraced by our nation, if the realities of our nation are still the chaotic traffic, rampant extortion, and scarcity of regulators who are loyal to their own rules.

It is the same with the effort to renew the curriculum of architectural education if the lecturers are still the old people. Moreover, it is not clear what can be called 'new'. It is very difficult to produce clear tears from the swamp. Following Merleau Ponty cited earlier: how can we claim the sweet meaning of the sour word? Because language (i.e., architecture or *wastu*) is a constitutive aspect of human beings.

How Do We Respond to this Matter?

There are three general attitudes:

1. To follow the wisdom of the Ancient Romans: *Lex Agendi Lex Essendi,* which means 'the law of action is the law of existences'. If the situation is chaotic, then just be logical and create architecture and spatial planning as a discussion that is chaotic as well, so that, in principle, the expression is objective. This approach can be found in the field of music and contemporary art, in the literature of Iwan Simatupang,[10]

4 Joglo is an iconic vernacular house roof type closely associated with Javanese upper-class households. Traditionally, a joglo roof is used for dwellings but also for the pavilion at the centre of a large housing compound.

5 *Burung-burung Manyar* ('Weaver Birds') is a historical novel written by Y. B. Mangunwijaya, first published by Penerbit Djambatan in August 1981.

6 *agad gede-jagad cilik* is a phenomenological concept in Javanese culture. *Jagad cilik* (microcosm) is represented by humans as the miniature of the universe, while *jagad gede* represents the universe itself.

7 The Youth Pledge (Sumpah Pemuda) was a declaration made on 28 October 1928 by young Indonesian nationalists in the Second Youth Congress (Kongres Pemuda Kedua). They proclaimed three ideas: one motherland, one nation, and one language.

8 'Earth, One Spaceship' (or 'Spaceship Earth' or 'Spaceship Planet Earth') is a worldview encouraging everyone on Earth to act as a harmonious crew working towards the greater good. The phrase was also popularised by Buckminster Fuller, the American architect who authored the 1968 book *Operating Manual for Spaceship Earth.*

9 Sutan Takdir Alisjahbana (1908–1994), was an Indonesian cultural practitioner, writer, and grammarian. His thinking tended to be pro-modernisation and pro-Western, which contradicted with the thoughts of several Indonesian intellectuals who were anti-materialism, anti-modernisation, and anti-Western. According to him, the Indonesian people must catch up by modernising their thoughts and studying Western sciences.

10 Iwan Martua Dongan Simatupang (1928–1970), commonly known as Iwan Simatupang, is an Indonesian novelist, poet, and essayist. As an author, he championed a new style in his essays, plays, short stories, and romances that abandoned conventional ways of thinking. The storyline and the appearance of the characters in his essays are not bound by logic to arrive at new basic values. Some critics refer to Iwan Simatupang's works as avant-garde works.

and so on. This attitude, which derives from logical formalism, can be considered consequential. To put it in contemporary terms: garbage in, garbage out; if you are talented as a bandit, be a bandit, but a high-quality one.

2. The second attitude rejects the contemporary logical principle above, but does not turn a blind eye to the current flow. Therefore, it is considered realistic. Not only in the sense of *Asal Bapak Senang* ('as long as it pleases the master'),[11] but as a basic principle, such an attitude is still admittedly wrong, like a bureaucrat who is languishing in corruption. This reflects the attitude of politicians: to achieve what is still possible in a situation that is not ideal. In other words: just go with the flow in order to be safe, yet still admit to having drifted away.

3. The third attitude is also aware of reality, knowing the strength of the current and one's own limitations. Here one has not drifted away, although in a certain sense, has 'lost against the current'. The steering wheel is still held tightly, and the oar is still paddling, trying to break free from the current. He can be saved or destroyed, but he stands up as a free human being and a man of responsibility. This attitude is also realistic, still striving for what is possible to achieve in a situation that is not ideal, but with an addition: pioneering to change the conditions, so that a non-existent possibility can become not-yet-existent, and the impossible can become possible. While the second attitude is that of politicians, traders, and technocrats, this third attitude is that of statesmen, true businessmen, and intellectuals. This is the attitude of the lotus that appears in the middle of the swamp.

The three attitude tendencies above basically exist in all professions, even in daily life at home and in the village. Architects are likewise faced with such choices. I do not feel qualified to suggest to the Indonesian Institute of Architects (IAI, *Ikatan Arsitek Indonesia*) congress which attitude should be taken by IAI members, especially in their endeavour to find a conception of Indonesian architecture or *wastu*. The important thing is that we are aware of the possibilities that come our way in the transition period we face today. Because a broken compass only endangers the ship and its captain as long as it is not known that the compass is broken. Even with a defective compass, as long as the captain knows where he went wrong and is aware of the problem, the danger is principally resolved.

III. Some Practical Advice

We know that it is not easy, not to say impossible, to find a concept of Indonesian architecture or *wastu* that is not imaginary but realistic. In doing so, there are several things we can still hold on to.

1. We should have a conception that is not only sectoral (e.g., architecture = building construction) but total, and comprehensive both in terms of planning the building and all processes that are wider and more complex regarding the objects of our profession. Indeed, the term 'architecture' does not really help us; it even leads to an understanding that is too narrow and wrong. The term *wastu* is more helpful, which encompasses the size of a true galaxy, in the sense of all forms. It covers aesthetics as an important principle, but not the only one, not even the most important one. *Wastuwidyawan*[12] works multidimensionally, both in terms of physical embodiment and the processes to create the finished results. In other words, one is not a pure specialist but a generalist, like a film director who cannot possibly dismiss filmmaking as a mere technique. However, he must admit his limitations and work with professional actors and the social structures in their community.

2. Thus, we also need to be aware of how macro-problems in technological civilisation and international industry or business are far more decisive than individual desires. On the other hand, we are responsible for giving feedback and preserving the highest human abilities, namely, creativity, which is like a lotus in the middle of the mud, which has functions to rejuvenate and increase the noble values in every interaction between humans. Creativity is always uniquely personal but not individualistic or wildly anarchistic. The lotus flower can also grow in a muddy environment.

11 *Asal Bapak Senang* or ABS (meaning 'as long as it pleases the master') is used as a political idiom to refer to subordinates who only want their superiors to be happy. This idiom first appeared in the Sukarno era as the name of a music group. During the Soeharto era, the term ABS became more popular due to the centralistic character of Soeharto's leadership, which fostered the tendency of many officials to make favourable reports to the president and cover up problems.

12 *Wastuwidyawan* is the term coined by Y. B. Mangunwijaya to replace the word 'architect'.

Our task is to examine how, in our poetic creations, we make explicit the most recent desires that already exist, even though it is implicit in the circles of the nation or community we serve.
3. Indonesian architects developed the task to formulate and especially manifest the idea of restructuring the regional planning, spatial planning, and governance that guarantees the equitable distribution of costs and benefits for the entire nation. Thus, it is possible to improve the systems of spatial order as we see in Latin America or the Philippines, where the difference between landlords and small people implies injustice. The legislation regarding all of this needs to be considered systematically, starting with the main issues and then the branches, twigs, and leaves. For example, the problem of understanding the cities and villages, the relationship between traditional agrarian networks and modern technological communication, as well as energy distribution still need to be investigated more thoroughly. For example, to what extent does the agrarian law apply to urban areas? Is our basic concept still based on the agrarian culture of the past, and is it simply being transposed onto our current situation? Or do we correctly embody the urban-rural structural relations, the industrial production system, and the agricultural/plantation production system with all their implications for the forests, rivers, and so on? Which 'world' of *wastu*-order are we consciously or unconsciously implementing in this country? To what extent do the realisation of the 1945 constitution (*Undang-undang Dasar 1945*), the Broad Outline of State Policy (*Garis Besar Haluan Negara*), and *wastu*-order still contradict each other, and how can we overcome these contradictions? The influence of architects is not limitless, but they do have the potential to develop ideas that are more objective and healthier.
4. Architects or *wastuwidyawan* on a global scale are very influential in the field of technology and the allocation of economic resources. For example, the glass, paint, and metallurgical industries are all needed to create new styles of buildings. There are close ties between the understanding of architects and that of various economic sectors at the national level. The problem of deforestation in developing countries is a direct result of ideas by international architects.
One question asked by the nation of our architects, for example, is this: Why do we always have to use or import steel that consumes our foreign exchange and upsets our balance of payments to foreign countries? Even though there are many structures with a wide span of up to 50 metres that can be realised with wood why make it unnecessarily complicated? Why can't wood, like cement, aluminium, and synthetic materials, be the most important domestic source of construction materials? Can the field of chemical engineering be stimulated by a distinctly indigenous notion of architecture based on wood (like in Canada) in the possibility of creating tropical glues and paints, which can also be a fire-resistant foam coating, and other basic materials that could grow the national economy and be a main export? Why do we still lose to Malaysia in terms of preserving forests? Why are there many loggers and wood industry experts from the Philippines? Are Indonesians not the same (i.e., in terms of intelligence and ability) as Malaysians and Filipinos?
Can wood in all forms (including bamboo) be used as a superior domestic material precisely because it can regenerate (unlike steel or aluminium)? Can we stimulate the industry of saw, planer, and polishing machines and so on for the market of a nation full of wood with 140 to 150 million people?
5. In fact, in addition to designers, we also need architects to build. If we observe the traditional Minang, Batak, Javanese, Sumba, Maluku, and Irian buildings, focusing on the principles of construction from Sumatra to Hawaii, from Java to Japan, then one characteristic stands out and seems to be eternal: the principle of structure – elastic structure. There is never a massive wall, but membranes, screens, and curtains. The reasons for them are closely related to the problem of earthquakes but also have deep and practical philosophical foundations.
Western people say: 'My house is my castle'. Indonesian people say: 'This is my hometown'. Phenomenologically, Japanese houses and the Nusantara[13] houses are siblings. They are the houses of happy people who live according to the principle *kandang langit kemul mega* ('the sky is my residence, the clouds are my blanket'), with a sense of openness, a people of three-dimensional space with two-dimensional separators. At the same time, such a construction method is practical, earthquake-resistant, elastic, easy to build and dismantle, flexible in structure, and ecologically sustainable.

13 Nusantara is the Indonesian name of Maritime Southeast Asia (or parts of it).

The notion of a house as a castle is far from it, and a house without a yard is impossible. Due to climate and nature, we live more outside than inside. Our nation also knows about privacy, but in a functional balance, not just as a goal. So, in its integration, the house is entirely open and forms a dialogue with human beings. This philosophy of life that manifests itself in traditional Indonesian architecture or *wastu* has been appropriated and utilised progressively by modern Western architecture. Why do we throw away one of the basic concepts that, apart from being beautiful and practical, signifies what is integral to our culture and reflects its true desires?

If Western people are able to create ancient principles to be *zeitlos* ('timeless'), and the indigenous from the Archipelago, Japan, and Hawaii follow modern desires, why can't we do the same?

In relation to the notion of an eco-conscious holistic philosophy I noted that the principle of the stilt house (*Rumah Panggung* or *Rumah Kolong*) is widespread in the cultures from the Archipelago to Japan and Hawaii as well.

Humans living on stilts feel like a king on a natural pedestal. At the same time, it is practical against moisture and wild animals. The hero of modern architecture on pilotis is Corbusier.[14] Corbusier is important for Indonesian people, not in his art of sculpture or exposed concrete, but in two basic principles of the philosophy of habitation that he learned from our world: the view through the columns of the stilt houses, which does not hinder the natural scenery (i.e., ecological needs), and the principle of the *unite d'habitation* – freely translated as the self-sufficient village system. Is the space under modern buildings considered an 'efficiency' loss? Does our nation philosophise about the whole human being, or is it merely concerned with floor efficiency?

Why does Jakarta panic every year when it rains? Because it has forgotten the system of houses on stilts. In this respect, famous architects and well-known institutions must also set an example. Why are we afraid of flat houses and verticalism when the Balinese meru tower has long demonstrated how the vertical dimension is a familiar semantic treasury? The people of Irian[15] (West Papua) have intelligently and logically built houses on tree stilts for centuries.

Perhaps it is because we always take things in the literal sense – the efficient sense. Yet who says that only horizontal development is efficient? The French, Germans, and Americans are able to translate the postulates of Japanese and Indonesian *wastu* philosophy into the context of modern Western life through recreation and reinvention in an innovative way.

We are all afraid that we are not innovative but tend to imitate. Maybe we are too lazy to take X-ray photos and, just like consumers, take easy-to-use colour photos instead. In fact, for architects or *wastuwidyawan*, there is a saying: 'Use your common sense and good manners too. And then: do as you please.' So does every jet plane builder.

6. Indonesians are not Japanese or Germans. We are the children of the equator and the waving palm trees. There are one or two scientists and money seekers who are insistent, but generally, our people are human beings who are good at enjoying the moment. Even the poorest people can make spontaneous, silly jokes with each other. To laugh, people don't need to drink whiskey first, and the *santri* girls[16] are also good at combining elements of piety with sexy clothes. Even in fighting, as in *pencak silat*,[17] people look more like they are dancing rather than displaying a technique for killing. We are *batik* people; we all like colours. Basically, our nation is a nation of adventurers.

Are we allowed to express these unique characteristics of our archipelagic people without getting carried away with the negative aspects, such as deceptive behaviour, laziness, deceitfulness, arrogance, boastfulness, and so on?

Swedes and the English love the cold and puritanical characters because that is how they are, without wanting to become too frozen and rigid. Just as the Italians and French are *de l'elegance*, flamboyant, and charming. Japanese architecture clearly reveals the roots of the Shinto soul. Our people are flexible, too: they enjoy watching performances, appreciating style, making jokes, and relaxing under a shady tree. The Dutch are

14 Le Corbusier (1887–1965), was a Swiss-French architect, designer, painter, urban planner, writer, and one of the pioneers of what is now regarded as modern architecture. One of the most famous of Le Corbusier's works, the Villa Savoye (1928–1931) became an icon of modernist architecture. The house is an elegant white box poised on rows of slender pillars.

15 The western part of the island of New Guinea, now West Papua

16 *Santri* are students at an Islamic boarding school.

17 *Silat* is a generic term for the traditional martial arts.

very aware of all of this. The influence of native philosophies of the countries they colonised strongly influenced Dutch houses and villages in the Netherlands, which is entirely different from Germany and England. At the same time, they did not lose their identity, for example, to the French style, which is unrelated to the Dutch. Urban planning in the Dutch East Indies was completely adapted to the *wastuwidya* philosophy of the indigenous people. Even in terms of dress, Dutch women also wore *batik* and *kebaya*,[18] complete with a hair bun.

7. Finally, our notion of Indonesian architecture is incomplete without paying great attention to the problem of our contribution, by the architects/*wastuwidyawan*, to address the needs of the majority of people in our nation who are still poor. Poverty can have two faces. The demonic face, as the fruit of social structures with evil aspects, and also the face that prioritises quality over quantity, an expression of quality in life. It is one of the incarnations of the philosophy of 'to be, not to have'. Of course, in everyday life, the two dimensions of 'to be' and 'to have' are always present in humans, because Rousseau's[19] paradise or romance is not a feature of our mortal world. However, it is not only the struggle to build new macro structures as infrastructure and superstructure that is very influential for us but also the micro aspects. For instance, how we can develop new designs that are more economical in trivial details such as hinges, latches, locks, doors, windows, blinds, roofs, and so on? So, there is a growing trend (and the industry to supports it) to further simplify construction systems and improve the production system itself. Semi-finished products, for example, allow a wider distribution of producing and finishing processes, more dedicated to the need for labour-intensive production processes.

How can we find a native system that is both simple and aesthetically pleasing precisely because logic and reasonableness shine through in it? So that the majority of people in our nation who are still weak and poor can be a mosaic of the meadow which, although small and simple, but as a whole can be a clean carpet? Poetically stated, small is beautiful, even when within the big. Or, more accurately, greatness in the devotion to the small.

18 *Kebaya* is a traditional blouse worn by Indonesian, Malay, and Singaporean women on formal occasions.

19 Jean-Jacques Rousseau (1712–1778) was a Genevan philosopher, writer, and composer.

It would be inappropriate to make an artificial division between architects who catch snappers and those who catch anchovies – the specialist of the Big and the specialist of the Small. As an ideal, somehow, we must be able to be both. The advocacy of the poor by architects or *wastuwidyawan* does not need to go through specific political skills, but in our professional field, there are still many opportunities and possibilities that non-architects may not see.

This is where we can contribute. Businessmen and industrial people are observant. They will be more meritorious if supported by the architects' new ideas. Because, after all, for the business world, a market of 140 million people is still attractive.

The *wastuwidyawan* can provide new inspiration to serve the majority of our poor nation in the innovation of construction systems, use of space, the distribution and equalisation of the production process, the introduction of new details that are more economical but do not sacrifice the aesthetic value, in the ideas behind select forms, establishing healthier and thoughtful concepts, and so on. And it can help convey the idea that architecture is not the domain of a new, quirky, glamorous, but meaningless profession, but rather an ordinary thing, the most normal, just like a human who talks. However, what invites us is that language (i.e., architecture/*wastu*) also comes from within humans themselves, which is why it needs to be nurtured and matured. It can be varied in diverse modern expressions, but the essence is the same, as believed by our wise ancestors:

Sipating ingkang alus, inggih punika alusing donya.
Yen karingkes, dados alusing redi Meru.
Yen karingkes malih dados alusing meru.
Yen karingkes malih dados alusing manungsa.

The subtle nature is the subtlety of the world.
If simplified, it becomes the subtlety of Mount Meru.[20]
If simplified again, it becomes the subtlety of a Meru building.
If still simplified again, it becomes the subtlety of human beings.

Translation: Siti Arfah Annisa

20 Also called Sumeru, the name of the mountain at the centre of the world in Buddhist cosmology.

Widyapura Editorials
Bianpoen

Indonesian architect Bianpoen was editor of Widyapura, a bi-monthly journal on urban and environmental issues that was published by DKI Jakarta Centre for Research on Urban and Environmental Problems (PPMPL) for many years. It contained scientific writings, research results, and essays on these issues. In this capacity, Bianpoen wrote many editorials for the magazine, some of which are printed here. They give an insight into the urban planning and architectural discourse of the time. The following editorials were translated from the original copies found in the National Library of Indonesia.

Footnotes by the translator.

Widyapura, vol. 1, no. 11/12, 1978
Just Passing Through …

It is with a heavy heart that the editors in this issue present the problem of low-cost housing. Heavy because it might be a bit boring and because we already understand what the problem is; what efforts have been made; and what is being done, both by the government and by the people themselves. But is it correct? Are we sure that all the efforts and sacrifices of the community/government in their attempts to meet these basic needs are on the right track?

In the 1970s, the *kampungs*[1] in Jakarta grew by about 100 hectares per year. Taking into account the completion of Perumnas[2] and other agency projects, it was assumed that by 1980, the villages in Jakarta would grow by approximately 514 hectares per year.

In 1976, the new villages expanded to 35 per cent of the built-up area of Jakarta. This relatively small area accommodates about 70 per cent of Jakarta's population growth. How will it be in the 1980s and after?

Does this not mean that what actually develops in Jakarta is the villages? We know what a village is: a place where the lower-income group resides. However, the target of developments by Perumnas and other government agencies is not this bottom layer. The real-estate industry is also unable to reach this layer. Thus, the housing construction provision only passes through this population group. 'That's a village repair business,' was the official opinion of housing officials, among other things.

The MHT[3] project only improved environmental conditions and built some basic facilities. However, it was also able to mobilise the residents to repair their own houses. Now the MHT project is almost finished, and in front of us is a sea of villages growing faster and faster.

This phenomenon has long attracted the attention of the Centre for Urban and Environmental Problems Research (PPMPL-DKI). From the bottom of the hearts of some of the research staff, feelings of anxiety and doubt have grown about how to provide infrastructure for the cheap houses that we know today; because it is very likely that this method will not be able to solve the housing problem in Jakarta, even in the narrowest sense.

In this regard, PPMPL tries to approach the settlement problem by looking for solutions where the problem is located, namely in the middle of the *kampungs* of Jakarta, in the middle of the city of Jakarta. One aspect of this effort was reflected in the 1977 Jakarta housing competition, the winners of which are listed in this issue.

1 *kampung* literally means village but in Indonesia it also refers to densely populated areas of poor and working-class communities in the centre and peripheries of the city.

2 The state-owned housing company Perum Perumnas (National Urban Development Corporation) was founded in the mid-1970s, during which time it developed large-scale subsidised housing projects.

3 The Mohammad Husni Thamrin (MHT) project was launched by Governor Ali Sadikin in 1968 and continued until the early 1970s. It aimed to improve basic infrastructure and sanitation in Jakarta's *kampungs*. It was named for Thamrin, a member of the Batavia (Jakarta) city council who wanted to improve conditions in the *kampungs* in the 1920s and 1930s.

Widyapura, vol. 2, no. 1, 1978
Poverty and Settlements

The general assumption about how to solve the housing problem for poor urban people is to build as many houses as possible in the shortest possible time.

For the situation in Jakarta, the issue of land must be considered, and therefore residential buildings in Jakarta must be multi-storey (four floors).

With such a rationale as above, all over the world, large-scale, low-cost housing development projects have long been initiated. Some have worked, and some have not. From the unsuccessful cases, several lessons can be learned.

First, it must be understood that the definition of a settlement is much broader than the notion of housing procurement. A settlement also concerns the problem of houses and their environment, along with all public and social facilities required for daily human needs. But if the facilities in question cannot be provided, the housing will not be able to meet the needs in question, and it will soon become slums and/or be abandoned by the occupants.

Second is the problem of location. For poor urban residents, their homes must be close to their workplaces. This is especially true for that part of the community consisting primarily of temporary and unskilled workers. In this case, developing a robust urban public transport system may be more helpful and beneficial than constructing low-cost housing.

Third is the problem of the ability of the poor to maintain buildings and their environment. This ability is very small, and what they can do will not be much different from the current conditions in their villages. This is not enough for permanent buildings, let alone for high-rise buildings. Inevitably, we are faced with the reality that the group of people we want to help can only live in the housing and environment we know today.

This brings us to the fourth 'lesson', namely the standard of living and income level. Faced with a series of housing problems, we may have to start by tackling the problem of poverty first. All efforts and funds should prioritise addressing that problem and 'side needs'.

It is more realistic to hope that once the problem of poverty is resolved (to a certain extent), the issue of the settlement will no longer automatically be a problem, instead of hoping that, by tackling settlements, the problem of poverty can also be resolved. These are some of the lessons we can take from those who have failed. The aim of the housing programme for low-income people in Jakarta was also so that Indonesia would not be considered a failed case. The working papers and the workshop results that are contained in this issue of *Widyapura* are enough to give us hope.

Widyapura, vol. 2, no. 4, 1979
Metropolis … Does it Apply?

Between 1975 and 2000, the population of the world's cities will grow by 1.3 billion people. Most of these cities consist of poor people. Indonesia is included in this calculation (World Bank, 1975).

Some concrete data is already available, especially for the island of Java. From 1975 to 2000, the population of cities on the island of Java will increase by 23.4 million people (Leknas/Lipi, 1976).

If calculated on the basis of the capacity of agricultural land, cities on the island of Java must accommodate more than 50 per cent of the total population or approximately 63.4 million people. This means one additional urban population of 47.2 million people. Whether the figures above can be reduced or not depends on the living conditions in the villages. In general, we think that the burden of urbanisation will be reduced if we succeed in improving the quality of life of the villagers. Maybe this is true. However, it will not last long or apply to all islands in Indonesia. Here we can draw lessons from other countries. South Africa and the People's Republic of China have long sought to prevent urbanisation and create an ideal agrarian state, but the result is not at all as desired. If dictatorships and communism, with their strict and harsh system of government, don't succeed, what can we really expect from democratic countries?

Meanwhile, there are other factors that come into play. Increased food production does not require more labour in rural areas, but quite the opposite. Colombia is a clear example. In order to fulfil food needs to a reasonable level, food production must be increased; for that, about 70 per cent of the rural population had to be relocated to urban areas. The largest food-producing countries in the world are also the countries with the highest levels of urbanisation.

How about now, with the island of Java? Does food production need to be increased with the consequences of massive urbanisation? Or can we find a recipe that allows increased food production, control of urbanisation, and improvement of the quality of life in villages and cities, to take place simultaneously? Can we create an urban system that avoids grouping the population with high density in some areas and, at the same time, maintains the preservation and harmony of the environment on the island of Java?

We must not be arrogant, and we must always be ready to face reality and not be easily carried away by rigid and possibly wrong traditional concepts. It is true that: '80 per cent of Indonesia's population lives in villages, our attention must be directed to rural problems, development must be equitable and balanced, and so on.'

However, the truth above is incomplete and only shows part of the problem. This issue tries to describe additional features so that the symptoms and problems of the metropolitan city can be seen in the context described above.

Widyapura, vol. 2, no. 5, 1979

The Role of Architects in Society …

'Immediately after the end of the tragedy of mankind (the Second World War), which caused destruction and sorrow throughout the world, architects from all countries deemed it imperative to unite in one federation of national organisations (Union Internationale des Architectes), which broke all political, economic, and aesthetic boundaries. By encouraging and developing relations between architects in a free manner, regardless of nationality, religion, education, and architectural doctrines, this union aims to provide architects with broad possibilities to exchange ideas, experiences, and knowledge and to benefit from the differences that exist between them. Under these conditions, architects can participate effectively in environmental improvement efforts that rebuild destroyed towns and villages, help improve the standard of living of the slum people, and give their share in the struggle to fulfil the physical and spiritual aspirations of mankind. Together with other professional organisations, they are determined to advance the welfare of human society and strengthen world peace.' This is an excerpt from the preamble of the Union Internationale des Architectes (UIA).

Since 1975 the Indonesian Architects Association (IAI) has been a member of the UIA and thus received the preamble above, which clearly outlines the working philosophy of architects, their obligations, responsibilities, and orientation of service.

The Urban Village Seminar organised by the IAI from 18 to 21 September 1979 embodied this philosophy. The chosen theme was very unusual for architects because no architect has ever planned a city village.

Indeed, the problems of life in urban villages are becoming increasingly serious. It is estimated that by the year 2000, approximately 2.1 billion people will live in the cities of developing countries. If we remember that the lives of people in urban villages today are still coloured by poverty, anxiety, overcrowding, and different kinds of pollution, it is impossible to imagine the condition of the urban village community approaching the year 2000. Can they still hope for a decent, happy environment that all levels of the population can enjoy? The working papers presented at the Urban Village Seminar try to provide the answer.

Widyapura, vol. 4, no. 3, 1983
To Do or Not To Do?

At a time when urbanisation in Western Europe was at its peak, the population growth rate for each country was approximately 0.5 per cent per year.

In the Third World, including Indonesia, the population growth currently ranges from two to three per cent, while the growth of cities in Indonesia reached 4.4 per cent per year from 1970 to 1980.

Therefore, it is not surprising that the leaders of many countries and cities in the Third World panicked to find solutions to the various problems that constantly arise and never seem to be resolved.

In such a mental atmosphere, the attitude that 'it is better to do something wrong than not to do anything at all' can be understood and appreciated.

However, it would be nice if we in Indonesia could do something wrong, and we need to know that, in many cases, 'doing nothing' is also the best way. Of course, all of this must be based on honest and bona fide research and both have one goal.

This is the spirit behind the National Habitat I seminar, which was organised by the Habitat Working Group of the Indonesian Architects Association from 24 to 26 March 1984 in Jakarta.

The editors express their deepest gratitude to the management of the Indonesian Architects Association that has allowed the publication of this special edition, which contains all the papers and results of the Habitat I Seminar in Jakarta.

Widyapura, vol. 4, no. 6, 1985
Don't Search for It

'Architecture' has now been taught in Indonesia for 35 years. It has been approximately 25 years since Indonesian architects have worked in Indonesia. From that time until now, architects have been busy looking for the shape/image of Indonesian architecture.

In this effort, many ideas, advice, and so on were received from various circles of society.

For example, (the late) Prof. Dr. Nugroho once stated to the architects assigned to design the Universitas Indonesia campus in Depok that the campus must have an Indonesian image, not one of Java or Toraja, or any other regions. As a guide, they could use one or more architectural elements that exists in all areas.

The results of the campus design can later be seen in Depok.

The congress of the Indonesian Architects Association, which was held in March 1985, addressed the main theme: 'Have Indonesian architects with professional skills been able to create Indonesian architecture?'

From the main theme, it can be concluded that the search for 'Indonesian architecture' is still actively being carried out.

The ideas raised at the congress are presented in this issue of *Widyapura*.

To the many ideas and opinions regarding the search for Indonesian architecture, it is necessary to add one more idea, namely: 'Look no further; the work of the Indonesian people in the field of architecture *is* Indonesian architecture.'

Translation: Fernisia Winnerdy

PHOTOGRAPHS

CONEFO building
Now DPR/MPR, The People's Representatives Council, Jakarta (1964–1934)

Architects: Soejoedi Wirjoatmodjo & Team
Photos: William Sutanto

MAJELIS
DEWAN
DEWAN

NUSANTARA

Ruang Rapat Paripurna I

Secretariat ASEAN
Jakarta (1978–1981)

Architects: PT. Gubahlaras / Soejoedi Wirjoatmodjo
Photos: William Sutanto

asean

Pusat Kehutanan
Forestry Centre, now Manggala Wanabakti – The Ministry of Environment and Forestry, Jakarta (1976–1983)

Architects: PT. Gubahlaras / Soejoedi Wirjoatmodjo and Noerpontjo
Photos: William Sutanto

KEMENTERIAN
LINGKUNGAN
DAN

04
02
02
02

ORIENTASI KEPRAMUKAAN DAN RAPIMNAS
SAKA KALPATARU DAN SAKA WANABAKTI
KEMENTERIAN LINGKUNGAN HIDUP DAN KEHUTANAN
"Pramuka Mengabdi Tanpa Batas"

Jakob-Andreä-House
Waiblingen (1964 / 1965 – 1968)

Architect: Jan Beng Oei
Photos: Moritz Bernoully

Urban Redevelopment 'Wohncity'
Fellbach (1966–1976)

Architect Collaboration: EOS, Kurt Ebinger,
Jan Beng Oei, Siegfried Schnell
Photos: Moritz Bernoully

prooptik

21/1
19
17

Lindenhalle Ehingen
(1978–1984)

Architects: Jan Beng Oei + Partner
Photos: Moritz Bernoully

Bürgerzentrum Waiblingen
(1979–1985)

Architect: Jan Beng Oei + Partner
Photos: Moritz Bernoully

Ghibellinen
Saal

Faculty of Literature, University of Indonesia in Depok
(1985–1987)

Architects: Mustafa Pamuntjak, Abdul Chattam /
PT. Han Awal & Partners
Photos: William Sutanto

Gereja Maria Bunda Perantara Cideng
Our Lady of Intercession Catholic Church, Cideng (1972–1974)

Architect: Bianpoen
Photos: William Sutanto

Gereja Salib Suci Cilincing, Jakarta
Holy Cross Catholic Church of Cilincing Parish, Jakarta (1983–1984)

Architects: Y. B. Mangunwijaya / PT. Han Awal & Partners
Photos: William Sutanto

House in Megamendung
West Java (1971)

Architect: Mustafa Pamuntjak
Photos: William Sutanto

House in Cilember
Jakarta (1997)

Architect: Mustafa Pamuntjak
Photos: William Sutanto

House in Jaya Mandala
Jakarta (1973)

Architect: Mustafa Pamuntjak
Photos: William Sutanto

House at Jalan Bangau
Jakarta (1992)

Architect: Mustafa Pamuntjak
Photos: William Sutanto

Bibliography

Al Radi, Abbad, 'Kampong Kali Cho-de, Yogyakarta, Indonesia: On-site Review Report', <https://www.archnet.org/sites/752> accessed 25 July 2022.

Arens, Esther Helena, *Neuordnungen. Westdeutsche und niederländische "Entwicklungshilfe" für Indonesien in den 1960er Jahren* (Dortmund: Westfälische Wilhelms-Universität, 2021).

Bahrdt, Hans Paul, *Die moderne Großstadt. Soziologische Überlegungen zum Städtebau* (Reinbek bei Hamburg: Rowohlt, 1961).

Beittinger, Verena, *'Zwietracht in der Vielfalt',* (Südostasien Working Papers, no. 24, Humboldt-Universität zu Berlin, 2004).

Bianpoen, *Research and Development for Urban Management: Case Jakarta*, trans. Carla Bianpoen (Rotterdam: Erasmus Universiteit Rotterdam, 1983).

Budihardjo, Eko (ed.), *Menuju Arsitektur Indonesia*, (Bandung: Alumni, 1983), pp. 43–60.

Butter, Andreas, and Hartung, Ulrich *Ostmoderne: Architektur in Berlin 1945–65* (Berlin: Jovis, 2005).

Dorn, Ralf, *Der Architekt und Stadtplaner Rudolf Hillebrecht. Kontinuität und Brüche in der deutschen Planungsgeschichte im 20. Jahrhundert* (Berlin: Gebr. Mann, 2017).

Drew, Jane, and Fry, Maxwell, *Architecture in the Humid Tropics* (London: B.T. Batsford Ltd., 1956).

Geist, Johann F., Kürvers, Klaus, and Rausch, Dieter (eds.), *Hans Scharoun, Chronik zu Leben und Werk* (Berlin: Akademie der Künste, 1993).

Gerken, Horst. (ed.), *Festschrift zum 175-jährigen Bestehen der Universität Hannover – Catalogus Professorum 1831–2006* (Hildesheim: Georg Olms, 2006).

Göderitz, Johannes, Rainer, Roland, and Hoffmann, Hubert, *Die gegliederte und aufgelockerte Stadt* (Tübingen: Wasmuth, 1957).

Grimm, Irina, *Zwischen Repression und Opposition. Indonesische Studierende in der Bundesrepublik (1965–1998)* (Berlin: regiospectra Verlag, 2019).

Haas, Ralph, *Ernst Zinsser. Leben und Werk eines Architekten der Fünfziger Jahre in Hannover* (Hannover: Inst. für Bau- und Kunstgeschichte, 2000).

Herlambang, Suryono, 'ATAP, Delft: 1953–1957 Kisah-kisah keciltentang Kelompok Diskusi; Perjalanan Arsitektur dan Persemaian Arsitek Modern Indonesia', in Pusat Dokumentasi Arsitektur Indonesia (eds), *Tegang Bentang* (Jakarta: Gramedia, 2007), pp. 97–107.

Hoffmann-Axthelm, Dieter, 'Germany 1945–80: Der Architekt ohne Architektur', *Arch+*, vol. 56, 1981.

Hoffmann, Hubert, 'Das Unternehmen Interbau', *Bauen + Wohnen*, no. 7, 1957.

Kusno, Abidin, *After the New Order* (Honolulu: University of Hawaii Press, 2013).

Kusno, Abidin (ed.), *Gunawan Tjahjono and Josef Prijotomo. Postcolonial Traditionality* (Delft: TU Delft Open, 2017).

Lindau, Friedrich, *Planen und Bauen der fünfziger Jahre in Hannover* (Hannover: Schlütersche, 1998).

Lindau, Friedrich, *Hannover. Wiederaufbau und Zerstörung. Die Stadt im Umgang mit ihrer bauhistorischen Identität,* 2nd edition (Hannover: Schlütersche, 2001).

Lukito, Yulia Nurliani, *Exhibiting Modernity and Indonesian Vernacular Architecture: Hybrid Architecture at Pasar Gambir of Batavia, the 1931 Paris International Colonial Exhibition and Taman Mini Indonesia Indah* (Wiesbaden: Springer VS, 2016).

Mangunwijaya, Y.B., *Wastu Citra: Pengantar ke Ilmu Budaya Bentuk Arsitektur Sendi-sendi Filsafatnya Beserta Contoh-contoh Praktis [Introduction to Cultural Sciences, Architectural Forms, Philosophy and Practical Examples]* (Jakarta: Gramedia, 1988); fourth edition published in 2009.

Napitupulu, Erwinthon P., 'St. Maria Assumpta Church', *World Architecture* 151 (Beijing), 1/2003.

Oesterlen, Dieter, 'St. Martin's Protestant Church, Hanover-Linden', *Bauen + Wohnen*, vol. 12, 11/1958, p. 378.

Oesterlen, Dieter, 'Parliament Building of Lower Saxon Diet in Hanover', *Bauen + Wohnen*, vol. 18, 2/1964, p. 79.

Pamuntjak, Mustafa, 'Persahabatan', in: Yori Antar (ed.) *Han Awal. Ayah Bagi Banjak Orang* (Jakarta, 2017).

Peters, Günther, *Kleine Berliner Baugeschichte* (Berlin: Stapp Verlag, 1995).

Redaktionsgruppe Kreuer 100 (ed.), *Willy Kreuer 1910–1984* (Kassel: Red.-Gruppe Kreuer100, 2012).

Roeder, O.G., Mahiddin Mahmud (eds.), *Who's who in Indonesia*, second edition (Jakarta: Gunung Agung, 1980).

Schulz, Stefanie, Schulz, Carl-Georg, *Das Hansaviertel: Ikone der Moderne* (Berlin: Braun, 2007).

Setiadi, Sopandi 'A Hundred Years of Architecture in Indonesia', in Armand, Avianti, Setiadi Sopandi (eds.), *Craftmanship: Material*

Consciousness (Jakarta: PT Imaji Media Pustaka, 2014).
Setyautama, Sam (ed.), *Tokoh-tokoh etnis Tionghoa di Indonesia [Ethnic Chinese in Indonesia]*, 'Liem Bian Poen' (Jakarta: Etnis, 2008), pp. 193–194.
Spengelin, Friedrich, 'Alt und Neu. Bauen im historischen Kontext', in Auffahrt, Sid and Pietsch, Wolfgang (eds.), *Die Universität Hannover. Ihre Bauten / Ihre Gärten / Ihre Planungsgeschichte* (Petersberg Michael Imhof, 2003), p. 251.
Thung, Po Hin, *Spontane nederzettingen begeleid / Enabled Squatter Settlements: Voorwaarden en criteria in Sri Lanka*, (dissertation, Technische Universiteit Eindhoven, 1993).
Tömmel, Till Florian, *Bonn, Jakarta und der Kalte Krieg* (Berlin: De Gruyter Oldenbourg, 2018).
Trisnawati, Vera, 'Dipl.-Ing. Hoemar Tjokrodiatmo: Suka menampilkan ukiran khas Indonesia', *Konstruksi*, November 1990, pp. 6–7.
tt, 'Projekt für ein Hallenbad', *Bauwelt*, vol. 37, 1963, p. 1057.
van Eyck, Aldo, 'Kinderhaus in Amsterdam', *Das Werk: Architektur und Kunst*, vol. 49, no. 1 (1962), pp. 16–23.
Zalewski, P. Paul, 'Rudolf Hillebrecht und der autogerechte Wiederaufbau Hannovers nach 1945', p. 92, in Rita Seidel (ed.), *Festschrift zum 175-jährigen Bestehen der Universität Hannover, vol. 1* (Hannover: Olms, 2006), pp. 89–102.
Zietzschmann, Ernst, 'Verkehrsplanung in Hannover', *Schweizerische Bauzeitung*, vol. 80, 4/1962, pp. 61–65.

Literature and sources for biography of Han Awal by Adelia Andani Djarot
Antar, Yori, Purwestri, Nadia, Suryaningsih, Febriyanti, Kosasih, Varani (eds.), *Han Awal: Ayah Bagi Banyak Orang*, (Jakarta: Pusat Dokumentasi Arsitektur Indonesia, 2017).
Astri, Lutik, *Pemikiran dan Karya Arsitektur Han Awal (1960–2003),* (Thesis. Bandung: Program Pascasarjana Institut Teknologi Bandung, 2004).
Herlambang , Soerjono, 'ATAP, Delft: 1953–1957: Kisah-Kisah Kecil tentang Kelompok Diskusi, Perjalanan Arsitektur, dan Persemaian Arsitek Modern Indonesia', dalam Pusat Dokumentasi Arsitektur Indonesia (eds.), *Tegang Bentang: Seratus Tahun Perspektif Arsitektural di Indonesia*, (Jakarta: PT Gramedia Pustaka Utama, 2012).
Subadyo, Junianto and Tutut, *Review Perjalanan Karya Han Awal*, (Malang: Jurusan Arsitektur Universitas Merdeka Malang, 2001).
Tjahjono, Gunawan, Agustananda, Putu Ayu P. (eds.), *Nyala Nirmala: 72 tahun Dipl.-Ing Han Awal,* (Depok: Jurusan Arsitektur Fakultas Teknik Universitas Indonesia, 2002).

Literature and sources for biography of Mustafa Pamuntjak by Gregorius Jasson, Nadira Adiswari, Siti Arfah Annisa (p. 125f)
Mahdi, Sharmi, *Rumah Tropis Tropical House* (Jakarta: Penerbit Djambatan, 1986).
Pamuntjak, Mustafa 'Persahabatan', in Antar, Yori, Purwestri, Nadia, Suryaningsih, Febriyanti, Kosasih, Varani (eds.), *Han Awal: Ayah bagi Banyak Orang*, (Jakarta: Pusat Dokumentasi Arsitektur Indonesia, 2017).
Sekhu, Akhmad, 'SOHO ala Mustafa Pamuntjak', *Indonesia Design* Vol. 4, No. 22, 2007, pp. 90–95.
Interview with Mrs. Endang Pamuntjak and Mrs. Sharmi Ranti by Gregorius Jasson, Nadira Adiswari, Siti Arfah Annisa.

Literature and sources for biography of Soejoedi Wirjoatmodjo by Angeline Basuki
Hidayat, Rahmi, 'Karya arsitek Soejoedi: Sarat Makna, Berkarakter, dan Bersejarah', *Konstruksi Magazine* no 199 / November 1994.
Kementerian Pendidikan dan Kebudayaan, 'Soejoedi Wirjoatmodjo, Pelopor Arsitektur Modern di Indonesia', *Indonesiana Platform Kebudayaan*, 17 December 2015. <https://kebudayaan.kemdikbud.go.id/ditwdb/soejoedi-wirjoatmodjo-pelopor-arsitektur-modern-di-indonesia/> accessed on 9 October 2022.
NBR. 'Karya Spektakuler Soejoedi Wirjoatmodjo', *Laras Magazine*, no. 71 / November 1994.
Saliya, Yuswadi, 'Pagi Hari dan Lekang Siang Seorang Sujudi', Tegang Bentang (ed.): *Seratus Tahun Perspektif Arsitektural di Indonesia*, (Jakarta: Gramedia, 2012).
Soejoedi, Hadijanto and Santoso, Interview by Nadia Rinandi, 15 November 2022.
Sukada, Budi A., *Membuka Selubung Cakrawala Arsitek Soejoedi*, (Jakarta: Gubahlaras, 2013).
Tanudjaja , F. Christian J. Sinar (ed.), *Arsitek dan Karyanya Dibalik Sosok Karya Soejoedi*, (Yogyakarta: Penerbitan Universitas Atma Jaya Yogyakarta, 1991).
Wiryomartono, Bagoes, 'Soejoedi and Architecture In Modern Indonesia: A Critical Post-Colonial Study', *Archnet-IJAR*, Volume 7, Issue 1, March 2013, pp. 177–185.

Literature for biography of Bianpoen by Fernisia Winnerdy, Adetania Pramanik, and Jesslyn Amanda
Awal, Han, 'Ketawa Belakangan: Beberapa Catatan Ringan Mengenai Bianpoen, Kawanku', pp. 4–8. Tjahjono, Gunawan, Kusumayanti, Mira, and Herlily (eds.), *Pelita Pura: 72 Tahun Dr. Ir. Bianpoen*, (Jurusan Arsitektur Fakultas Teknik Universitas Indonesia, 2002).
Balai Pelestarian Cagar Budaya Jawa Timur, 'Klenteng Hok Sian Kiong Mojokerto', *Kementerian Pendidikan Kebudayaan Riset dan Teknologi.* Direktorat Jenderal Kebudayaan website <https://kebudayaan.kemdikbud.go.id/bpcbjatim/klenteng-hok-sian-kiong-mojokerto/> accessed 5 Juli 2019.
Bianpoen, *Research and development for urban management: case Jakarta = Onderzoek en ontwikkeling voor stadsbestuur: de case Jakarta,* (Erasmus Universiteit Rotterdam, 1983).
Bianpoen, *'Untuk Apa? Untuk Siapa? Rangkaian Pemikiran Lingkungan Berkelanjutan'.* UPH Press, 2011.
Dr. Bianpoen, dipl.ing, 'Bismo yang Saya Kenal', pp. 5–14. Lantera, Laras, Sukada, Budi, and Harahap, Yulia Nurliani (ed.), *72 Tahun Prof. Suwondo B. Sutedjo*, (Jurusan Arsitektur Fakultas Teknik Universitas Indonesia, 2000).
Febriani, Sarie, 'Sarang Bernaung Bianpoen', *Kompas,* 29 August 2010, p 27.
Khoiri, Ilham, 'Bianpoen, dan Jakarta yang Krisis', *Kompas*, 11 February 2007, p. 12.
Suwondo B. S. 'Dipl. Ing. Bukan B.I.', pp. 31–40, Tjahjono, Gunawan, Kusumayanti, Mira, and Herlily (ed.), *Pelita Pura: 72 Tahun Dr. Ir. Bianpoen*, (Jurusan Arsitektur Fakultas Teknik Universitas Indonesia, 2002).

Literature for biography of Suwondo by Hedista Rani Pranata
Kan Wan Tjin, 'Bismo dan Suwondo, Yang Saya Kenal dari Cerita dan Anekdot yang Beredar di Keluarga dan Teman-temannya', pp. 34–61, Sukada, Budi A., Harahap, Yulia Nurliani (eds.), *Laras Lantera: 72 Tahun Prof. Suwondo B. Sutedjo,* (Jurusan Arsitektur Fakultas Teknik Universitas Indonesia, 2000).

About the Authors

Adelia Andani is an academician, researcher, and writer. She received her bachelor's degree in architecture from Universitas Tarumanagara in Jakarta and her master's degree in architectural history and theory from Universitas Indonesia in Depok.

Adetania Pramanik received her MSc in architecture from Texas Tech University and in environmental behaviour from Colorado State University. She is experienced in research and master planning.

Angeline Basuki holds an MA in heritage management from the University of Kent and a bachelor's in architecture from Universitas Pelita Harapan. She is a project manager at the Jakarta Old Town Consortium and works in the field of cultural and natural conservation.

Eduard Kögel is a curator and independent researcher based in Berlin, Germany. He received a PhD from Bauhaus Universität Weimar. He is one of the initiators of the international platform *Encounters with Southeast Asian Modernism*, which explores the legacy of postcolonial modern architecture and contemporary urban development in Southeast Asia.

Fernisia R. Winnerdy earned her MA in architectural history at The Bartlett, University College London, and a bachelor's degree at the Architecture Department of Universitas Pelita Harapan, where she currently teaches. She is also an architect at the firm Monokroma Architect.

Gregorius Jasson graduated from Tarumanagara University in 2019 with a degree in architecture and has since worked in architecture and other related fields. He is currently a research officer for the non-profit organisation Yayasan Kota Kita, focusing on urban food systems, community climate resilience, and other urban issues.

Hedista Rani Pranata received her master's degree in architecture and sustainability at Universitas Indonesia in 2020 and joined the architecture department at Multimedia Nusantara University as a full-time academician. She is actively involved in diverse research, books, and other publications on architecture, planning, and sustainability.

Jesslyn Amanda received her bachelor's degree in architecture at Universitas Pelita Harapan. She works at the architectural firm Monokroma Architect.

Moritz Henning is an architect, writer, and independent researcher based in Berlin, Germany. He is one of the initiators of the international platform *Encounters with Southeast Asian Modernism*, which explores the legacy of postcolonial modern architecture and contemporary urban development in Southeast Asia.

Nadira Adiswari earned both her bachelor's and master's degrees in architecture from Universitas Indonesia, where she has been assisting lecturers and partaking in research. Besides pursuing her interests in architecture, history, and media and popular culture, she has been developing an educational family-based project.

Setiadi Sopandi is a practising architect based in Bogor, Indonesia, and an architectural historian by training. He is a co-founder, curator, and director of Yayasan Museum Arsitektur Indonesia – the first and only online architecture repository in Indonesia.

Siti Arfah Annisa earned her bachelor's degree in architecture from Institut Teknologi Bandung and her master's degree in architectural history and theory from Universitas Indonesia, where she currently researches and teaches.

Making of

Prof. SUWONDO BISMO SUTEDJO
Dipl.-Ing., Arsitek IAI
Stadtbüchereien Hannover
DIPL. – ING. SUWONDO BISMO SUTEDJO I.A.I.
Jalan Daksinapati Timur I No. 12
JAKARTA – Timur.
Fahrtberechtigungsausweis für Studenten
30.4.1962
Hannoversche Verkehrsbetriebe (Üstra) Aktiengesellschaft

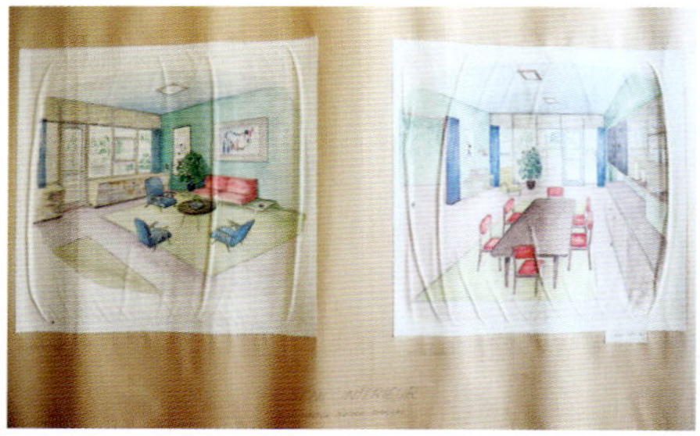

Aufenthaltserlaubnis
Hauptstadt Hannover
Ordnungsamt
Einwohnerabteilung
Empfangsbescheinigung

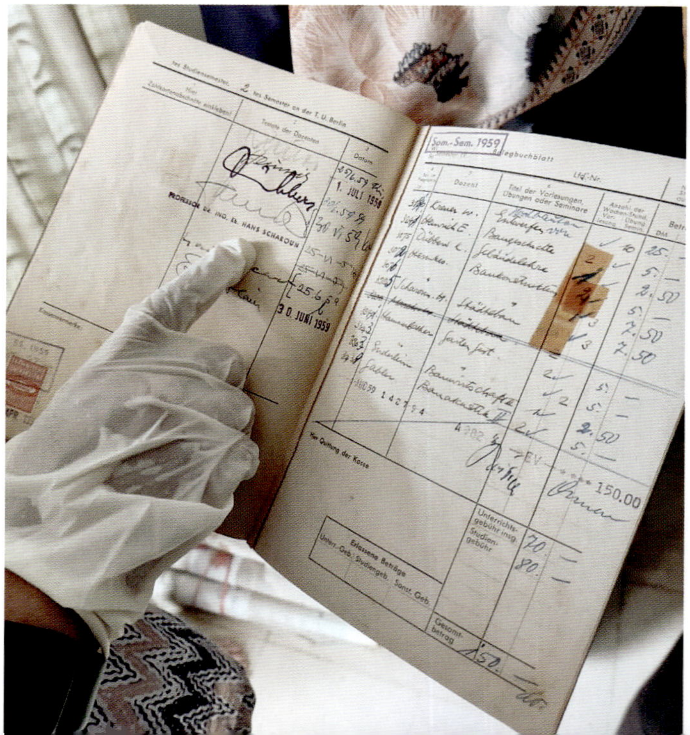

Som.-Sem. 1959
PROFESSOR DR.-ING. EH. HANS SCHAROUN

GC
GC

26.10.1992

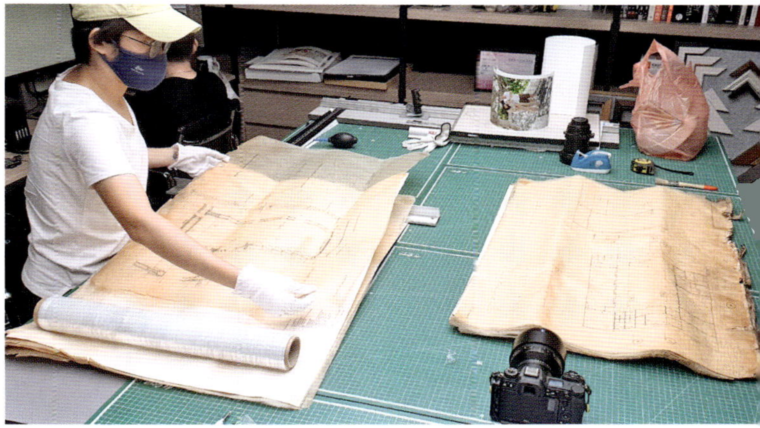

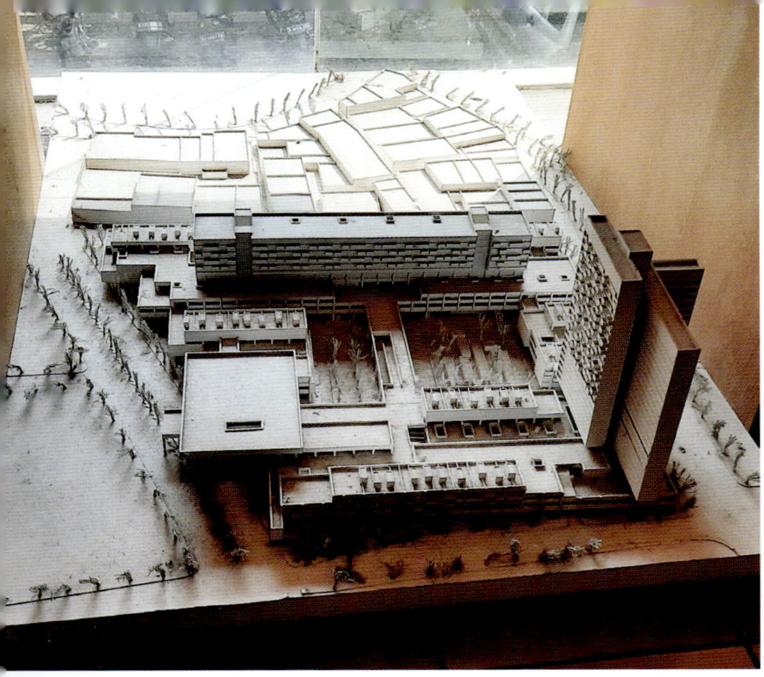

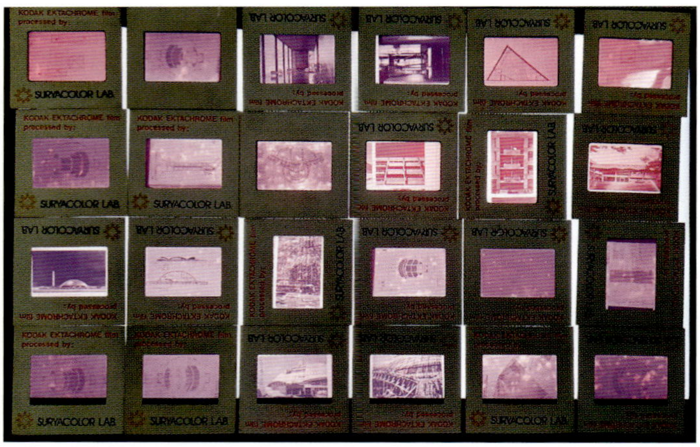
KODAK EKTACHROME film
processed by:
SURYACOLOR LAB

MAKET GEDUNG ASEAN. Gedu:ng seharga US$ 35 juta ini adalah maket gedung markas besar Sekretariat Tetap ASEAN, terletak di sudut Jl. Sisingamangaraja/Trunojoyo Kebayoran Baru. Seluruh biaya pembangunan dan tanah ditanggung Pem. RI. Gedung bertingkat 9 itu nanti akan terdiri dari tiga ruangan konperensi yg luas, ruangan pers dan dua tingkat khusus untuk sekretariat. Sementara lima tingkat teratas khusus untuk masing2 anggota ASEAN. Pada waktu ini Sekretariat Tetap ASEAN masih menggunakan bekas gedung Deplu di Jl. Sisingamangaraja. Anggaran belanja sekretariat tetap ASEAN tahun 1976 mencapai US$ 335 ribu dan tahun ini diperkirakan US$ 1 juta, dibagi sama rata antara kelima negara anggota. — Foto : TST —

DESAIN

Arsitektur Neogotik Gereja Katedral Jakarta

Oleh Han Awal

Procter&Gamble

Nikah Tamasya

LOWONGAN

Sales Executive (SE)
Sales Counter (SC)
Fleet Sales (FS)

"Gebt unsren(n) Kuchn urbanes Gruen" "Berikan 'para sapi' kita hijau kota" (Kuebn = Prof Kuebm = pakar dan penganjur penghijauan kota-kota. YBM dengan rekan mahasiswa sedang berdemo mendukung usaha Prof. Erich Kuebn untuk menghijaukan kota-kota Jerman, kira-kira tahun 1964. (Kub = sapi Kuebn = sapi-sapi).

ASIAN ARCHITECTS VISIT LA ARCHITECT

Two Indonesian architects were recent visitors in the Los Angeles offices of Victor Gruen and Associates through sponsorship of the Asia Foundation.

Oei Jan Beng and Oen Poo Hauw, seniors at the University of Architecture and fine arts in Bandung, Indonesia, will remain with the Gruen firm for two months studying American architecture and construction.

The Deutsche Bibliothek lists this publication in the *Deutsche Nationalbibliografie;* detailed bibliographic data is available on the internet at *http://dnb.d-nb.de.*

ISBN 978-3-86922-866-2

www.dom-publishers.com

Consultants
Avianti Armand, Sally Below, Setiadi Sopandi

Translations and copy editing
Alisa Kotmair, Paul Cohen
Yayasan Museum Arsitektur Indonesia

Proofreading
Sandie Kestell

Design
Nicole Wolf

Printing
Tiger Printing (Hong Kong) Co , Ltd.
www.tigerprinting.hk

DOM
publishers

Dipl.-Ing. Arsitek: German-trained Indonesian Architects from the 1960s is funded by the German Federal Foreign Office on the occasion of the 70th anniversary of diplomatic relations between the Federal Republic of Germany and the Republic of Indonesia.

Federal Foreign Office

Partners:

TECHNISCHE
UNIVERSITÄT
BERLIN